LIFT

LIFT

THE FUNDAMENTAL
STATE OF LEADERSHIP

Second Edition

RYAN W. QUINN
and **ROBERT E. QUINN**

BK
Berrett–Koehler Publishers, Inc.
a BK Business book

Berrett-Koehler Publishers, Inc.
1333 Broadway, Suite 1000
Oakland, CA 94612-1921
Tel: (510) 817-2277   Fax: (510) 817-2278   www.bkconnection.com

Ordering Information
Quantity sales. Special discounts are available on quantity purchases by corporations, associations, and others. For details, contact the "Special Sales Department" at the Berrett-Koehler address above.
Individual sales. Berrett-Koehler publications are available through most bookstores. They can also be ordered directly from Berrett-Koehler: Tel: (800) 929-2929; Fax: (802) 864-7626; www.bkconnection.com
Orders for college textbook/course adoption use. Please contact Berrett-Koehler: Tel: (800) 929-2929; Fax: (802) 864-7626.
Orders by U.S. trade bookstores and wholesalers. Please contact Ingram Publisher Services, Tel: (800) 509-4887; Fax: (800) 838-1149; E-mail: customer.service@ingrampublisherservices.com; or visit www.ingrampublisherservices.com/Ordering for details about electronic ordering.

Berrett-Koehler and the BK logo are registered trademarks of Berrett-Koehler Publishers, Inc.

Printed in the United States of America

Berrett-Koehler books are printed on long-lasting acid-free paper. When it is available, we choose paper that has been manufactured by environmentally responsible processes. These may include using trees grown in sustainable forests, incorporating recycled paper, minimizing chlorine in bleaching, or recycling the energy produced at the paper mill.

Library of Congress Cataloging-in-Publication Data
Quinn, Ryan W.
  Lift : the fundamental state of leadership / Ryan W. Quinn and Robert E. Quinn.
    pages cm
  Revised and updated edition of the authors' Lift : becoming a positive force in any situation, published in 2009.
  Includes bibliographical references.
  ISBN 978-1-62656-401-5 (pbk.)
  1. Leadership—Psychological aspects.   2. Influence (Psychology)   3. Self-actualization (Psychology)   4. Success.   I. Quinn, Robert E.   II. Title.
BF637.L4.Q56 2009
158—dc23

                                                                    2015009343

Second Edition
20 19 18 17 16 15   10 9 8 7 6 5 4 3 2 1

Cover designer Leslie Waltzer, Crowfoot Design

To Jane Dutton and Kim Cameron,
two pioneers in the scholarship of the
positive who have lifted us to higher
and more meaningful levels of life.

CONTENTS

HARNESSING THE POWER OF LIFT

On August 18, 1941, officer John Gillespie Magee Jr. of the Royal Canadian Air Force took a new airplane, the Spitfire Mk I, on a test flight.[1] Magee had just received his wings as a pilot. As he flew the Spitfire to new heights he felt inspired to write a poem that is now the official poem of the Royal Canadian Air Force and the British Royal Air Force. The poem has inspired short films, songs, inscriptions on headstones, presidential addresses, museum displays, and eulogies. Some have even used this poem as a prayer.

High Flight

Oh, I have slipped the surly bonds of earth
    And danced the skies on laughter-silvered wings;
Sunward I've climbed, and joined the tumbling mirth
    Of sun-split clouds—and done a hundred things
You have not done—wheeled and soared and swung
    High in the sunlit silence. Hov'ring there,
I've chased the shouting wind along, and flung
    My eager craft through footless halls of air.
Up, up the long, delirious blue
    I've topped the windswept heights with easy grace
Where never lark, or even eagle flew.
    And, while with silent, lifting mind I've trod
The high, untrespassed sanctity of space,
    Put out my hand, and touched the face of God.

It is hard to read this poem without feeling at least a bit of the exhilaration that Magee must have felt.[2] His momentary thoughts and feelings inspired words that continue to move others generations after his death. Magee's experience, and the poem it generated, have "slipped the surly bonds of earth" and "done a hundred things" because Magee "trod the high, untrespassed sanctity of space" with a "lifting mind." If Magee's experience had this kind of impact, what impact might we have if we slip the surly bonds of earth with a lifting mind?

This is a book about how we can do just that: slip the surly bonds of earth by lifting our hearts and minds, and in the process lift other people as well. Like Orville and Wilbur Wright, who used physical science and practical experience to build the first airplane, thus making it possible later for Magee to rise above the bonds of earth, we can use social science and practical experience to learn to rise above the constraints of life and lift others around us. The tool that the Wright brothers developed to help people harness the aerodynamic force of lift was the airplane; the tool that we have developed to help people harness the social and psychological forces that "lift"—or exert a positive influence upon—themselves and others is called the fundamental state of leadership.

The fundamental state of leadership is a psychological state: a temporary pattern of thoughts and feelings in which we are (1) purpose-centered (the results we want are not weighed down by needless expectations); (2) internally directed (our personal values guide our actions); (3) other-focused (we feel empathy for the feelings and needs of others); and (4) externally open (we believe that we can improve at whatever it is we are trying to do). When we experience these thoughts and feelings, we feel uplifted and, consequently, lift others around us.

In aerodynamics, *lift* is the name for the force that pushes an airplane (or a boat, or any object traveling in a liquid or a gas) upward. We use the metaphor of *lift*, and of heavier-than-air *flight*, to frame our discussion of the fundamental state of leadership. There are many parallels between how airplanes harness "lift" and how the fundamental state of leadership helps people to harness their potential to lift themselves and others to greater heights of achievement, integrity, learning, and love.[3]

The fundamental state of leadership lifts us and others, but daily living often drags us into more normal states. In normal states we (1) seek comfort, (2) react to situations automatically, (3) focus on our own wants, and (4) believe that there is little we can do to improve. In a normal state, our leadership is less positive and it can be hard to change.

We offer four questions that anyone can use to experience the fundamental state of leadership, and we use scientific research to explain how people who ask themselves these questions tend to lift themselves and the people around them:

1. What result do I want to create?
2. What would my story be if I were living the values I expect of others?
3. How do others feel about this situation?
4. What are three or more strategies I could try in learning how to achieve my purpose?

These questions are simple, but their power is in their simplicity. We considered each word carefully, comparing it against scientific research. For example, the question "How do others feel about this situation?" may seem like it is simply repeating the old adage, "Walk a mile in another person's shoes," which encourages people to consider other people's perspectives. As we will discuss in chapter 8, however, simply considering others' perspectives is often not enough; we must understand the feelings behind those perspectives. And research suggests that including such words as *others* and leaving out such questions as "How would I feel?" are also important for different reasons.

Scientific research gives us insight into why the fundamental state of leadership is important, what its characteristics are, how it influences others, and how to formulate questions that can help us experience it.

These questions are, however, not the only means for experiencing the fundamental state of leadership. When we teach people about the fundamental state of leadership, most people can remember times when they have experienced it, often in moments of crisis. Questions derived from science enable us to experience the fundamental state of leadership intentionally, and we offer other potential questions as well.

This book is rich in scientific detail, but it is not possible to include every detail. We try to make the research that we share as practical and as engaging as possible. Therefore, in addition to using science to explain the fundamental state of leadership, we provide practical illustrations: stories from our own lives and from the lives of people we know.[4] We take you into corporate offices where executives make decisions that affect the lives of thousands of people, and into our living rooms where we make decisions that affect our families. We take you into community organizations where people work to help others, and into the library where we study alone. We take you onto the basketball court and into neighborhoods; on television shows and into classrooms; into the marketplace and onto the front lawn. We take you to all of these places to illustrate how leadership matters in most situations. We have also included exercises for personal application at the end of chapters 1, 4, 6, 8, and 10; these exercises contain lists of practical ideas. We want the book to be interesting and useful to people who want to lead, whatever their circumstances may be.

Chasing the Shouting Wind Along; Or, Writing the Second Edition

Kendara, an MBA student, was taking Ryan's class on leadership. As part of the class study, she had to read the first edition of this book and had to pick specific times to practice leadership every week. (We describe this learning process in chapter 12.) By the time Kendara got to the penultimate week, she said that she had only applied the leadership principles to "some simple issue, never really using it on something 'serious,'" and she had no intention to do so. She had a serious matter weighing on her mind when she sat down to complete that week's reading assignment, however: she needed to let her boss know that her workload exceeded her capacity. She had a meeting scheduled to discuss it, but Kendara had spent the entire morning wondering if her boss would think that she was incompetent and her career would be ruined.

As Kendara read her assignment from the book that morning, she said that it was like a lightbulb had turned on. She focused on her boss's concerns instead of her own, had a clear intuition about what she should say, and walked into the meeting with confidence. She laid out her points. In turn, Kendara's boss said she was impressed, and that it took a big person to admit being in over her head. Because Kendara had been honest with her, the boss now felt more comfortable trusting her. Kendara, in turn, left the meeting energized, relieved, and confident about her career prospects.

Kendara's story illustrates why we wrote a new edition of this book and is itself a metaphor for this second edition. Kendara's story is a story of second chances. Other students in her class had used the first edition of *Lift* to address serious leadership challenges and had benefited from doing so. Kendara did not mention any negative feelings toward the book and its principles, but when she gave the book a second chance, this helped her approach her class assignments more productively. In turn, her boss gave her a second chance, and everyone involved was better off for these second chances.

For the past six years, people have read and used this book, and we have used this book in our teaching and consulting, and many of the reports we have received suggest that it has had a positive effect. At the same time we have also learned many things about the book, and about teaching these principles, that suggest that if we give this book its own second chance we can enhance the positive impact it has upon the world. As Kendara's story and many others suggest, we have been pleased with the book's impact. But we do think that we can further enhance the book and its impact; hence this second edition.

The changes we have made are threefold. First, we have made hundreds of little revisions throughout the book: we clarified a point of research here, explained a story more fully there, and otherwise used six years of feedback to improve little things about the book in every way we could. Second, we added two new chapters. Chapter 12 provides a description of a method for teaching leadership that we have developed, refined, and digitized in the years since the first edition was published. We are seeing all kinds of exciting possibilities open up with regard to this learning method, and we wanted to share it with readers. In the new chapter 13 we have described some of our own personal learning that has occurred since the first edition was published. This has been one of the most delightful things about the first edition: how much learning it has created in us and in others.

The third major change was to clarify throughout that this is a book about leadership. To do this, we changed the subtitle, changed language, and even added icons to the chapters to help readers stay clear about the overall purpose of the book even when they are reading detailed chapter accounts. In the first edition we used the word *influence* more than *leadership* because we were worried that some people might not think of themselves as leaders, and therefore might not see the book as relevant. In this second edition we have decided to focus more squarely on leadership because we do in fact use this book to train and develop leaders, we offer a new and unique perspective on leadership, and we want everyone to rise to the call of leadership, whether it be in the boardroom or on the factory floor, in the company or in the home, on the sports field or in the backyard. As the subtitle of the first edition suggested, we want to help anyone and everyone to be a positive force in any situation. As the subtitle of this new edition suggests, we want people to realize that the choice to be a positive influence is a choice to lead.

CHAPTER 1

THE FUNDAMENTAL STATE OF LEADERSHIP

Ron, a colleague of ours, became a bit of a legend in his company after only a few months of working there. Like many of the executives in his company, Ron got projects done well and on time. Unlike many of these executives, Ron's employees loved working together and were excited about their projects, even if they began the projects disagreeing with each other. Some executives managed to push their projects through in spite of problems and disagreements; some executives managed to work well with people but did not accomplish quite as much. In contrast, Ron's leadership always increased harmony while bringing exceptional results. He became one of the most influential people in his company.

One day Ron walked out of a staffing meeting and said something that surprised his coworkers. The meeting had occurred in a stuffy, windowless room at the end of a long week; Ron and everyone else in the group had felt grumpy. They had discussed whether or not people from other units in the business should be moved into Ron's department. He did not want anyone else transferred in, so Ron argued his point and won; it seemed like a normal business meeting. Yet when Ron walked out, he told his coworkers, "I have given away my power."

Ron's coworkers did not believe him. He was one of the most influential people in the company, and he had gotten what he wanted out of the staffing meeting. How could he have given his power away? Even Ron could not answer this question, but he could tell that something had changed and that his ability to lead had changed as a result.

A Different Kind of Power

When Ron was one of the most influential people in his company, his leadership did not depend on a position of authority. And when he "lost his power" his formal authority had not changed. Leadership may be exercised by a CEO who is trying to implement a strategic change in a multinational corporation, but it could also be exercised by a player on a soccer team who inspires his teammates to play less selfishly, a teacher who motivates the children in her class to exceed all standards of academic proficiency, a father who stirs a desire in his children to cooperate with each other, or an employee who convinces her boss to change a policy that impedes her colleagues from giving their best performance.

Many scholars agree that leadership does not depend on position. They define leadership as a process of social influence that involves determining collective goals, motivating goal pursuit, and developing or maintaining the group and culture.[1] We agree that leadership is a process of social influence and that it often involves setting goals and motivating people to pursue those goals. However, we also propose one implicit difference and one explicit difference from this definition. Implicitly, this definition of leadership suggests that leadership is intentional. In this book we show how leadership also involves motivating people without intending to, and sometimes even involves motivating them to do things that we never intended to motivate them to do. Sometimes our leadership is intentional, but it may not always be so. For example, Ron sometimes took action in which he intended to create productivity and harmony, but other times the people he inspired came up with ideas of their own that were much better than what Ron thought they would do.

We also propose an explicit difference from the standard definition of leadership. In particular, we propose that leadership occurs when people *choose to follow* someone who *deviates* from at least one accepted cultural norm or social convention. If a person complies with accepted norms, that person is not blazing a new trail but is simply following convention. And even if the person breaks cultural norms, if no one follows that person there is no leadership. Leadership challenges convention *and* inspires others to follow. The impact of such leadership is most positive and effective when cultural deviations inspire people to enhance their ethical contributions and the welfare of the people who hold a stake in the situation. We often saw this in Ron—before the grumpy staffing meeting—when he would take action that defied what people accepted as possible, appropriate, or real. Defying accepted conventions can offend or alienate others, but when people understood the intentions and effects of Ron's actions, they often contributed to his efforts, rather than feel offended or alienated.

Most of us, when we want to lead, use rational arguments, appeals to duty, rewards, punishments, or any number of other tactics to try to persuade others.[2] Sometimes these approaches succeed, and if they succeed we often feel satisfied. But most of us have also experienced moments of exceptional leadership—moments such as Ron's—even if these moments were fleeting. And because of these experiences our intuition tells us that more is possible even if it feels elusive. This elusiveness is the feeling Ron experienced at the end of the staffing meeting.

Ron got what he wanted in the staffing meeting, but he did not feel satisfied. He struggled to explain his feelings. The tactics he used in the staffing meeting worked, but he also began to see that he had created "collateral damage." In contrast with his usual experience in the company, at the end of the staffing meeting people felt hurt and relationships had suffered. People felt weighed down rather than lifted up, and because they did not feel committed to the decisions made in the meeting, the same problems may reemerge. Although Ron had wielded influence successfully, he wanted to be a leader again. He wanted the kind of social influence that comes from challenging a cultural norm in a way that inspires others to want to participate in pursuing a meaningful, collective good. He could tell that he had "lost" the ability to do this because something had changed inside him, but he could not explain why. All he could think to say was that he "was in a different place."

Psychological States

Ron learned later that the different place he was in was a different psychological state. A *psychological state* is a current, temporary condition of our mind. It is the pattern of thoughts and feelings we experience at a given point in time.

A person's psychological state can be simple or complex. A simple psychological state, for example, could be described by a single emotion, such as "happy" or "sad." A complex psychological state can include many thoughts and emotions at the same time. For example, if a teenager receives an invitation to take the last spot on the school soccer team but received the invitation because a good friend was kicked off the team, then that teenager's psychological state might involve a complex blend of happiness about the good news, a resolve to succeed, concern for her friend's feelings, fear of the challenge, and guilt for accepting the position.

Scientists who study psychological states seek to understand what kind of states people experience, what leads people to experience particular states, and how these particular states influence other people. This last question is particularly important; as researchers come to understand the answers to it, they are discovering that our psychological states can influence other people in surprising and sometimes even dramatic ways.

Bill, a colleague of ours, told us a personal story that is a good example of this. Bill and his mother did not get along, let alone enjoy each other's company. It had been this way for a long time. In any situation Bill knew what his mother would say, he knew how he would respond, and he knew how the argument would unfold. He hated it, but he could not stop himself.

Bill went to a retreat and ended up working with a counselor. The goal was to improve his relationship with his mother. After much effort he began to feel more positively toward his mother. By the end of the retreat he was anxious to see her. He reports the following experience:

> I took a deep breath and walked into the kitchen. I saw her before she saw me. I thought about the sacrifices she made and how much I loved her. She turned and looked at me. She opened her mouth. My stomach tightened and I thought, "Here it comes." She paused and smiled. Then she went on with what she was doing. I was stunned. That was not what she was supposed to do. I was different and now she was different. From then on the relationship totally changed. I had not said a word, but I was different, and somehow she sensed it.[3]

Bill's relationship with his mother changed without his saying a word because Bill was in a different psychological state. At the retreat he had worked hard to consciously appreciate her positive characteristics and the sacrifices she had made over many years. This less angry and more loving orientation was probably communicated in his facial expression, his posture, and other nonverbal ways. These nonverbal signals of love and appreciation provided Bill's mother with a new set of cues to interpret. When people receive unexpected cues from others—particularly unexpected emotional cues—they have to make sense of them in new ways.[4] Thus, without saying a word to his mother, Bill had begun to construct a new relationship. The change in his relationship began with a change in his psychological state.

Our psychological states, whether they influence others positively or negatively, do so in at least four ways:

1. Our facial expressions, body language, and tone of voice send new and unexpected cues that people interpret and react to in new and different ways.

2. The emotions that are part of our psychological states are contagious. In other words, people often unconsciously mimic and then adopt our feelings.[5]

3. Psychological states sometimes lead us to make different decisions or act in different ways than we would if we had been in a different psychological state, and other people are influenced by these decisions and actions.[6]

4. When we take different actions and perform them in different ways, we also generate different results—results that may be more or less effective, creative, or beneficial. People pay attention to and try to make sense of unusual results.[7]

Ron's leadership exhibited all of these forms of influence. For example, when Ron felt positive, his coworkers had to make sense of his positive feelings—especially when Ron was positive during difficult times. The energy he brought to his activities was contagious, and it lifted others. Because of how he felt toward others, he might listen carefully in situations where others would feel compelled to argue their points. And because he achieved exceptional results, people wanted to learn from him or be a part of his team.

Our psychological states influence other people, and their psychological states influence us; we are relational beings.[8] Our psychological states are the sum of who we are at a given moment as we play out the stories of our lives in relation to others. Therefore, who we are at any time depends on who the people around us are, and who they are depends on who we are. The psychological state that Ron experienced in the staffing meeting affected how he experienced himself and acted as a manager, a coworker, and a friend. It also affected how positively other people experienced themselves in similar roles.

Typically, the influence that we exert upon each other tends to reinforce the conventions and norms to which we are already accustomed. However, if we experience a positive psychological state that defies some convention or norm, we may lead people into entirely new ways of relating and performing.

Our purpose in this book is to propose a specific psychological state that can make us a positive influence upon those around us in any situation. We call this the *fundamental state of leadership*. When we experience the fundamental state of leadership, we tend to lift both ourselves and those around us.

Learning to Lift with Mason

When people experience the fundamental state of leadership, they are purpose-centered, internally directed, other-focused, and externally open. To understand each of these characteristics, we share a story about Ryan and his son Mason that illustrates both what the fundamental state of leadership is and what it is not. Ryan begins this story in a normal psychological state. A normal psychological state is not bad; it is simply common. Sometimes a normal state leads to negative influence, and sometimes it does not, but it does not achieve the same type of influence that comes from the fundamental state of leadership. In this story Ryan experiences a change from the normal state to the fundamental state of leadership.

> **Ryan:** Shortly before Mason turned six years old he and I fell into an unhealthy pattern. Mason would do something wrong, such as provoke his sister or refuse to clean up. In response, I would tell him that I would put him in a time-out. He would scream, "I hate you! I wish you weren't part of our family! Go away and never come back!" I would then try to calm him down and explain why he should clean up or leave his sister alone and why the time-out was the consequence. In spite of this, Mason would scream more and sometimes even hit me. Often I would have to pick him up and take him to his bedroom kicking and screaming. I had no idea how to break out of this pattern.
>
> One reason Mason and I were unable to break out of this pattern was that I was treating Mason's behavior as a problem; I did not like Mason's tantrums and I wanted him to behave the way he had before. His old

behaviors were comfortable for me: I was *comfort-centered*. This desire to stay comfortable is a characteristic of a normal psychological state. In my desire for comfort I never considered that perhaps Mason was behaving differently because of changes that had happened in his life, such as starting kindergarten. If his circumstances were different, that meant that my circumstances were different as well. Trying to make people behave the same way under new circumstances is often not the most appropriate way to influence them.

Eventually, I decided to become more *purpose-centered* with Mason. This focus on purpose is one characteristic of the fundamental state of leadership. Instead of trying to make Mason behave as he had before, I asked myself what result I wanted to create. I decided that my purpose was to help Mason learn how to make responsible choices of his own volition. Once I made this decision, I was no longer interested in whether he was behaving in a way with which I was comfortable. Instead, I was wondering how I could help Mason learn to make responsible choices.

As I thought about this I realized that Mason was already making many responsible choices. He often made responsible choices, for example, when he was clear about what the consequences of his choices were in advance. He was also better at making these choices when my wife Amy or I had spent quality time with him that day. Based on these insights, I changed the way I interacted with Mason. I tried to anticipate opportunities for Mason to make decisions—such as when bedtime was approaching or when it was time to clean up—and I made a point of helping him understand his options and the consequences of each option in advance. Then I would let him make his own decisions. I also made an explicit effort to spend more quality time with him.

My efforts to help Mason understand his choices and consequences and to spend more time with him improved the situation somewhat. He appreciated the time I spent with him, and in some cases made better choices. But, there were still times when I was not able to anticipate decisions ahead of time, when he made poor choices even when he understood the consequences, or when I was not able to spend as much time with him as I would have liked. In situations such as these he threw tantrums when he had to do many of the things I asked him to do.

Another change came to my psychological state one day when Mason started to badger me about something while I was changing his little sister's diaper. I was fully occupied and told him to wait. Suddenly, it occurred to me that I was not willing to let him interrupt me, and yet when he was doing something, I had no problem telling him to stop what he was doing. Sometimes this was legitimate, but often there was no reason why I had to insist that he stop what he was doing at that moment. It became clear to me that my impatience was the cause of many of his tantrums. This lack of patience and respect was a sign that I was *externally directed*. External direction is a characteristic of a normal psychological state. When people are externally directed, they let circumstances (such as the drive to interrupt Mason to get him to do what I want) drive their behavior instead of their values (such as patience and respect).

When I realized that I was being externally directed, I decided that I would become *internally directed*. Internal direction is a characteristic of the fundamental state of leadership in which people experience the dignity and integrity that comes with exercising the self-control necessary to live up to the values that they expect of others. In Mason's case I became internally directed by showing him and his activities the same respect that I wanted from him. For example, when it came to interrupting one of his activities, I would ask him how much time he needed to finish what he was doing, and then ask him to do the chore that I wanted him to do after he had completed the activity. As I showed Mason increased patience and respect, his tantrums decreased significantly.

One day while I was making dinner for Mason and his sister Katie, I offered to read him a book while he ate. Mason was excited. When I put the meal on the table, though, Mason started hoarding the food, leaving Katie with none. Katie started to cry. I asked him why he was hoarding the food; I tried to help him understand his choices and the consequences that would result from each choice. Even so, he just screamed at me, saying that he would not be my friend anymore. I was shocked by the intensity of his reaction. I was planning to spend time with him; I was trying to help him see his choices and consequences; I was trying to show him patience and respect. I did not know what to do. In spite of all of my efforts, Mason was screaming again. Bewildered and exasperated, I almost told Mason to stop immediately or I would put him in a time-out.

When I was about to threaten Mason with the time-out I felt *self-focused* and *internally closed*. Focusing on ourselves and closing ourselves off to feedback are characteristics of a normal psychological state. When we are self-focused, we are concerned only with our own needs, feelings, and wants. We see other people as objects that either help us or impede us in our goals. In my case, Mason was an object that was preventing me from my goal of showing that I was a good father.

When we are internally closed we ignore and deny feedback, such as the feedback that I was getting from Mason that said all my efforts to show that I was a good dad were not working. We ignore or deny feedback out of fear that the feedback says something about our worth as human beings. Because of this fear, and the frustration I felt, my first instinct was to get angry.

In my anger I was about to threaten Mason with a time-out. Before I did, however, I remembered my purpose: to teach Mason how to make responsible choices. I also remembered that in my previous efforts with Mason I thought I was doing the right thing and yet I was not showing him the respect I wanted him to show me. I had been at least somewhat wrong in those situations, and I could be wrong here as well. So, just as I was about to react, I caught myself and considered the possibility that I might be wrong here as well. And as I opened myself to that possibility, I also opened myself up to what Mason was feeling, and to what his needs might be. I became *other-focused*.

A focus on others' needs and feelings is another characteristic of the fundamental state of leadership. When we focus on others we feel empathy and desire to be compassionate. When I focused on Mason, I realized that Mason's screaming was rather extreme. He must be hurting, I felt, to have such an extreme reaction. Maybe his lashing out was the only way he knew to deal with some pain he felt inside, and if Mason was hurting inside I wanted to know why. I was no longer interested in proving I was a good father. Instead I wanted to understand why Mason might be hurting. And once I realized this, my desire to avoid feedback disappeared; I wanted feedback so that I could learn why Mason was feeling this way. Instead of being *internally closed*, I became *externally open*.

Openness to external cues—to feedback—is the final characteristic of the fundamental state of leadership. When we are open to these cues we learn, grow, and adapt ourselves to the situation unfolding before us. In my experience with Mason, my focus on purpose, my commitment to act respectfully, my empathy, and my desire to learn from feedback created an entirely new situation. And because I was in a new situation, paying attention to new cues, the unconscious, automatic part of my brain began noticing new patterns in those cues and coming up with new responses faster than the controlled, conscious part of my brain. In other words, I began to have a feeling—an intuition—about what I should do.[9] The intuition I felt was to read to Mason anyway.

My conscious reaction to this unconscious intuition was to think that reading to Mason was a crazy idea. Why would I want to reinforce his bad behavior? Somehow, though, it felt like the right thing to do, so I took a chance. I sat down and asked Mason if he would still like me to read to him.

My question to Mason was honest. It was not an attempt to bribe him into letting Katie have her share of the food. I could make more food for Katie or find another way to make her happy if I needed to. If Mason said yes and listened to the story without sharing the food, I would have found another solution for Katie. I was acting on how I genuinely felt at that moment.

When I offered to read the story to Mason he melted. He found a piece of paper and a crayon and wrote, "I AM SORY. I AM YOUR FREND. I WANT TO BE YOUR FREND." He handed me the paper. I told him that of course we were friends. Mason threw his arms around my neck and burst into tears. Then he let Katie have her share of the food. I read him the book while they ate their dinner.

I am not sure why he responded the way he did; I suspect that Mason, who was not even six years old at the time, could not have explained it himself. Perhaps he felt guilty because he knew what he was doing was wrong but he was scared to admit it. Perhaps he wanted to feel he had control over his own life, and once he knew he had control he no longer felt a need to exert it. Perhaps he simply needed to feel loved. Maybe it was all of the above.

Based on the scientific research that we will discuss throughout this book, I believe that Mason wanted to change because I connected with his deepest feelings and helped him work through those feelings in a purposeful, respectful way—even if neither of us could put those feelings into words. What I know for sure is that in a normal psychological state, my intuition was to punish Mason, but when I experienced the fundamental state of leadership, my intuition was to read to him. By acting on that intuition, I changed my relationship with my son. Offering to read to him was only a part of what inspired Mason to change. Offering to read a book, or to do any nice thing, may not inspire any change in another situation. In fact, in a different situation I might have had an intuition to punish Mason for his behavior. The intuition was less about what I *did*, and more about who I *was*.

In the weeks following this event, Mason's tantrums ended almost completely. Sometimes he still did things that I wished he would not do, but his behavior improved and so did mine. I still sometimes act in ways that are comfort-centered, externally driven, self-focused, or internally closed, but I am learning how to experience the fundamental state of leadership more often. When I do, Mason tends to be lifted by my efforts, as do I.

The fundamental state of leadership, as illustrated in the story of Ryan's relationship with Mason, is a psychological state in which a person is (1) centered on purpose, (2) directed by internal values, (3) focused on the feelings and needs of others, and (4) open to external cues that make learning, growth, and adaptation possible. We named this book *Lift* because this is what happens when people experience the fundamental state of leadership: they lift their own thoughts, feelings, actions, and outcomes and, in turn, those of others. Lifting ourselves and lifting others are interrelated experiences. We are unlikely to lift others without lifting ourselves, and we are unlikely to lift ourselves without lifting others.

The changes we need to make in order to experience the fundamental state of leadership depend upon our current situation. We may experience the state and lift others in one situation, but then the situation changes and we, like Ron, suddenly discover that we are no longer experiencing it. New circumstances often pull us into more normal psychological states, where we focus on problems rather than purpose, react to our circumstances rather than use our values to drive our behaviors, dwell on our own agendas rather than empathize with others, and avoid the feedback that could enable us to learn and grow. When we do, we weigh people down rather than lift them up. The circumstances of everyday life create strong pressure to fall back into normal states, even after the most uplifting of experiences. Even so, scientific research and practical experience teach us how to lift ourselves and others once again. Based on this research, we offer four questions that we each can use to lift ourselves and others, becoming a positive force in any situation.

The Four Questions

Ron struggled to explain his claim that he had given his power away, but he was unable to do so. He knew things intuitively that he could not explicitly explain. A few weeks after the meeting Ron attended a training program for business executives titled "Leading the Positive Organization." In this program he learned about an area of research called positive organizational scholarship that examines the best of organizations and the best of human behavior in organizations.[10] It is similar to positive psychology, in which researchers seek to understand positive emotions, strengths, and virtues and how human strengths can contribute to better communities.[11] The professors and participants in the training program that Ron attended discussed topics such as how to create a culture that helps organizations and their people to thrive, tools for fostering high-quality relationships in the workplace, ways to energize the organization, and new ways to think about positive leadership. Ron learned about the fundamental state of leadership in this program.

The fundamental state of leadership drew Ron's attention because he recognized it in his own experience: such a state of leadership was the "place" that he was no longer in, and was the "power" that he had given up. He also recognized that the reason he had experienced the fundamental state of leadership so often in his work prior to the staffing meeting was that a series of difficult life events had pushed him to rise to the occasion and be his best self. This worried him; what if he could only experience the fundamental state of leadership when critical circumstances called him to do so? What about the rest of his work and life? Given this concern, Ron felt empowered when he learned four questions, developed from scientific research, that could help him experience the fundamental state of leadership in any situation:

1. **What result do I want to create?** When people answer this question they become less comfort-centered and more purpose-centered.
2. **What would my story be if I were living the values I expect of others?** When people answer this question they become less externally directed and more internally directed.
3. **How do others feel about this situation?** When people answer this question they become less self-focused and more other-focused.
4. **What are three or more strategies I could try in learning how to accomplish my purpose?** When people answer this question they become less internally closed and more externally open.

These are not magic questions. There are other questions, methods, or circumstances that can also help you experience the fundamental state of leadership. We offer examples of such questions in table 1.1. But we use these four questions throughout this book because they are carefully worded to reflect the scientific understanding we have of this psychological state. Our purpose for writing this book is to give you these questions. When people ask and answer them, they tend to move out of a normal psychological state and into the fundamental state of leadership, lifting themselves and others.

When Ron learned that he could experience the fundamental state of leadership by answering the four questions, he began using them to experience the state as often as possible. For example, after the training, Ron was supposed to attend a meeting in which he and his coworkers would make decisions about employee pay. These decisions were more complicated than usual because Ron's company had just been acquired by another company. The two companies had different forms and procedures for paying people, but there were no directions about

TABLE 1.1

Alternate Questions for Experiencing the Fundamental State of Leadership

Becoming Purpose-Centered

What result do I want to create?
What is my highest purpose for this situation?
What goal would be the most challenging and engaging?
What outcome would be most meaningful to me?
What would be the most ambitious and exciting goal I could pursue?

Becoming Internally Directed

What would my story be if I were living up to the values I expect of others?
What would I do if I had 10% more integrity than I have right now?
How can I live my core values in this situation?
What could I do right now to be more authentic?
If I were not worried about negative consequences, what would be the right thing to do?

Becoming Other-Focused

How do others feel about this situation?
What might be the deepest, unmet needs of those who care about this situation?
How could I explain others' behavior if I assume that they think they are good people?
How would I feel about others if I could empathize with their truest selves?
How and what could I sacrifice for the common good?

Becoming Externally Open

What are three or more strategies I could try in learning how to accomplish my purpose?
What would I do differently if I were heeding all of the relevant feedback for this situation?
How would I act if I were not concerned about my role, expertise, or need for control?
How might I approach this situation if I saw it as an opportunity to learn?
How might I approach this situation if I saw it as an adventure with challenges to overcome?
How could I reframe negative outcomes as feedback from which I should learn?

how to handle the different forms and procedures. In fact, these forms and procedures were just one of many problems caused by the acquisition of Ron's company. There were no instructions for dealing with any of these problems, and Ron's boss—who was their contact with the parent company—was afraid to ask for directions. Ron worried that all these problems would make the compensation meeting a frustrating waste of time.

Ron prepared himself for the meeting by asking himself the four questions. The agenda for the meeting was to decide how to pay employees, but this agenda was problem-focused given the companies' conflicting procedures and lack of direction. When Ron asked himself the first question, he decided that the result he wanted to create was to come up with an approach for working with the new company regarding how to pay employees that people in both companies could stand behind and work on together.

Ron then asked himself the second question, determined not to react automatically and get frustrated with people while he was in the meeting. When he did he realized that the value that he expected from his boss was candor: he wanted his boss to have a straight conversation with the people in the other company so that they could find out what they needed to know. As a result, he decided that he should speak to his boss with as much candor as he expected the boss to speak with when he met with people in the parent company.

When Ron asked himself the third question he stopped seeing his boss (and others in the meeting) as either tools to help him achieve his goals or as obstacles preventing him from doing so. Instead he empathized with the pressure that his boss probably felt in approaching the people in the company that had just acquired theirs. Because of this empathy he wanted to support his boss as well as to be frank with him.

When Ron asked the fourth question, he stopped worrying about what feedback he might get for taking initiative in the meeting, or what feedback he and his coworkers might receive from the other company. Instead he was open to using many different strategies for developing new approaches to paying employees and was eager to learn which approach might be the best.

When Ron entered the meeting, his boss began to work through his agenda. He suggested that the group should make the best decisions they could with the information they had. Ron asked if he could stop the meeting. He asked if the group could discuss what they needed to achieve that afternoon. He suggested that the group try to come up with an approach for paying employees that would work out well for both companies and their employees in the long run. As they did this, Ron's boss remembered new and relevant information that he learned from the parent company but had forgotten to share. This helped the group to more clearly adapt and specify what additional information it needed to move forward. Once the group was clear about what it needed, Ron's boss agreed to ask the managers in the parent company for more information. When he talked to the managers from the acquiring company, the conversation went well. They were impressed by the boss's clarity and objectives.

Before Ron's boss brought their questions to the managers in the other company, Ron and his colleagues had believed that the managers from the acquiring company displayed a demeaning attitude toward them. After Ron's boss talked to these managers, however, the feeling changed. Employees from the acquiring company began to invite people from Ron's company to give input and to help them design the integration of the two companies.

Ron was thrilled by this experience and others like it. He now uses the four questions on a regular basis. He is increasingly purpose-centered, internally directed, other-focused, and externally open, lifting himself, his coworkers, and his organization.

Anyone can do what Ron did. Social science and practical experiences help us understand how people can lift themselves and others, how people can experience this more often, why asking these four questions can change a person's psychological state, and how one person's psychological state influences that of other people. Our first step in learning the answers to these questions begins with a description of the metaphor behind the science we present and an explanation for why the four characteristics are all necessary for a person to lift themselves and others. This step of the journey occurs in chapter 2.

FUNDAMENTAL STATE OF LEADERSHIP PRACTICES

Sometimes during the swirl of daily life people struggle to pause and ask themselves the four questions or to remember what they are. Here are some suggestions that people have used to deal with these challenges:

1. **Identify critical activities and schedule a preparation time.** One of our colleagues decided that he wanted to be a positive leader in his meetings at work. On his calendar he scheduled ten minutes before every meeting to ask himself the four questions. We can use the same principle in any recurring activity. You can also do this using the Breakthrough tool on Lift Exchange (http://www.liftexchange.com/breakthrough). This tool enables you to join either a public and free or private and paid community of people who practice the fundamental state of leadership, to make plans, to report on your efforts, and learn from others' reports.

2. **Put a coin in your shoe.** Another way to remember to pause and ask the four questions is to create a spontaneous reminder. You could put a coin in your shoe and ask the four questions whenever you feel the coin move. You could also wear a bracelet, a ring, or tie a string around your finger.

3. **Pay attention to tense emotions.** If we feel strong, tense emotions like anger or fear, and we are not facing any physical danger, then there is a good chance that our influence in that situation will not be positive. Strong, tense emotions are often a good signal for telling us when we should stop and ask the four questions.

4. **Print the four questions on an index card.** If you have trouble remembering the questions, you can print them out on a card. Carry it with you in a wallet or purse, or tape it to your computer or your refrigerator.

5. **Give other people permission to call you out.** If it is hard to be a positive influence in particular types of situations, and there are people you trust who are often involved in those situations, tell them about your desire to be a more positive influence. Give them permission to ask you to pause if they think you are in that type of situation and you are not being a positive influence. This technique not only has the advantage of helping you to pause but can also help you to be more accountable for the influence you have on others. It can help other people feel like it is okay to learn from mistakes because of the example you are setting.

6. Use a mnemonic. You can also use a LIFT mnemonic to remember the questions, such as:

List strategies: "What are three or more strategies I could try in learning how to accomplish my purpose?"

Increase integrity: "What would my story be if I were living the values I expect of others?"

Feel empathy: "How do others feel about this situation?"

Think of results: "What result do I want to create?"

Legacy: "What result do I want to create?"

If . . . : "What would my story be if I were living the values I expect of others?"

Feelings: "How do others feel about this situation?"

Tactics: "What are three or more strategies I could try in learning how to accomplish my purpose?"

CHAPTER 2

THE LIFT METAPHOR

Bob: When I was in my second year of college I became increasingly depressed. When I realized what was happening I decided to find some direction in my life. I started by trying to determine my major. Despite months of agonizing, I made little progress.

One day I was walking across campus when a question popped into my mind: "What is the most meaningful thing you have ever done?" I knew the answer instantly. During my life I had had a number of opportunities to help other people make significant and positive changes in their personal lives. These experiences were the most meaningful things I had done. A moment passed, and then something inside me said, "Major in *change*."

That was a great answer. The only problem was that there was no major in change. I wrestled with this problem, and eventually approached my education differently. I became proactive. I read books that were not assigned, I went to public lectures, and I took classes from many fields that I thought would help me understand change. My formal major eventually became sociology, but I graduated with a body of knowledge about how to help people change. Then I went to graduate school and focused on this same question as it related to groups and organizations. I studied change, taught change, and helped people and organizations make change. As I did these things I realized that I was not interested in change for change's sake; I wanted to understand how people and organizations change for the better. To do this I needed to understand why some organizations, groups, and people were more effective than others, including why some people were more effective in leading more positively than others.

Bob's experience in discovering his passion was the beginning of our process for discovering the ideas that led us to develop the concept of the fundamental state of leadership. In this chapter we will describe how we have learned through our research, teaching, and professional practice to conceive of leadership in terms of psychological states, and to bring together what we have learned into the concept of the fundamental state of leadership. We use the work and the principles of Orville and Wilbur Wright as metaphors for our own work and principles. The Wright brothers' efforts to build an airplane are similar to our own efforts. And the four principles used to harness the aerodynamic force of lift mirror the four characteristics of the fundamental state of leadership that socially and psychologically lift us and the people around us.

Four Principles for Harnessing Lift

Orville and Wilbur Wright began their quest to develop a manned, sustainable, heavier-than-air flying machine in 1896.[1] They were running a small chain of successful bicycle shops when they heard that Otto Lilienthal, a German engineer who built and successfully flew manned gliders, had died while flying. Lilienthal's death was a shock to the world, because "the flying man" had been studying aeronautics for over two decades, had amassed extensive experimental data in his "lift tables," and had made two thousand brief flights in sixteen different gliders. The Wright brothers wondered why a man as knowledgeable and experienced as Lilienthal had died; they were also restless to expand their work beyond their bicycle shops.

The Wright brothers' research into aeronautics began in earnest in 1899, when they requested all of the information that the Smithsonian Institution could provide them on flying and began devouring materials on the topic. They learned that to build a machine that could harness the power of lift the machine would need

1. forward *motion*
2. through the *air*
3. *properly designed wings*
4. flight controls—a means of *adapting* to flight conditions

Scientists discovered the first two principles centuries before the Wright brothers began working on the problem: if the particles of a fluid substance such as air move over the top of an object at a faster rate than the particles moving under the bottom of the object, then the particles under the bottom of the object put pressure on the object, lifting it upward.

Lilienthal worked extensively on the third principle, compiling data on how different wing designs would generate different degrees of lift. Lilienthal's problem, however, came from trying to adapt to the changes that occurred in the air. Airplanes need to achieve a degree of stability while in the air, but the circumstances in the air often change. Airplanes, then, must adapt to these changes. Lilienthal tried to solve this problem by moving his body around on the surface of the glider. This was an unreliable means of adapting, so it was here where the Wright brothers began to focus their attention.

Many scientists and enthusiasts in the Wright brothers' day thought that flying machines would achieve stability through features of the machines' design. They did not think that humans could adapt to changes in wind currents swiftly enough. In contrast, the Wright brothers believed that humans could adapt because of their experiences with bicycles, which are unstable yet remain controllable. Thus, to make a flying machine that was unstable but controllable, they would need controls that would allow a pilot to adapt. And because air currents can change along three dimensions (raising one side of the aircraft while lowering the other, raising and lowering the nose of the aircraft, and turning the nose of the aircraft right or left), they would need controls for all three dimensions. The problem was figuring out how to create these controls.

Four Lenses on Organizational Effectiveness

Bob: I can relate to how the Wright brothers felt when they had to figure out how to create controls. When I finished graduate school and took my first job as an assistant professor, I was trying to understand organizational effectiveness. Organizational scholars realized that effectiveness must involve more than one measure of performance, but they did not agree on which measures they should use to determine their effectiveness. To learn how to make a heavier-than-air machine fly, the Wright brothers requested literature to read from the Smithsonian Institution. To solve the problem of understanding and measuring effectiveness, I devoured the research literature on organizational effectiveness. Reading the literature from the Smithsonian led the Wright brothers to realize that a heavier-than-air machine would not be able to fly until the problem of flight controls had been addressed. Reading the literature on organizational effectiveness led me to realize that we could not understand what makes organizations effective if we could not even agree on what effectiveness was. The Wright brothers recognized the need to reframe the problem as one of building an unstable-but-controllable machine, but they had to figure out how. I recognized the need to think differently about effectiveness, but I did not know how.

The Wright brothers found the inspiration they needed to solve one of the problems when Wilbur was absent-mindedly twisting a rectangular cardboard box. As he twisted it he realized that the box retained its stiffness from side to side. If that was true of a cardboard box, then it would also be true of the wings of a biplane. If one set of wings met the oncoming air at a different angle than the wings on the other side, then each side of the wings would experience a different degree of lift, banking the aircraft to one side or the other and enabling the pilot to maintain balance and to turn the aircraft. The Wright brothers built a large model aircraft with this design and flew it like a kite in the summer of 1899. To their delight, the model responded to their controls immediately and exactly, suggesting that a full-size aircraft might do the same.

Bob: My colleague John Rohrbaugh and I had an insight that reframed the problem of organizational effectiveness in a way that was similar to the Wright Brothers' reframing of the problem of controlling an unstable airplane. In a conversation with John, I explained that everyone studying organizational effectiveness was using different definitions and measurements. John replied, "Instead of studying organizational effectiveness, why don't you study how people perceive organizational effectiveness?" This idea had never occurred to me. But like Wilbur Wright twisting a cardboard box and coming up with an idea that nobody else had thought of, this new question enabled John and I to come up with an entirely new perspective.

We became excited as we discussed this question. We realized that the effectiveness of an organization depends on who is judging that effectiveness, and that meant that we should study the people who study organizations. This would help us to see if there were any patterns in all of the different claims about what effectiveness was. If there were patterns, then we would be able to have a much more informed conversation about what makes an organization effective and what needs to be done to accomplish that effectiveness.

To study how people perceived effectiveness, John and I identified the criteria that we found in the research literature (such as *profit*, *quality*, or *growth*, as shown in figure 2.1).[2] We asked experts to rate how similar they thought each criterion was to each of the other criteria. Analyzing these ratings we found that all of the criteria could be mapped along two dimensions. One dimension (the vertical line in figure 2.1, labeled "Flexible Structures" in the top half and "Stable Structures" in the bottom half) describes how flexible or stable an organization's structure is. The second dimension (the horizontal line in figure 2.1, labeled "Internal Focus" in the left half and "External Focus" in the right half) describes the degree to which an organization focuses on internal or external issues. When we lay these two dimensions one on top of the other, they create four quadrants: four ways in which we can understand an organization's effectiveness: competitiveness, collaboration, control, and creativity.

The competitiveness lens defines effectiveness in terms of how productive and competitive an organization is, using criteria such as profit, goals, and efficiency.

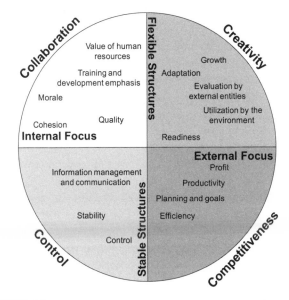

FIGURE 2.1
The Competing Values Framework of Organizational Effectiveness

The collaboration lens defines effectiveness in terms of how collaborative and developmental an organization is, using criteria such as morale, quality, and training.

The control lens defines effectiveness in terms of how reliable and accountable an organization is, using criteria such as information use, stability, and control.

The creativity lens defines effectiveness in terms of how adaptable and innovative an organization is, using criteria such as adaptation, growth, and utilization.

Using these four lenses we can identify the underlying values in anyone's approach to organizational effectiveness and help him or her take a more complete approach. Researchers who studied topics related to effectiveness tended to use many criteria from one lens (such as the competitiveness quadrant), a few criteria from the two lenses next to the first lens (such as the control and creativity quadrants), and no criteria (or almost no criteria) from the opposite quadrant (such as the collaboration quadrant). In other words, we found that most researchers were systematically biased in their beliefs about effectiveness: they would exhibit favoritism for the values represented by one quadrant and prejudice against the values represented by the opposing quadrant, even though values in all four quadrants were positive ones.

We find that most people, without knowing anything about this framework, behave just like the researchers who studied organizational effectiveness. They apply negative labels to values in the quadrants that are on the opposite side of the framework from the values they prefer. For example, people who favor competitive values tend to call collaborative values "soft" or "unproductive," whereas people who favor collaborative values tend to call competitive values "cutthroat" or "selfish." Because of this tendency, we called the framework created by these four lenses the *competing values framework*. Like the Wright brothers after trying their ideas out with their model glider, we were now ready to begin using this framework to help lift people and their organizations to higher levels of effectiveness.

Becoming Scientists

Heartened by successful trials with their model glider, the Wright brothers spent the year between the summer of 1899 and the summer of 1900 building a full-size glider designed for manned flight. The Wright brothers used the research and experimentation of the people who preceded them, but also introduced a number of their own innovations. In addition to designing wings that could "warp" (or twist like Wilbur Wright's box), they also moved the high point of the arc in the wings toward the front edge of the wings and mounted an elevator (a movable horizontal surface) to the front of the glider to help counteract upward or downward pitching. They went to Kitty Hawk, North Carolina, to test their full-size glider because the area had steady winds, wide open spaces, and sandy landing surfaces. They tested the glider a number of times as a kite, and then flew the glider a few times. By the time their stay in Kitty Hawk in the summer of 1900 was complete, the Wright brothers were pleased to learn that many of their designs, including the warping wings, the arc, and the elevator, worked well. The glider did not achieve as much lift as they hoped it would, but it had at least flown three hundred feet.

The amount of lift the aircraft generated seemed to be the only problem. So, based on tables that Otto Lilienthal had created for predicting how much lift a wing would generate, the Wright brothers increased the size and curvature of their wings. They had high expectations for their return to Kitty Hawk in 1901. The results, however, were disappointing; the new glider not only had problems with lift but also problems with its controls—both the elevator and the wing warping. The Wright brothers reduced the arc of the wings, which helped somewhat, but the glider still crashed and Wilbur was thrown into its elevator mechanism, receiving a black eye and bruises. After that, the brothers only flew their glider as a kite. The brothers were baffled by these results, and on the train ride home to Dayton, Ohio, a dejected Wilbur said that he did not think that people would learn to fly in his lifetime—perhaps not even in a thousand years.

When the brothers arrived home there was a letter waiting for them from Octave Chanute, a civil engineer, inviting them to come to Chicago to speak to the Western Society of Engineers. This was an intimidating request; the Wrights had done one thing that no one else had—compared actual flight data with Lilienthal's experimental data—but their flight data did not match the experimental data, and they were not sure why. What would they say to a body of learned scientists?

Just before Wilbur left to give his speech to the society, he and Orville built a wind tunnel out of a soap box and ran some preliminary experiments that convinced them that Lilienthal's tables were wrong. Wilbur gave his talk, which was received well, and upon returning to Dayton he and Orville made a fundamental change in their approach to harnessing lift: they transformed from practitioners (well-read enthusiasts who were trying to build a flying machine) into scientists (systematic empiricists who were trying to understand fundamental principles for harnessing lift). Throughout the winter of 1901–2 they created a better wind tunnel, built as many as two hundred different model wing shapes to test, measured lift and drag more accurately, and ran experiments using these measurements. Based on their experiments they were able to create more accurate tables and equations and designed a glider based on these. As a result, in the summer of 1902 their new glider responded well to its controls, flew over seven hundred times and sometimes for over six hundred feet, allowed them to land safely, and enabled them to develop the most advanced piloting skills in the world. By transforming themselves from practitioners to scientists, they built a fully controllable aircraft.

Becoming a Practitioner

Like the Wright brothers and their glider from the summer of 1900, we were thrilled with the possibilities the competing values framework (CVF) presented. It turned out to be even more useful than we thought it would be. It improved our understanding of organizational effectiveness, but it also helped us to clarify our understanding of leadership, organizational life cycles, culture, presentations, innovation, value creation, and management skills.[3] We also discovered that other scholars with no knowledge of the CVF were developing frameworks that were very similar to it. For example, Paul Lawrence and Nitin Nohria later found that humans have four biologically determined drives (for bonding, learning, acquiring, and defending) that map perfectly onto the quadrants of the CVF.[4] Shalom Schwartz found that cultural values across societies can be mapped onto two dimensions that are nearly identical to the two dimensions of the CVF.[5] Katherine Benziger identified four thinking styles that are similar to the CVF quadrants and mapped them onto activation in the four quadrants of the human brain.[6] Alan Fiske identified four models that people use for relating to others in his review of the anthropological literature of cultures across the earth that are similar to the quadrants of the CVF.[7]

And philosopher Ken Wilbur's *A Theory of Everything* posits that the whole universe can be summarized in a four-quadrant framework that maps nicely into the CVF.[8] We are not so ambitious in our own claims, but we do believe that this converging evidence suggests that there is something fundamental about the CVF.

Social scientists were not the only people who got excited about the competing values framework. Laypeople often come to us as well; they tell us their problems, tell us what they think the solution should be, and express frustration over the fact that their solution is not working. When this happens we often draw a picture of the CVF and show them how the solutions they are proposing fall into only two or three of its quadrants; we then suggest that they try a solution that incorporates values from one of the missing quadrants. More often than not, people understand their omission, see new solutions, and return to work feeling energized about the possibilities.

> **Bob:** I was thrilled with the opportunities that the CVF gave me to help people and organizations change their cultures, develop their leaders, or make strategic decisions. I learned how to help people do this along the way. One of the things I learned was that in order to help people change, I often had to change myself as well. Similarly, I learned that if people wanted their organizations, communities, or families to change they would also need to change themselves. I developed a number of insights into this phenomenon, and eventually decided that I should write a book about it. When I tried to write the book, though, I could not; every time I sat down to write I failed.
>
> At this point I felt like the Wright brothers after the failure of their glider in the summer of 1901. In contrast to the Wright brothers, however, my personal transformation had to occur in the opposite direction: rather than transform from a practitioner to a scientist, I had to transform from a scientist to a practitioner. As I struggled to write a book about the things I was learning, I realized that I was writing a book to help others change, but I was not changing myself. I was trying to write this book academically and scientifically, which was not likely to be interesting or accessible to the people for whom I was writing. I was afraid to write in a way that would be interesting and accessible for

practitioners because I was worried about what my academic colleagues would think of me. Eventually I realized my problem, gathered the courage, and wrote the book in the way that I knew it should be written.

The result for me, as for the Wright brothers, was profound. I named the book *Deep Change*. After it was published I was humbled by how well the book was received; I became flooded with requests from people asking me to help them with their lives and organizations. What was even more meaningful to me was the letters I received from people telling me how the book had changed their lives. That would not have happened if I had given in to my fears. The lessons I had been learning since the day I decided to study change as my college major were beginning to come together.

From a Controllable Glider to Powered Flight

Things began to come together for the Wright brothers when they moved from developing a fully controllable glider to developing a powered aircraft. Between the summer of 1902 and December 1903 the brothers calculated the power that an engine would need to propel their glider through the air and generate enough lift for flight. Along with adding an innovative new engine, they continued to improve the wings, designed and built propellers, and built a launching rail in Kitty Hawk for the now much heavier flying machine. Weather and technical problems provided a few setbacks, but on December 17, 1903, the Wrights made four flights in a fully controllable, heavier-than-air, self-propelled flying machine, including one flight of 852 feet for fifty-nine seconds. The Wright brothers had harnessed the power of lift.

From Deep Change to Lift

In the decade after Bob published *Deep Change*, he and his colleagues drew on the insights of others and a few innovations of their own to add power to the principles they were discovering, much as the Wright brothers had done. During this decade Ryan began a graduate program and eventually became a management professor as well. Also during this decade, both Ryan and Bob had the opportunity to participate in

and to interact with scientists in both the fields of positive psychology and positive organizational scholarship—fields that ask unabashedly positive questions about human beings and human societies. For example, in the field of positive psychology, scholars ask questions about topics such as learned optimism, authentic happiness, optimal experiences, human strengths, and positive emotions. These are unusual topics for a field that has historically focused on depression, disorders, dysfunctions, and decision errors. Similarly, those in the field of positive organizational scholarship study topics such as high-reliability organizations, authentic leadership, psychological safety, high-quality connections, and organizational virtues. Both fields generate exciting insights into how we live and work.

In graduate school Ryan spent much of his time studying psychological states such as energy (a feeling of positive activation) and flow (high performance experiences that people describe with phrases such as "I was in the zone"). Although much of the research on topics such as these focus on how people come to experience these states, Ryan was equally interested in how an individual's subjective experience comes to affect others. As we discussed these types of states we also began to see how some of these states mirrored the quadrants of the competing values framework. We examined whether positive but competing psychological states could be captured by the CVF, and how people integrate these states in their daily experiences. We found that the CVF works very well for this purpose, as shown in figure 2.2. A *purpose-centered* state mapped well onto the competition quadrant because of its focus on results and achievement. An *internally directed state* mapped well onto the control quadrant because of its focus on the self-control required to live with integrity to one's values. An *other-focused* state mapped well onto the collaboration quadrant because of its focus on the feelings and needs of other people. And an *externally open* state mapped well onto the creativity quadrant of the CVF because of its focus on coming up with new approaches and learning from feedback. We began to share this framework with others, and it had a powerful impact,

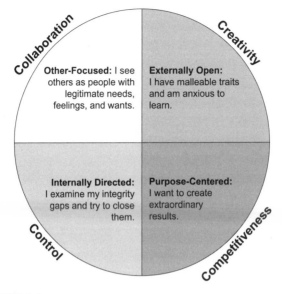

FIGURE 2.2
A Competing Values Framework for Psychological States

as the stories throughout this book illustrate. Evidence from research that Ryan is currently conducting with Bret Crane and Ned Wellman lends further support to the idea of treating leadership as a psychological state and of using questions to help oneself experience these states.[9]

Putting It All Together

The Wright brothers harnessed lift by creating a flying machine that could (1) propel itself forward, (2) through the air, (3) with properly designed wings, and (4) control systems that allowed a pilot to adapt to changing conditions in the air. Our framework of psychological states helps people to harness lift by showing people how to become (1) purpose-centered, (2) other-focused, (3) internally directed, and (4) externally open. Figure 2.3 shows how the aerodynamic principles for harnessing lift serve as a metaphor for the way in which the fundamental

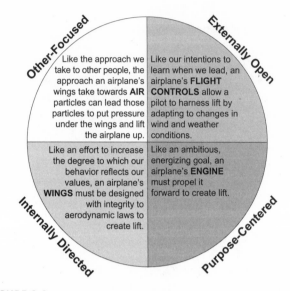

FIGURE 2.3

Psychological States and the Four Aerodynamic Conditions for Lift

state of leadership lifts the person who experiences it and others whom that person influences.

First, when people are purpose-centered, their purposes motivate forward motion, or action, similar to how forward motion is necessary for an airplane to harness the aerodynamic force of lift. Second, when people are internally directed, they act with integrity to their values. This is similar to having wings that are designed in consistency with the appropriate measurements for harnessing lift. Third, the forward motion and wings of an airplane must turn the particles of air through which it passes in the right way, or those particles will not create upward pressure on the bottom of the wings. Turning air particles correctly is similar to being other-focused because people respond to the empathy we feel for them, causing them (or failing to cause them) to be lifted and to lift others in return. Fourth, airplanes' flight controls enable them to adapt to changing air conditions in a manner similar to how a person who is externally open will adapt in response to feedback.

Four Requirements for Positive Influence

When Otto Lilienthal tried to pilot a glider without effective flight controls, he lacked the ability to adjust to changing conditions, crashed, and died. When the Wright brothers used Lilienthal's incorrect tables to design the wings of their glider in the summer of 1901, Wilbur crashed and hurt himself. Without flight controls, properly designed wings, an engine, and air, an airplane is in danger of crashing. Similarly, when a person is not purpose-centered, internally directed, other-focused, and externally open, that person is in danger of exerting negative or neutral influence rather than positive influence.

To understand how these four characteristics of the fundamental state of leadership work together to increase how positive a person's influence is, imagine a real estate agent who is showing homes to a family. If she is purpose-centered, internally directed, and other-focused but not externally open, then even though she wants to find the family a home, acts with honesty and integrity, and wants the family to be happy in their new home she will ignore or deny feedback as the family goes through the process and will be less likely to learn the nuances of what the family wants. If she is not other-focused, she will not care about the family and will place them in the first house she can find that will make her a profit. If she is not internally directed, she will not try to live her professional values, perhaps investing less than her full effort into the project or cutting corners with the family, the sellers, the mortgage broker, or others. If she is not purpose-centered, her work will be less clear and meaningful, making the family's need for a home a problem to be solved rather than an opportunity to contribute to the family's lifestyle, security, and happiness. Any of these omissions can diminish the positivity of the real estate agent's influence.

The reason why omitting characteristics from the fundamental state of leadership would diminish the positivity of our real estate agent's (or anyone else's) influence is that each of the four characteristics of the fundamental state of leadership embodies a particular type of moral

responsibility. They are grounded in prominent moral philosophies. For the sake of accessibility we will not discuss these philosophies in detail, but we will note the connections. For example, the purpose-centered characteristic is grounded in teleology because it involves an inquiry into possible and appropriate ends. The internally directed characteristic is grounded in Aristotle's virtue ethics because of its focus on living our values. The other-focused characteristic is grounded in relational ethics such as Immanuel Kant's categorical imperative and Martin Buber's relational attitudes because of its focus on seeing others as valuable in and of themselves. The externally open characteristic is grounded in pragmatism because of its focus on learning from and adapting to particular situations.[10]

Each moral philosophy brings important insight into our understanding of appropriate ways to be, to act, and to influence others, but each philosophy has also been criticized as having specific weaknesses. The benefit of embedding them in the competing values framework is that it enables us to figure out how, in practical experience, to integrate these philosophies in ways that amplify their benefits while compensating for or overcoming their weaknesses. The philosophies that fall on opposite sides of the CVF represent competing—or even opposing—values. In other words, the externally open characteristic is the opposite of the internally directed characteristic, and the results-centered characteristic is the opposite of the other-focused characteristic. But these are not opposites in the way we normally think of them.

Usually we think of opposites in terms of positive and negative. The CVF, in contrast, suggests that we can have positive opposites. For example, the negative opposite of *humble* is *arrogant*, but the positive opposite of *humble* is *confident*. Similarly, the negative opposite of *confident* is *timid*, whereas the positive opposite of *confident* is *humble*. Confidence and humility are positive; we keep our confidence in check with our humility. Otherwise our confidence might become arrogance and our humility might become timidity.

In a similar way, we need to keep our own desires (the results we want to create when we are purpose-centered) in check with our concern for others (the empathy we feel when we are other-focused) or we will become self-focused, and we need to keep our focus on others in check with our purposes or we will become comfort-centered (trying only to find comfortable solutions to problems that others define for us). The same is true for the relationship between the externally open and internally directed characteristics. It is by keeping all four of these characteristics in play that our real estate agent can be a positive influence in finding a home for her clients and we can be a positive influence in the situations we encounter.

The CVF, and the four moral philosophies its quadrants represent, help us understand why we need four characteristics, and why we need *these* four characteristics in particular, to lift ourselves and others. Like the engine, wings, air, and flight controls of an airplane, if we leave any characteristic out we are in danger of decreasing the positivity of our influence. To experience these four characteristics, however, we need to understand each individually. Thus, our next step is to examine what each characteristic consists of, why we don't experience the characteristics more often, and what effect they have on us and on the people around us.

The next eight chapters review each of the four characteristics of lift in sequence. The final three chapters describe the fundamental state of leadership as the integration of these four characteristics. To help you keep track of which characteristics we are reviewing and how it fits into the overall framework, we will use the following icons at the beginning of each chapter.

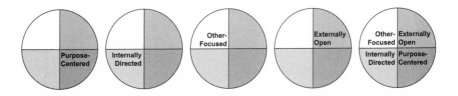

GROUNDED:
BEING COMFORT-CENTERED

Bob: I was once talking to my friend Mindy, who was upset at the leader of a local community organization. This leader said that Mindy's son would be expelled from the organization because he had violated some of its most important rules. Mindy raged on about what an unjust person this leader was, and she listed things that she might do to take action against him. As I listened it was clear that if she actually did the things that she said she was going to do she would make the situation worse. It was also clear that if I told her this she would likely turn her anger toward me. I wondered if there was something I could say that would lift her out of this angry and vengeful state.

As I listened to Mindy complain I remembered a question that I read in Robert Fritz's book *The Path of Least Resistance*.[1] Fritz argues that to move from a reactive state to a creative state, a person should ask the question, "What result do I want to create?" This question focuses us on results and creation rather than on resolving our disrupted expectations. It changes those expectations, creating new purposes that are not inhibited by our existing expectations.

With these ideas in mind, and after having listened for a long time, I asked Mindy, "What result do you want to create?"

Mindy looked at me for a moment. Baffled by my question, she said she wanted justice and she began complaining again. I listened for a few more minutes, and then I asked again, "What result do you want to create?" I got the same response. After I waited a few more minutes I asked the question a third time. Finally, she stopped and asked, "What do you mean by that?"

"If you could have all of your hopes and dreams for your son come true, what result would you want to create for him?"

Mindy looked at me in silence for a time. Then she slowly described how she wanted him to have a happy life, to be a responsible and productive citizen, to serve others, and so on.

I asked how the actions that she was threatening to take would bring about the result she desired. She paused for a long time. Then she began to speak more softly, saying, "He has made some bad decisions, he needs to recognize that and pay the consequences."

As she said this, her disposition seemed to change. The anger dissolved. She seemed more peaceful and more determined. She had new expectations. She said she was going to go home and have a conversation with her son. As she turned and walked away, I was struck by the dramatic change. In her traumatic situation, she had stopped trying to solve the problem and had clarified what result she desired. When she did, the most appropriate strategy became obvious. By asking and answering this basic question, she lifted herself into a new and more positive state, and she was now more likely to lift others.

Mindy's reaction to her son's expulsion was a normal one. Good people sometimes react unproductively to negative situations. The fact that they do this relates to the first characteristic of the fundamental state of leadership. Mindy was approaching the situation in a comfort-centered way, and comfort-centered approaches sometimes lead to unproductive actions.

The alternative to a comfort-centered approach is a purpose-centered approach. Often we are comfort-centered rather than purpose-centered; we are content with a situation, so when problems disrupt or threaten to disrupt the situation we try to solve them. Sometimes this can be appropriate, but often it is not. Sometimes we spend our lives solving

problems and never find purpose. Eventually, with Bob's help, Mindy was able to become purpose-centered. In this chapter we will explore how a question such as "What result do I want to create?" can help us transform our problems into purposes. However, before we do, we will examine why good people such as Mindy—or any of us—can have such strong tendencies to focus on problems.

Problems and purposes have some similar elements. For example, they both can grab our attention and motivate us to action. Some of the actions we take, the things to which we pay attention, or the things about which we feel motivated are more likely to lift us into a state of leadership and lift people around us as a result. For example, Mindy's problem at the beginning of her story and Mindy's purpose at the end both focused her attention and motivated her to act, but the focus of her attention and her motivations was much more likely to lift herself and others when she had a purpose at the end of the story. Problems and purposes are like engines. Any engine could, in theory, propel an airplane forward. But as Orville and Wilbur Wright learned, some engines are much more useful for harnessing lift.

Building a Better Engine

When the time came for them to build an engine that could propel their glider through the air, the Wright brothers faced a situation that was analogous to Mindy's. At that time, many engines existed, but the engines that could generate enough power to propel the glider as fast as the brothers needed also weighed too much. Their weight would push the airplanes down with greater force than the lift that these engines could help generate. To address this problem the Wright brothers performed calculations for the power, speed, thrust, and weight of the engine that they would need. They sent these numbers to the various companies that manufactured engines and asked them to build the engine they required. Ten companies responded, but none of them could make the engine—at least, not for a price that the brothers could afford.

It may have been fortunate that engine companies could not produce the engine that the Wright brothers needed. They were determined enough to build an airplane that they were willing to figure out how to do it themselves, innovating new ways if they had to. For example, in order to help meet the weight requirements, they developed an aluminum crankcase for their engine. It was the first time people used aluminum to build an engine, and aluminum is still a standard material in airplane construction today. They also had the idea to create propellers as if they were rotating wings. This propeller design creates a horizontal force (or thrust), similar to the way that wings produce vertical force (or lift). They used a chain-and-sprocket mechanism—like the ones familiar to the Wright brothers from their bicycles—to transfer the power from the engines to the propellers. With these and other innovations, the brothers built an engine that could propel their aircraft in a way that would generate lift.

If the Wright brothers had used an engine that the engine companies of their day were selling, they could not have generated sufficient lift (the aerodynamic force) to make their glider achieve flight. Similarly, there are many social and psychological "engines" that will propel a person forward, but not all of them are sufficient to generate lift. Like Mindy, who was upset about her son, people often have problems that focus their attention and propel them to action, but their forward motion does not lift them or others. In cases such as these, the poor designs of our psychological "engines" tend to weigh us down rather than lift us up. Many of the problems that move us forward also weigh us down with inappropriate expectations.

Mindy was weighed down with inappropriate expectations because she expected her son to continue to participate productively in an organization from which he was to be expelled. She was angry because she was comfortable with those expectations and they had been disrupted. She invested enormous energy into trying to return things to the way they had been before. However, when a new situation disrupts

our previous expectations, it is often more productive to change our expectations rather than to try to make the world conform to our old ones. If the expectations we have created or learned from past experience are not appropriate, either because we have developed inappropriate expectations or because the situation has changed, we are unlikely to lead—to lift ourselves and others—until we change those expectations.

Inappropriate Expectations

To understand how inappropriate expectations weigh us down, imagine that you are an airline pilot, flying to Las Palmas in the Canary Islands. You expect to drop off your passengers, pick up new passengers, and return home. If all goes well you should be able to complete this process without coming too close to the number of flight hours to which you are limited for the month. This is important because pilots who exceed the legal limits for flight hours in your country can be fined, lose their licenses, or even be imprisoned. As you approach Las Palmas, however, you find out that a bomb has exploded at the airport. You need to fly to the airport in Los Rodeos, Tenerife, instead until the situation in Las Palmas is resolved. The extra time that these new orders add to your trip will put you dangerously close to exceeding the legal limits for your flight time this month. How would you feel?

Most people faced with this type of situation would feel anxious or tense. In turn, these feelings would affect how they perform. Physiologists Timothy Noteboom and his colleagues, for example, have studied how sources of tension (such as mild electric shocks) decrease the steadiness and precision with which people are able to grip a machine between their fingers and thumbs.[2] Psychologists Mark Ashcraft and Elizabeth Kirk have shown that anxiety lowers people's performance on such activities as math tests.[3] And neuroscientists Bernet Elzinga and Karin Roelofs have examined how increases in cortisol—a stress-related

hormone—can decrease people's working memories when they engage in stressful activities such as giving public, evaluated speeches with only five minutes of preparation.[4]

The ability to remain steady, be precise, and keep up one's working memory can have a significant impact on performance in many activities—including piloting an airplane. A little bit of tension may improve performance by activating people's nervous systems, focusing their attention, and motivating them to eliminate the tension they feel, but as tension increases these same biological processes can cause people to focus to the point where they lose perspective, decrease the efficiency of complex thinking, and make actions more habitual or more erratic.[5]

Most of the negative effects that come with higher levels of tension can be seen in the actual story of airline pilots who were diverted from the Las Palmas airport. On March 27, 1977, two flights were told to go to Los Rodeos because of an explosion at Las Palmas. This diversion was not the only source of tension; the pilots on one airplane were in danger of exceeding their legal limits for flying hours, the airplanes were bigger than the airport was equipped to handle, and a cloud floated over the runway in Los Rodeos, reducing visibility. As a result the pilots and the controllers made many mistakes that are typical when people experience higher levels of tension. The pilots focused too much on getting to Las Palmas. They struggled to process instructions, asking what they were supposed to do only a few seconds after they had received instructions. Controllers issued orders erratically, changing some and refusing to be questioned on others. One pilot—who had spent more time training other pilots over the past ten years than actually flying—resorted to habit and authorized himself to take off rather than wait for permission to take off. When he did the wheels of his airplane hit the right wing and rear cabin of the other airplane, the fuel in his own airplane ignited, and 567 of the 586 people on board the two airplanes died.

Karl Weick, an organizational scholar, used research on tension to analyze the events that occurred at the Los Rodeos airport.[6] He pointed

out that people—like the pilots and controllers in Los Rodeos—usually feel tense when they expect events to turn out one way but those events turn out another way instead. Our nervous systems are designed to rally our effort and attention toward resolving disrupted expectations such as these,[7] either by removing the disruption or by finding some other way to make events turn out the way we have expected them to. The longer it takes to do this, the more tension we feel. In Los Rodeos, tragedy occurred largely because disrupted expectations became harder and took longer to restore with each additional disruption. This increased tension and decreased the quality of pilots' and controllers' thoughts and actions.

The experience of disrupted expectations, increased tension, and decreased performance is not limited to dramatic events such as the tragedy in Los Rodeos. Our colleague Mindy had this same experience regarding her son's pending expulsion: it disrupted her expectations, and she was not able to remove that disruption. She felt anger and fear, two emotions that are high in tension. As a result she had trouble focusing on anything else, thinking through the situation carefully, and acting constructively. In this new situation her old expectations were like a poorly designed engine: they kept propelling her forward, but as they did so they also weighed her down—as well as everyone else with whom she interacted.

Expectations and Problems

Disrupted expectations create a gap between the situations people expect and the situations people actually encounter. Gerald Smith, a decision scientist, points out that if we experience a gap such as this, the gap matters to us, and if it is difficult to close the gap we are likely to label it a problem.[8] For example, Mindy thought of her situation as a problem because her son was to be expelled from an organization in which she expected him to participate productively and happily. The pilots had a problem because they expected to fly to Las Palmas and

back but were unable to do so. These gaps mattered, and they were hard to close.

Once we think of gaps such as these as problems, the *problem* label implies that the appropriate response to that gap is to solve it—to restore the situation to its expected state. Therefore, Mindy felt compelled to restore her son's membership in the community organization and the pilots felt compelled to complete the flight plan that had been disrupted.

Sometimes, it is appropriate to label the gap that an interruption creates a problem. This is true when it is possible, desirable, and ethical to try to restore a situation to its previous or its expected state. Many situations, however, cannot or should not be returned to their previous or expected states. For example, when Mindy's son violated the organization's rules, he created a new situation; he had taken actions that had consequences, he was fully aware of those consequences, and all of the other members of the organization were aware of the consequences. To restore him to his previous state would undermine both the rules and the consequences for him and for the other members of the organization. In Los Rodeos, completing the flight as quickly as possible was an unsafe expectation. Trying to solve these problems did more harm than good. It would have been more productive to question the validity of these expectations given the new situations that had emerged.

A Bias for Confirming Evidence

One reason people try to restore their situations to match previous or expected situations, rather than to update their understanding of the new and unfolding situation, can be seen in an experiment conducted by Mark Snyder and William Swann.[9] Snyder and Swann told the participants in their experiment that they would be interviewing people to find out if the other person was an introvert or an extrovert. On the surface this seems like a relatively easy task: introverts tend to be

more distant and quiet, whereas extroverts tend to be outgoing and talkative. Introverts often get energized by a good book or a conversation with a single friend, whereas extroverts get energized by parties and large social gatherings. Traits such as these—it would seem—should be relatively easy to discern when conversing with another person.

Snyder and Swann found, however, that the ease with which the participants in their experiment discerned a person's introversion or extroversion depended significantly on the instructions they were given. For example, rather than ask participants to find out if a particular person was an introvert or an extrovert, Snyder and Swann told half of their participants that they needed to interview people to find out if they were introverts, and told the other half that they needed to interview people to find out if they were extroverts, but they gave these participants no data to indicate whether the people they were going to interview were introverts or extroverts. They then gave the participants a list of ten questions that largely made sense only to ask of people who are already known to be introverts, eleven questions that largely made sense to ask of people who were already known to be extroverts, and five neutral questions.

Snyder and Swann asked the participants to select twelve questions from the list for their interviews. On average, the people who were told to find out if the person they were interviewing was extroverted selected a high number of questions designed for people that are known to be extroverted and the people who were trying to find out if the person they were interviewing was introverted selected a high number of questions designed for people that are known to be introverted. These differences were significant, suggesting that people tend to look for evidence that confirms what they are looking for rather than look for disconfirming evidence, even when there is no data to suggest that a person should look for confirming evidence.

Snyder and Swann followed this first experiment with others. They had participants actually conduct the interviews rather than just pick the questions. They gave the participants data on how likely it was that

the person they interviewed would be an introvert or extrovert so that the participants would know to look for disconfirming evidence. They even offered to pay participants money for making more accurate assessments. Even so, in every case, the simple instruction to find out if a person was an introvert or an extrovert led participants to look for—and sometimes to even create—evidence that confirmed the personality trait that had been mentioned in their instructions.

The tendency for people to look for evidence that confirms their expectations has been found in experiments of all kinds. For example, in one experiment, participants were given an article to read that presented evidence for the deterring effect that capital punishment has on violent crime and an article to read that presented evidence suggesting that capital punishment does not deter violent crime. Although both articles were written with equal rigor, people hailed the article that supported their beliefs as a highly competent piece of work and were hypercritical of the article that refuted their beliefs, looking for minor flaws and enlarging them.[10]

In another experiment, scientists presented people with information about the current Republican and Democratic presidential candidates. As they read the information the scientists monitored responses in the participants' brains using functional magnetic resonance imaging. They found that when participants were presented with information that disconfirmed their expectations, the reasoning areas of the brain were hardly activated at all; in other words, people put no mental effort into understanding any evidence that disconfirmed their beliefs, dismissing it out of hand. In contrast, when people were presented with information that confirmed their expectations, the emotional areas of the brain were activated pleasantly; in other words, their brains rewarded them for finding confirming evidence.[11] The tendency for people to seek confirming evidence crosses all political boundaries and all domains of life.

The human tendency to seek confirming evidence is an efficient thing for our brains to do. If evidence confirms our expectations, we can continue acting the way we have been acting, and we will not have to invest

the energy that is necessary for thinking consciously about what we should do differently. Our brains need to manage our actions with as little conscious thought as they can, or they would be overwhelmed with energy demands and information overload. We therefore create simple expectations for our experiences and act as if those expectations are correct, sometimes even when we receive overwhelming evidence that they are not. Our unconscious minds cling tightly to our expectations, searching for and even creating data that confirms those expectations and ignoring or discounting data that does not.

The tendency to seek data that confirms our expectations explains why Mindy did not realize that her anger and her intentions were unproductive. Her son's potential expulsion confronted her with two options: she could fight it, or she could change her expectations. The tendency to seek confirming evidence suggests she was not likely to change her expectations. It is more comfortable to solve problems than it is to admit that we have inappropriate expectations. Because of this, Mindy said the organization's people and processes were unfair; she created arguments to back up her claims, and these arguments made it "obvious" to her that she should fight the leaders of the organization over her son's expulsion.

From Problem Solving to Purpose Finding

Mindy is normally a pleasant and peaceful person. When she was complaining to Bob, she was caught in a trap in which most of us get caught: her expectations had been disrupted and she labeled this disruption a problem. By trying to solve the problem, she was about to create more problems. Her expectations, like the engines from which the Wright brothers had to choose before they created their own, weighed her down. Until she dropped the dead weight of her inappropriate expectations she could not lead, feel uplifted, or in turn lift others.

To drop the dead weight of her inappropriate expectations, Mindy needed to stop thinking about her situation as a problem. When people

think of a situation as a problem it implies that a person should solve the problem. Karl Weick points out, however, that if a situation can be labeled a problem, "then one could also say things like, that is an issue, manage it; that is a dilemma, reframe it; that is a paradox, accept it; that is a conflict, synthesize it; that is an opportunity, take it."[12] In other words, the labels that we use determine how we see our situations, and how we see our situations affects how we respond to them. For Mindy to change her expectations she needed to think in terms of different labels. When Bob asked her what result she wanted to create, he helped her find new labels. She saw the world differently, and she became purpose-centered.

CHAPTER 4

IN FLIGHT:
BECOMING PURPOSE-CENTERED

Bob: A few years ago some of my colleagues and I were appointed to serve on a committee that was assigned to design the new executive masters of business administration (EMBA) program for our business school. The marketplace for EMBA programs was already competitive, and we needed to design this program with a high degree of excellence. In other words, this assignment presented an opportunity to lift ourselves and lift the school by being very clear about the result we wanted to create.

I was not able to make the first meeting of the committee, but when I arrived at the second meeting, my colleagues briefed me on what had happened. They showed me their design and asked, "What do you think?"

"Would you mind closing your eyes?" I asked. This was not a standard procedure; after some resistance, my colleagues closed their eyes.

I asked them to envision the first graduating class. "After the first graduate collects a diploma and walks off the stage, this graduate comes to you, hugs you, and says, 'Thank you, this was the most powerful educational experience of my life!'"

I told them to imagine the second, third, and fourth persons doing the same thing. Then I told my colleagues to open their eyes. I asked them

how the program they had begun designing would generate the results they just imagined. There was an uncomfortable silence. One of them changed the subject and the discussion moved on. I was being ignored.

I could understand how my colleagues felt. I know how hard it can be to shed inappropriate expectations. Knowing this, I chose to remain purpose-centered but patient. I mostly remained quiet, only occasionally asking questions, but when I did I asked radical questions, though I asked them quietly and respectfully. For example, at one point my colleagues mentioned grades. I asked, "Why are we having grades?"

One colleague patiently explained what grades were and why we needed them. I nodded. Later we talked about books, and I asked why we were using books. I received a less patient response: one colleague said, with some anger, "Because without books, we would overwhelm document processing."

Document processing is an administrative function that makes course packs full of readings and case studies; we use course packs when we do not use books. My colleague was telling me that if we did not use books, that administrative function would be overwhelmed.

At that point I finally gave some input: "So, what you are telling me is that we are not designing this program for excellence, we are designing it for administrative convenience."

Again I was ignored, but within a few minutes the meeting took an unexpected turn. No one articulated a new strategy; people just began to talk about the program in new ways: "What if we tried this?" and "How would it work if we did that?" My colleagues began to question their own expectations. In a short period of time a new design began to emerge on the whiteboard. It was not driven by one person; at various points in the conversation different people would chime in with insights that were exciting and perfectly timed. People worked together to create a program they were beginning to believe in.

When we finished designing the program one colleague leaned back in his chair and said, "Over the years, I have thought about what it would be like to go back to school. I have always thought, 'I would not want to do that again.' But this program—this program has"—he struggled to find the words—"it has *commitment*."

Our program *did* have commitment. It went to the next committee, where some of our design was taken out because it was "too radical."

That was fine, because other elements remained and the commitment still showed. When the magazines began to rank our EMBA program, *US News and World Report* ranked ours as the best among all US public institutions, the *Wall Street Journal* ranked it among the top three programs, and *BusinessWeek* ranked it the fourth best program in the world. These results depended on much more than just the decisions of the initial design committee, of course; hundreds of people contribute to outcomes such as these. Even so, those of us who were on the committee are proud of the way in which we could generate a design that truly served the students and set a tone of commitment to excellence. Today the program continues to be ranked among the top ten in many if not most magazines' EMBA rankings.

For me there has always been something even more impressive than the rankings. For a number of years I had the opportunity to teach in the first week of the program. I would watch some of the finest people I have ever met enter the classroom, and they did so with excitement. Part of the excitement was due to the fact that they were beginning a new program; another part came from associating with faculty and staff who believed in what they were doing. The students could sense that they had become a part of something special. They radiated confidence in the program.

The approach Bob used to challenge his colleagues was unusual. He could, after all, have just suggested that they be more purposeful. Bob had two reasons for asking them to visualize the first graduating class, though. First, he knew his colleagues had worked hard on their design. Rethinking the purpose of the program might have required them to start designing it again from scratch, and they would be reluctant to do that. Second, he knew that people often think they are pursuing outstanding results when they are just reproducing something they are already familiar with. It is not just faculty members in a university who act this way; most of us choose comfort over purpose, more often than we realize. If Bob had said this to his colleagues, however, he probably would have made them defensive rather than inspire them to change the design.

A visual image can sometimes inspire people to lead. For example, it inspired the EMBA committee to defy cultural assumptions—such as beliefs about how to design an EMBA program—in a way that inspires others to choose to follow. But when Bob asked his colleagues to envision the first graduating class they resisted him because such a visualization might provide them with disconfirming evidence about their design. Consistent with the research on the confirming evidence bias, it was more comfortable for Bob's colleagues to resist him than to change their expectations and create excellence.

The other members of the committee did not resist Bob because they disagreed with his approach. His colleagues are good, competent people, and their design was a good and logical one. But the design was based on accepted cultural expectations about what an EMBA program should be, not on leadership as we have defined it. After the dean had asked them to design an EMBA program, Bob created a gap between his colleagues' current situation (no EMBA program) and their expectations (an EMBA program). Designing the program became a problem to be solved, not an opportunity to be purpose-centered. It was an important problem, but a problem nonetheless. They did not ask themselves what result they wanted to create; they just designed a solution for the problem as it was given to them.

Our work and lives are filled with presumed constraints that prevent us from setting and pursuing goals we truly want to achieve, whether we are designing a program, cleaning our house, performing surgery, deciding how to enter a new market, or attempting any other activity. The sociologist Harold Garfinkel used to teach this principle to his students by giving them homework assignments designed to test their cultural assumptions about how the world works.[1] For example, one time he sent his students to a grocery store and told them to try to negotiate the prices of the products. People in the United States almost never try to negotiate the prices of products in grocery stores; they expect grocery store prices to be fixed and nonnegotiable. To the surprise of Garfinkel's students, however, they found that in most cases

they were able to negotiate lower prices for the products they wanted to buy. Garfinkel was well known for such "natural experiments," and one idea we learn from his work is that many expectations that we think are true are often constraints that weigh us down rather than lift us up.

The expectations that Garfinkel's students had about grocery store prices were similar to Bob's colleagues' expectations about designing an EMBA program. Before we can understand how his colleagues were influenced to question their expectations and consider a loftier purpose, though, it is useful to understand what it means to be purpose-centered.

The Impossible Lawn

Richard Thurman tells a story that illustrates the experience of being purpose-centered. During his youth in the early 1900s, a rich woman moved into his small town whom the townspeople came to call the Countess. She asked Thurman to mow her lawn. On his first day, she made him mow the lawn three times before she said that he was finished. She paid him $2, and told him that if he did the job with the same quality the next time, without supervision, she would pay him $3. He could earn up to $5, and he would evaluate his own work. A job that was so good that he would "have to be something of a fool to spend that much time on a lawn" was worth $4. A $5 lawn was so good that it was "impossible."

Thurman resolved to earn $4, and tried to do so for a number of weeks. He eventually completed $3.50 jobs, but never reached the $4 mark. He lay in bed at night dreaming of completing a $4 job when "one Thursday night I was trying to forget that day's defeat and get some sleep . . . the truth hit me so hard I sat upright, half choking in my excitement. It was the five-dollar job I had to do, not the four-dollar one! I had to do the job that no one could do because it was impossible."[2] When he realized that he "had" to do the $5 job Thurman became purpose-centered. He was not purpose-centered when he

was pursuing the $4 job, even though he had a goal to do that job. This is a subtle but important distinction. Like the students who thought that prices in a grocery store could not be negotiated, and like professors who thought that EMBA programs had no options other than books or document processing, Thurman accepted the Countess's claim that a $5 lawn was impossible and focused on solving the problem of a $4 lawn. A purpose is more than a goal. When people are purpose-centered,

1. they envision and pursue extraordinary results that are not constrained by previous expectations or by the expectations that they receive from others
2. the results they pursue are energizing because they are self-chosen, challenging, and constructive
3. they provide a clear definition of the situation, focusing people's attention

These components of being purpose-centered are illustrated well by Thurman's experience.

Energizing Goals

When Thurman realized that he could mow a $5 lawn, he chose his own purpose rather than accept the $4 goal. The $4 goal was a social convention—created by the Countess—that implied that $4 was the best he could do. Before he set a goal to mow a $5 lawn, Thurman mowed the lawn the way the Countess had shown him. She had pressed him into service. He was being paid for his work, and the Countess had even told him he might be fired when his first few jobs only met a $2 standard. Rewards (such as money) and punishments (such as the threat of being fired) are what psychologists call *extrinsic motivators*. They motivate us, but they are outside pressures rather than end results that we want to create ourselves. Goals that we want to achieve ourselves are much more energizing.

Imagine, for example, that someone asks you to play a game. This game is designed to test the flexibility of your thinking. You have a deck of cards with pictures of different shapes, numbers, and colors. An instructor asks you to sort the cards into piles based on particular combinations of numbers, shapes, and colors. She also changes the combinations from time to time to see how quickly you can adjust. After each card, the instructor tells you if you placed it in the right pile. The challenge of this game, then, is to try to understand, recognize, and keep up with the patterns. Such a game could be a fun diversion for a few minutes.

Contrast this game with another scenario. In this case, imagine that you are playing the same game, but this time the instructor does not tell you to sort each card into particular combinations, but instead tells you that the cards need to be placed in a certain order. She gives you explicit instructions on where to place each card, and then tells you if you did it right or wrong. This game, in contrast to the previous one, is not a test of your mental flexibility but a test of your ability to follow detailed instructions.

The interesting thing about these two games is that they are designed so that the correct sequence for card placement is exactly the same in both games (for example, square, 10, blue, red, green, 9, 4, circle, and so on). The difference between the games, then, is that in the first game you get to try to figure out the sequence for yourself, and in the second game someone tells you how to do it. Which version of the game would you find to be more energizing?

These two games were performed in an experiment by Glen Nix and his colleagues.[3] As you might expect, the energy that people felt in the first game remained high from the beginning to the end, whereas the energy that people felt in the second game dropped precipitously. These psychologists conducted similar experiments involving word-finding puzzles and in selecting classes. In each case, energy was highest when people were able to choose for themselves what they wanted to do.

Sociologist Stephen Marks has observed that people get energized by freely chosen purposes.[4] The energy we feel toward an activity, he notes, affects how much physical energy we expend in that activity. Marks points out that, at least in developed societies where people have adequate food to eat, the physical energy we have in our bodies is plentiful for all of the activities we engage in on any average day. The reason we sometimes do not feel energy for activities is usually not because of a lack of physical energy but because of a lack of subjective energy: we are simply not interested. When we are intrinsically interested in an activity, we not only have energy for it but we easily translate the energy we feel into physical effort.

The energy we feel toward the activities in which we participate is influenced by how positive and challenging our goals are as well as by how freely chosen they are. A positive goal is one in which a person strives to achieve such outcomes as increasing sales by 5 percent in a given quarter, maintaining a healthy lifestyle, or mowing a $5 lawn. Negative goals involve striving to avoid such outcomes as losing market share, keeping from getting fat, or preventing being fired by the Countess. Research suggests that people experience more positive emotions when they remember experiences with positive goals versus experiences with negative goals.[5] If other influences are not present to dampen one's energy, it is plausible that people will feel more energized pursuing positive goals than negative ones.

A challenging goal is a goal that people believe will stretch their resources and their abilities to their limit in order to accomplish it. If, for example, you were challenged to count out aloud and backward from 1,528 by thirteens, you might consider this to be a challenge or even a threat. Joe Tomaka and his colleagues asked people to participate in activities such as these.[6] The heart rate, strength of heartbeat, blood vessel activity, and other physiological measures of participants who saw this activity as a challenge indicated that they were mobilizing increased energy to complete the task. When Tomaka and his colleagues compared participants who saw this activity as a challenge with

those who saw it as a threat, they found that those who saw it as a challenge felt less stress and performed better than those who saw it as a threat.

Such studies explain why Thurman "sat upright, half-choking in [his] excitement" when he decided to mow a $5 lawn: it was a self-chosen, positive, challenging goal. Self-chosen goals increase our energy because of our intrinsic interest; challenge increases our energy because we need energy to generate the required effort; and positivity increases our energy because we are attracted to the desired result.

Focus and Direction

The question "What result do I want to create?" energizes people because it leads them to pursue results that are self-determined ("What . . . do *I* want . . . ?") and that challenge them in positive ways (". . . to *create*?"). Creating implies doing something positive, difficult, and new rather than relying on existing expectations about what can and cannot be done. Energy alone, however, is not sufficient. People need to know how and where to exert that energy, which is why this question also focuses us on creating *results*. Self-chosen, challenging, positive goals help people focus their attention as well as energizing them.

Consider, for example, a study Ryan conducted with nuclear scientists and engineers in which he had participants report daily activities and their goals for those activities.[7] In one activity, a scientist said his goal was to write new software that would enable a system to test the connections across its subsystems. This goal focused his attention on the algorithms he needed to learn to test connections across subsystems, the books or papers that would be useful to him in finding algorithms, and what to look for when perusing these books and papers. Without this goal he would have been less able to identify which algorithms, books, data sets, and other items he should pay attention to, or how to use those tools and information.

The scientist could also use his goal to judge how much progress he was making. For example, by reviewing a book's table of contents or

index he could tell if that particular book would bring him closer to or farther from achieving his goal. Other research suggests that goals direct people's actions even to the level of the movements that people's eyes make when they have a goal to assess characters' personalities in a movie.[8] Goals, then, direct people's attention and focus it on extracting relevant information and responding to that information appropriately.[9]

The goal to mow a $5 lawn redefined Thurman's situation, redirected his attention, and focused him on new activities. Once he realized that he should mow a $5 lawn, there was a change in the information he paid attention to and the actions he planned to take:

> I was well acquainted with the difficulties ahead. I had the problem, for example, of doing something about the worm mounds in the lawn. The Countess might not even have noticed them yet, they were so small; but in my bare feet I knew about them and I had to do something about them. And I could go on trimming the garden edges with shears, but I knew that a five-dollar lawn demanded that I line up each edge exactly with a yardstick and then trim it precisely with the edger. And there were other problems that only I and my bare feet knew about.[10]

Worm mounds, yardsticks, and trimming with an edger were all aspects of the situation that were not relevant when Thurman's goal was a $4 lawn. But with the goal of a $5 lawn, he suddenly had new directions in which to invest his energy.

The next week Thurman set out to mow a $5 lawn. He ironed out worm mounds. He mowed the lawn four times—twice going one direction and twice going perpendicular to that. He used an edger and a yardstick to trim the edge precisely. He smoothed sod with his hands and cleared grass out of the walkway. He worked from early in the morning until the sun began to set. He knocked on the door and announced to the Countess that he had mowed a $5 lawn.

The Countess was surprised, and wanted to see "the first five-dollar lawn in history." She walked around the lawn with him, admiring what

he did. When she asked him what inspired him to do such an incredible thing, Thurman had no answer. The Countess guessed,

> "I think I know . . . how you felt when this idea first came to you of mowing a lawn that I told you was impossible. It made you very happy when it first came, then a little frightened. Am I right?"
> She could see she was right by the startled look on my face.
> "I know how you felt because the same thing happens to almost everybody. They feel this sudden burst in them of wanting to do some great thing. They feel a wonderful happiness, but then it passes because they have said, 'No, I can't do that. It's impossible.' Whenever something in you says 'It's impossible,' remember to take a careful look. See if it isn't really God asking you to grow an inch, or a foot, or a mile that you may come to a fuller life."[11]

Thurman then summarized what the moral of this story was for him: "Since that time some 25 years ago when I have felt myself at an end with nothing before me, suddenly with the appearance of that word 'impossible' I have experienced again the unexpected lift, the leap inside me, and known that the only possible way lay through the very middle of the impossible."[12]

The Leadership of a Person Who Is Purpose-Centered

When we, like Richard Thurman, create new purposes that shed the inappropriate expectations that come with being comfort-centered, we lift ourselves with new ideas, new direction, and new energy. We assume leadership, and we lift others. For example, Bob knew what kind of program he wanted to create when he went to the second design meeting for the EMBA program. As a result he knew how he wanted to respond when his colleagues asked him what he thought of their design. By asking them to envision a result that he knew they would claim that they wanted to create, and then asking them how their first

design would bring the desired outcome, Bob revealed that they were not, in fact, designing an extraordinary program. They were simply reproducing the existing MBA program with minor modifications. Bob's colleagues, like most people, did not like disconfirming evidence, so they chose to ignore him.

Lifting through Enactment

This process, in which (1) Bob acted in pursuit of a goal, (2) his colleagues saw his actions and had to make sense of them, and (3) the colleagues responded to and even participated in the goal, is an example of what Karl Weick calls *enactment*,[13] the process of taking actions that create at least part of the situation that we are acting in.

Enactment does not have to be intentional and does not have to compete with other people's views of the world. For example, when an earthquake occurred in southern Italy in 1980, a social scientist named Giovan Lanzara observed that many people's actions created new realities that had not existed before.[14] One man set up a coffee stand on the piazza of a devastated village. On the day after the earthquake he started distributing free coffee to anyone who wanted it. People began to meet, rest, exchange information, and organize activities next to his stand. On the second day two additional people joined the coffee stand, helping the first man and adding services such as providing milk for children.

The first man on the piazza simply set out to serve coffee to people who were in need. But whether he intended it or not, other people made sense of his actions. Some made sense of his actions as a coffee stand, drinking his coffee, some made sense of his actions as creating a place for people to gather, and some made sense of his actions as a vehicle for their own service: they helped him serve coffee and introduced their own complementary innovations (such as serving milk). And some people may have made sense by ignoring the coffee stand.

No matter how people made sense of the actions of the first man on the piazza, his purposeful actions influenced others whether the influ-

ence was intentional or not. And because the earthquake left people with limited options for understanding and responding, it was a natural response for people to accept and participate in the world that he was creating—at least until the third day after the earthquake. On the third day the government agencies arrived, set up formal rescue and aid procedures, and the coffee stand disappeared.

People create new realities all of the time, and often do so unintentionally. Even so, we are likely to have a particularly significant influence on others when we are purpose-centered because we usually act differently from how comfort-centered people would act in the same situation. People are more likely to try to preserve the status quo or to remain inactive than to intentionally seek to create extraordinary realities.[15] Also, we perform these unusual actions with more energy, focus, and persistence when we are purpose-centered because our purposes are self-chosen, challenging, positive, and specific. When one person acts in energized ways that persistently disrupt others' expectations, other people are likely to pay attention.

Imagine, for example, that Bob had taken a comfort-centered approach to designing the EMBA program. If he had, he probably would have accepted his colleagues' first design, suggesting only minor changes. As a result, Bob's colleagues would not have shared their own innovative ideas. Similarly, if the man making coffee on the Italian piazza had been comfort-centered he might have chosen to stay home and watch the response to the earthquake on his television, and the other people in the devastated village would probably not have offered other services or have rested and planned at that central location. People do not put effort into making sense of others' actions unless the actions that others take are unexpected in some way.

The fact that people feel a need to make sense of another person's unusual actions is documented in research on minority influence. Imagine, for example, that you are sitting in a room with four other people. A sixth person, with a slide projector, is projecting blue slides onto a screen. After each slide the person with the slide projector asks

each of the other five people in the room, including you, to tell her what color she is projecting. Three of the other people in the room say that the slide is blue. But one person says the slide was green. What would you say?

Ninety percent of the people who participate in experiments such as these say that the blue slide is blue. Ten percent of the participants, however, tell researchers that the blue slide is green.[16] If one person can convince others that a blue slide is green 10 percent of the time, what impact would individuals have if they said or did unusual things in situations that are more ambiguous than watching slides on a screen?

To answer this question Linn Van Dyne and Richard Saavedra conducted a study in which groups were assigned to come up with creative and sophisticated answers to problems that could have many correct answers of varying quality.[17] In half of the groups they assigned one group member to take a minority viewpoint on issues that the group discussed. After working on these problems for ten weeks, Van Dyne and Saavedra found that the groups with a member who was assigned to take a minority viewpoint had considered more alternative approaches along the way and ended up with more creative solutions (as rated by independent judges) than the groups that did not have a member assigned to take a minority viewpoint.

This is a common finding in research where people take unexpected actions: those who observe unexpected actions generally end up thinking more, more complexly, and sometimes even more creatively in their efforts to make sense of the actions. The people who take the unusual actions sometimes feel stress about being different, but if they are consistent in expressing their opinions, they not only help others to think more complexly but the people who observe them often come to respect and admire them as courageous, even when the observers think that the people who do unusual things are wrong.[18] Note how this description is similar to our definition of leadership as actions that deviate from cultural expectations and which others choose to follow. We also saw this when Bob and his colleagues designed the new EMBA

course. As Bob consistently asked questions that challenged their expectations, his colleagues' inputs became more thoughtful, more complex, and more creative. They began to enact a new reality.

Consistency is necessary for minority influence to occur, including that of Bob's experience in the EMBA design meeting. If individuals do unusual things randomly or sporadically rather than consistently, other people are less likely to truly question their own expectations. Consistency is a characteristic that generally describes people who are purpose-centered,[19] and this consistency is one of the things that make such people influential.

The energy and focus that people experience when they are purpose-centered also make them influential. In fact, when Jeffrey Pfeffer—one of the world's leading researchers on the topic of power—listed personal characteristics that have a tendency to make a person influential, the first two characteristics on his list were *energy* and *focus*.[20] One reason energy and focus are so influential, he pointed out, is that when people see a person focused and energized, they think that the goal must be really important for that person to focus so intently and to invest so much energy. Thus, when people see an individual take unexpected, energized, focused, and persistent actions, they are likely to question some of their own expectations, think more complexly, adopt some of the ideas of the individual taking unexpected action, and perhaps even offer ideas that build on and contribute to that individual's actions.

Leadership through Contagion

Erika James, a friend and colleague of ours who is currently the dean of Emory University's Goizueta Business School, is consistently uplifting in her interactions with others. When she and Ryan worked together, she never failed to look up with the brightest of smiles when he would come by her office. That smile always made him feel welcome and energized, even if he felt concerned or hesitant before coming to her office.

Erika's influence is an example of what Elaine Hatfield and colleagues call "emotional contagion," a process through which people begin to feel the same way as the people around them. Contagion often happens without people realizing it is happening. We notice each other's facial expressions and other emotional cues, mimic those cues, and then feel the emotions that generally accompany those expressions. This happens to people all over the world.[21] Muscles in the face tend to move to particular positions involuntarily, or automatically, when people feel particular emotions.

Because of the commonality and clarity of facial expressions for conveying emotion, children learn early on to pay attention to facial expressions. For example, in the "visual cliff" experiment, researchers place an infant on a surface that is half solid and half clear Plexiglas.[22] An infant who crawls along the surface and comes to the Plexiglas experiences an ambiguous threat: the Plexiglas feels solid but looks like a cliff. When this happens, the infant's first, instinctive response is to look at her mother's face. If the mother's face is calm, most infants will crawl over the Plexiglas. If the infant detects fear, the infant is likely to shy away.

Over a lifetime of scanning people's faces to learn about the world, people scanning others' faces becomes a habitual way of making sense of our world. The conscious conclusions we draw from others' faces may not always be accurate, but the tendency to scan faces is habitual, and we often unconsciously mirror others' emotions when we scan their faces. We wince in pain when we see someone hurt, open our mouths with babies when feeding them, and yawn when we see or hear other people yawn. This mimicking is instinctive—it happens in milliseconds without us realizing we are doing it. And when people mimic others' facial expressions they also tend to feel the emotions associated with those expressions. In other words, facial expressions not only express emotions but also cause them.

Imagine, for example, that someone told you to hold a pen between your teeth without letting your lips touch it while you watched a

cartoon. Fritz Strack and his colleagues gave these instructions to a number of people participating in an experiment.[23] When people hold pens between their teeth without letting their lips touch them, their mouths form a smile. By giving people these instructions Strack and his colleagues got people to smile without telling them to smile. Then they had the participants in their experiment watch a cartoon. The participants who watched a cartoon with the pens in their teeth found the cartoons to be funnier than the people who watched the cartoon while holding a pen with their lips (a facial position that makes it nearly impossible to smile). This experiment, and others like it, shows that our facial expressions have as much effect on our feelings as our feelings have on our facial expressions.

When one person exhibits a facial expression and a second person notices that expression, mimics it, and begins to feel the same way, that is emotional contagion. It is what Ryan feels, for example, when he walks into Erika's office. People usually feel energized when they are purpose-centered, and their energy tends to be contagious, making other people feel energized as well.

Positive Emotions

As Bob and his colleagues considered designing a more innovative EMBA program, the committee became more energized about what it was doing. The energy that people feel when they are purpose-centered influences the energy of others around them; it also influences the number and types of thoughts and actions people consider and the resources they have to work with. Barbara Fredrickson, a psychologist from the University of North Carolina, has shown this impact in her research on positive emotions.

One example of this research is an experiment in which Fredrickson and her colleague, Christine Branigan, showed film clips that evoked positive, negative, and neutral emotions in their participants.[24] After the participants saw the clips, Fredrickson and Branigan asked them to write down a list of all of the things they would like to do right

now. Those who felt positive emotions listed more things they would like to do than those in the neutral and negative conditions, suggesting that those who felt positive emotions had more thought and action options than those who felt neutral or negative emotions.

Fredrickson and her colleagues have confirmed this finding in multiple studies, showing that people with positive emotions think more broadly about their social world. They include other people when they think of themselves (for example, using the word *we* to describe themselves instead of *me*).[25] They even lose the pervasive and well-documented bias that people have to favor people from their own race (for example, white people become just as good at recognizing the faces of black people as they are at recognizing the faces of white people).[26] Positive emotions also appear to have a positive effect on how creatively people think.[27]

Bob and his colleagues broadened their thought and action options as they designed the EMBA program, and their ideas led to the creation of new and enduring resources. The effect of positive emotions on resource creation is another of Fredrickson's findings: people who have more thought and action options are more likely to try more things, develop more skills, learn more principles, gather more information, and so forth. For example, Fredrickson and her colleagues offered a free wellness program to employees in a computer firm. As part of the program, employees practiced daily meditations in which they focused on feelings of love, tenderness, and kindness. Half of the employees were given the program right away, and the other half had to wait. All of the employees filled out surveys, though, examining the mental, psychological, social, and physical resources that they had available to them before and after the first group participated in the program. Those who participated in the program experienced an increase in mindfulness, savoring, agency, growth, relationship quality, social support, and sleep quality, and a decrease in symptoms of illness, in comparison to those who did not participate.

Energy Networks

We have described how positive emotions increase the thoughts and actions available to people and help them build enduring resources. Because emotions are contagious, one energized person can help other people think more broadly, act more creatively, and create more resources. With more options and more resources, people can accomplish more than they would otherwise, both through their own efforts and through mobilizing others.

People generally mobilize the people with whom they have relationships first. These people, in turn, mobilize others. In other words, people use their social networks to mobilize others. Wayne Baker and colleagues found that the degree to which one person is energizing to other people does more to explain that person's performance than factors such as the person's use of information.[28] Erika James, for example, usually energizes people in her social network and is a high performer. Bob and his colleagues designing the EMBA program became energized about creating something extraordinary and ended up creating a program that was recognized as a leader in its industry.

Leadership through Results

One reason Bob's colleagues changed the way they approached their program design was because of the results they began to achieve as they tried out new ideas. People achieve higher performance on the results they pursue when they have clear and challenging purposes.[29] On the EMBA design team, each time one person shared an idea and other people saw how the idea could work, those other people got excited about the idea. Excitement and agreement are types of positive feedback. These were moments of success: each idea that excited the group made the overall purpose seem more feasible. People like to be a part of successful endeavors—especially if their endeavors are creating something extraordinary. As more of Bob's colleagues embraced the purpose, the purpose became more attractive.

Each time the EMBA design committee agreed upon and got excited about a new solution, it became what Karl Weick calls a "small win." People achieve small wins when they succeed at some discrete step on the way to achieving their larger purpose. When people become purpose-centered, they often experience more small wins because they are focused on discrete situations, but they use larger purposes to guide their thinking and acting in those discrete situations. The small wins that they achieve in these situations then attract people's attention without intimidating them (because their size is not threatening) and get integrated into other people's agendas (because their size makes them easy to include). "Once a small win has been accomplished," notes Weick, "forces are set in motion that favor another small win. When a solution is put in place, the next solvable problem often becomes more visible. This occurs because new allies bring solutions with them and old opponents change their habits. Additional resources also flow toward winners, which means that slightly larger wins can be attempted."[30]

In the EMBA design meetings one person would propose an idea that other people saw as both exciting and feasible. Then another person proposed an idea. Each idea deviated a little from cultural expectations (i.e., it was an attempt at leadership), and each idea's success in furthering the design goals made their purpose a little more legitimate, a little more feasible, and a little more exciting (i.e., others chose to follow). Soon no convincing was needed; the whole group was energized about the common purpose.

A similar phenomenon occurred at Proctor & Gamble when Claudia Kotchka tried to instill innovation practices throughout the company. Claudia and her team began by working with a team that was focused on Mr. Clean, a once popular brand that had lost much of its luster. Using new innovation practices the team introduced a product for making it easier to clean bathrooms: Mr. Clean Magic Reach. The new product sold well, even if it wasn't a hit, and that was enough of a

win to increase the confidence in Claudia's team, launch it into the development of the Mr. Clean Magic Eraser (a household cleaning pad that became a true blockbuster as a product), and get other branches of P&G to try out the new innovation practices.[31] If enough small wins can be achieved toward a larger purpose, they can eventually fuel a virtuous cycle, creating a culture that makes the scaling of excellence nearly habitual.[32]

Actions, Energy, and Results

When people are purpose-centered, other people must make sense of the new realities they are creating. They must also make sense of how focused, energized, and persistent purpose-centered people are in creating those realities. Their energy is contagious, and their new actions and positive emotions lead others to think and act more broadly and to build enduring resources. They achieve small wins that accumulate over time and add legitimacy to their purposes; they practice leadership. This is what happened in the EMBA design team meetings.

Limits to Possibility and Positivity

A purpose-centered state can lift the purpose-centered person and others around that person. People become purpose-centered by asking and answering the question "What result do I want to create?" This question helps us to shed inappropriate expectations and set goals that are clear, challenging, positive, and self-chosen. The question can lift us, and we can in turn lift others.

Two questions should be addressed before we move on. First, can it be dangerous to shed one's assumptions about what is possible and what is not? After all, some things really are impossible, aren't they? And if they are, isn't it foolish to pursue impossible goals? Second, is the setting of extraordinary goals necessarily a positive thing? After

all, a person could set goals that are unethical. And even if the goals are ethical, does that necessarily mean that the person with positive goals will have a positive influence?

Impossibility

In his book *The Path of Least Resistance* Robert Fritz discusses the role of impossibility in determining what result you want to create. He shares the following story:

> Once I was leading a workshop for the Easter Seal Foundation. The people with whom I was working were all suffering from lung ailments such as emphysema, lung cancer, and asthma. In one section of the workshop, the objective was for participants to practice separating what they really wanted from what they thought was possible.
>
> One elderly woman was having particular trouble with the exercise.
>
> "Remember, the exercise is to separate what you want from what you think is possible," I said to her. "So, what do you want?"
>
> "I can't say," she replied. "It really isn't possible."
>
> "Well," I said, "for the moment, don't consider whether or not what you want is possible. What do you want?"
>
> "I can't say what I want because I can never have it."
>
> "I can tell you what you want," I said.
>
> "You can?"
>
> "Sure," I replied. "What you want is good health."
>
> "But I can never have it."
>
> "But isn't that what you want?"
>
> "But I can never have it," she repeated.
>
> "Well, if I were a magic genie and could wave a wand and give you perfect health, would you take it?"
>
> "She paused for a moment, and quietly said, "Yes."
>
> "If you would take it," I said, "You must want it. Furthermore, Even if it doesn't seem at all possible to you—even if it is NOT possible—the real truth is that you want perfect health."
>
> "Yes," she said, "That's so."
>
> "So, now tell yourself the truth about what you want," I said. "It's never wrong to tell yourself the truth about what you want, even though you think it's not possible to have it."

She paused. Then, looking down at the floor, she said quietly, "The truth is I want to be healthy."

"What just happened to you when you said that?" I asked.

"I don't understand this," she replied, looking very different than she had looked up to that point. "I feel physically lighter. As if a weight has been lifted off my shoulders. I feel clearer. It's almost as if there is an energy flowing through me right now."

Whether or not her illness persisted, she no longer had to bear the additional burden of feeling obligated to misrepresent to herself the truth about her desire for health.[33]

The result a person desires may not be possible. But as Fritz points out, one reason to ask ourselves what result we want to create, and to answer honestly, is to be free not only of incorrect expectations but also of expectations for what we allow ourselves to admit. Sometimes the healthiest option may be to change our desires, but we cannot change them if we are not honest about what those desires are. And if we can put aside questions of possibility just long enough to ask ourselves and honestly answer what result we want to create, then we will often discover that what appears impossible may not be impossible after all.

History is riddled with stories of people who overcame disabilities or disease, who accomplished extraordinary feats that no one else believed possible, or who discovered technologies that enabled people to do things that no one could do before. Some things are impossible. Some things become less desirable or wise as we work on them. But we tend to pick up so many limiting expectations that asking "What result do I want to create?" is almost always worthwhile, even when we eventually discover something is impossible.

Negativity

A second concern we could raise is whether being purpose-centered is necessarily positive. The answer, of course, is no. People can be as purpose-centered when they try to create extraordinarily negative results as they are when they create extraordinarily positive results. Even

people who pursue positive purposes can still do negative things or have a negative impact if they are inaccurate or wrong. For example, if the minorities in the minority influence studies can convince others that a blue slide is green, then what effect might we have when the issues have real consequences on people's lives?

Possibilities such as these are what make the other characteristics of the fundamental state of leadership so important. People who are vigilant about the integrity with which they pursue their purposes (being internally directed) are likely to detect and correct personal mistakes and errors. People who pursue their purposes with empathy for others (being other-focused) are likely to take actions that will help others as well as themselves. And people who desire to learn and grow (being externally open) are likely to develop increasingly effective and ethical ways to pursue their purposes.

The other characteristics of the fundamental state of leadership can affect people's purposes. Consider, for example, how Bob persisted in trying to get his colleagues to adopt a more lofty vision for the EMBA program. When they ignored him he could have insisted that they pay attention, called them hypocrites, or demanded answers from them. Responses such as these would have been just as *focused, energetic,* and *persistent* as the approach he took, but they would have also been less likely to have had a positive influence or to have enabled him and his colleagues to create a powerful EMBA program.

The reason Bob persisted patiently, quietly, and respectfully in his goal rather than insisting, blaming, or getting angry is because he was internally directed, other-focused, and externally open as well as purpose-centered. In short, he experienced the fundamental state of leadership. His internal direction led him to be vigilant about living his core values and to not let others shut him down. Because he was other-focused, he empathized with their struggle to give up their expectations. He did not judge or criticize; he simply asked questions. Because he was externally open, he listened deeply to their feelings and

their words, considered their feedback, and updated his strategy as he learned. We next discuss internal direction in chapter 5.

PRACTICES FOR BECOMING PURPOSE-CENTERED

When we want to become purpose-centered, we often struggle to come up with exceptional purposes that are not limited by expectations. The following practices can help:

1. **Use zero-based budgeting.** When managers create their budgets they often adjust last year's budget to reflect what their plans are for the coming year. In zero-based budgeting, managers start with a blank page. A blank page forces us to think harder about what we want to do and what we need to do it. We can use this process in many activities: "If I started with a blank page, how would I approach this?"
2. **Recite the mantra, "Why not?"** Sometimes we habitually look for obstacles rather than possibilities. When this happens we can ask ourselves again and again, "Why not?" This question invites us to look for possibilities and not just obstacles.
3. **Expand the scope or the time frame.** Problems tend to focus us on immediate issues. One way to escape this focus is to ask ourselves what the problem will mean months or years from now. In addition, thinking of more people, resources, locations, and other forms of scope can help us to put the problem in context and develop new purposes.
4. **Imagine scenarios.** When creating purpose it can be useful to imagine what the purpose might look like if you achieve it. Visualizing purposes can make them more or less appealing, or can suggest changes in what we want those purposes to be.

GROUNDED:
BEING EXTERNALLY
DIRECTED

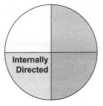

Ryan: When I was nineteen years old, I left home for two years to serve a mission for my church. A mission is both the period of time that a mission-ary spends in service and the name of the organization that missionaries serve in, located in a particular place. In my mission I taught, prosely-tized, did community service, and helped people make life changes, such as overcoming addictive habits or developing better patterns for family life. I was excited to serve.

The mission in which I served had many management positions. It consisted of about two hundred young women and men, but it was led by a couple in their sixties who served as mission presidents. The mission president had two assistants. These assistants supervised twelve zone leaders, the zone leaders supervised about thirty district leaders, and the district leaders supervised the rest of the missionaries. The assistants, zone leaders, and district leaders were all young missionaries. When there were changes in these leadership positions, missionaries often speculated about who the next person to fill a management position might be.

Consistent with the theme of this book, I believed that when a person assumes a management role, the positivity of that person's leadership depends significantly, if not overwhelmingly, on their reasons for seeking or accepting that position. Sometimes and in some organizations, members should seek management positions if they have skills that can benefit their organization or if they can learn from serving in that position. In my mission, however, the positions were filled with capable and appropriate people, there was plenty for me to learn in any position, and my purpose for serving a mission was to serve other people, not win promotions. If I was truly motivated by love for the people I was serving then I would not have cared what position I was in; I would only have cared about whether or not the people I was serving were blessed by my service.

I worked hard. Five months into my mission I was asked to serve as a district leader. Three months later I was asked to serve as a zone leader. One year into my mission, another missionary and I were asked to become partners and tour the mission helping other missionaries improve their teaching skills. When we received this assignment, many missionaries speculated that my partner or I would be asked to be the next assistant to the president. I tried to ignore all of this talk, but it was hard. Two weeks later, the mission president asked my partner to be the new assistant.

I was devastated that I was not asked to be the next assistant. I was also depressed because I had spent the past year telling myself that all I cared about was serving others, but the fact that I felt devastated was undeniable evidence that I wanted more than just to serve. I had been lying to myself, but now I had to admit that I wanted to be the assistant to the president. I wanted to write to family and friends and tell them that I was the assistant so that they would see how special I was. I wanted to be the assistant because I thought it would validate what a good person I was and prove that others should listen to my opinions. Instead, by realizing that my hard work was motivated by self-promotion as much as it was by love for other people, I had to admit to myself that I was not as good of a person as I had convinced myself I was. That hurt deeply.

Now that I could not deny that I was motivated by self-promotion, I looked back over the past year. I could see how I had, at times, behaved in ways that were more consistent with my desire to win admiration or approval than with my love for the people I was serving. Sometimes

I had worked hard more to show myself and others how hard I was working and less because I cared about the people I was serving. When I did this my behavior would change in small but real ways. Instead of pooling insights and efforts with the other missionaries to come up with optimal collaborative solutions, I might force my own idea on them. I did not consciously decide to do such things so that I could become the assistant. I really wanted to be a good missionary. But even though my errors were subtle, I was shocked, upon reflection, at how often my actions had been inconsistent with the values that I wanted to live. When I failed to live my values, I also failed to lift myself and others, and I failed to lead because I submitted blindly to cultural expectations and inspired no one to follow.

As painful as it was to recognize how I had been failing both to live up to my values and to recognize my failure, I eventually learned to appreciate this realization. Without it I had not even recognized that I had shortcomings to improve, but with it I was empowered to make changes. I have learned, and continue to learn, how to recognize activities in which I am tempted to try to win others' attention and approval, stop, question my integrity, and make changes that help me to live with ever-increasing consistency to my values. I find this to be liberating and empowering. Before I could experience liberation and empowerment, however, I had to understand the human tendency to be blind to our gaps in integrity, which is the topic of this chapter.

Building Wings That Work

Acting in a way contrary to one's values is like building an airplane with poorly designed wings: valueless actions and poor designs both lack integrity. Poorly designed wings were among Orville and Wilbur Wright's problems that we discussed in chapter 2. The glider they built in 1900 did not generate enough lift, so in 1901 they used Otto Lilienthal's lift tables to build larger wings with more curvature. Based on Lilienthal's tables, they thought this would increase lift. Instead, their new wings had almost the opposite effect.

Lilienthal's tables gave the Wright brothers problems for two reasons. The first reason was that the Wright brothers were using wings

that had a different shape from the wings that Lilienthal used. The amount and the controllability of the lift that wings generate depends on their shape, their size, the angle at which the wings approach the oncoming air, and the angle of the wings relative to the body of the aircraft, among other factors. Lilienthal, however, created his lift tables using gliders that only used one wing shape, so when the Wright brothers made adjustments to their wings—which did not have the same shape as Lilienthal's—their adjustments generated less lift and less controllability.

Another reason the Wright brothers had problems with Lilienthal's table is that the numbers in it were not sufficiently accurate. Part of this could be fixed with more precise measurements. Lilienthal, however, had also measured the forces on the wings relative to the direction the wings were facing, but the Wrights recognized that they should measure pure upward force ("true" lift) and pure backward force ("true" drag) instead. To fix this, the Wright brothers built a wind tunnel, instruments for collecting the data they needed, and as many as two hundred different model wings of varying shapes and sizes. Using these they created new tables using true lift and true drag for about four dozen different wing shapes as well as other, more accurate numbers for their equations. Using this data they selected a wing design for their glider that generated the lift that they needed. This new design had integrity because it was consistent with correct principles for harnessing lift.

The Wright brothers needed wings with designs that were consistent with correct principles to be able to harness lift and make their airplane fly. Prior to collecting data that were accurate representations of these principles, they could not harness the aerodynamic force of lift. This required them to question their beliefs in a critical, thorough, and uncompromising way. Similarly, Ryan was unable to lift himself or others when his actions were based on a desire for self-promotion rather than on love for the people he was serving. In order to lift the people he was serving and his fellow missionaries, Ryan needed to question his motivation in a critical, thorough, and uncompromising

way. It was only when he was honest with himself that he could change his motivations and act consistently with his values. As long as he remained convinced that he had pure motives when he did not, he kept slipping into behaviors that were not consistent with his values, no matter how he tried to pretend otherwise.

Ryan is not the only person who has thought he was living his values when he was not. We all do this in more ways than we realize. In fact, in the book *Blind Spots: Why We Fail to Do What's Right and What to Do About It*, Max Bazerman and Ann Tenbrunsel review a sobering list of studies documenting how shockingly unaware you and I are about the ways we fail to act ethically, or even to recognize ethical issues when we encounter them.[1] Sometimes we act in ways that are inconsistent with our values because we have learned inappropriate but automatic reactions to particular life experiences without even realizing we have learned them. Sometimes we simply give in to temptations. But once we do either of these, if we do not have some means to question ourselves there is a good chance that we will repeat those actions until they become habit: automatic, unconscious responses to other, similar experiences.

We need to respond automatically in order to keep from being overwhelmed by all of life's experiences. The problem is that many of our responses are inconsistent with values that we claim to hold. When people respond automatically to their contexts in ways that are inconsistent with their values, we describe their psychological state as *externally directed*.

External Direction

Human history is littered with examples of people acting in externally directed ways. On a grand scale, we have examples such as the Holocaust, in which government officials, military leaders, and citizens tortured and killed millions of innocent people. On a less grand scale we regularly have public figures—many of whom claim to have high

standards—caught taking bribes or cheating on their spouses. And, in our everyday lives, average citizens ignore people in need, break their word, speak poorly of others, or fail to exercise self-restraint. These may be examples of deviation from cultural norms, but they are unlikely to be examples that inspire others to follow. When other people act in externally directed ways we are often surprised or even outraged. Actions such as these are surprising because, as researchers who study values have found, most people consider values such as compassion, honesty, self-control, or the preservation of life to be important human values.[2] Why, then, do people fail to live these values?

A more troubling question for each of us may be, "Why do I fail to live my own values?" All human beings—that is, all of us—have strong tendencies to be externally directed. Our personal values may include courage, wisdom, friendship, compassion, honesty, or self-restraint, but research suggests that whatever our values may be, we live up to them less than we think we do. Like Ryan discovering that he was motivated by self-promotion, we may be just as surprised and disappointed when we discover our own failures. A small sampling of relevant research follows.

Compassion

One of the most famous researchers to examine the question of why people act in ways that are inconsistent with their values was Stanley Milgram,[3] who wanted to understand how the Holocaust could have occurred. As part of an experiment, he built a machine with a row of switches across the front and an electrode coming out of the back. Each switch was marked with a number, indicating how many volts of electricity would be sent through the electrode if a person flipped the switch. The first switch was labeled "15 volts" and had a verbal description of "SLIGHT SHOCK." The remaining switches increased by 15 volts each ("30 volts," "45 volts," "60 volts," and so on), with the final switch labeled "450 volts" and "DANGER—SEVERE SHOCK."

In Milgram's experiment a person in a gray lab coat brought two people, a "teacher" and a "learner," into the laboratory. The learner was

actually one of the research assistants, but the teacher did not know this. The teacher was a volunteer from the local community. The person in the lab coat would tell the teacher and the learner that he was studying the effects of punishment on learning. He would lead the learner to a chair, strap his arms to the chair, and attach the electrode we described above to the learner's wrist. The learner's job was to learn a list of word pairs. The teacher's job was to test the learner. If the learner answered a question correctly, the teacher was to read the next question. If the learner made a mistake, the teacher was to flip the next highest switch on the box, administering higher and higher levels of electric shock to the learner for each wrong answer.

The learner in this experiment did not actually receive an electric shock, but he acted as if he did. The learner grunted when he received the 75-volt shock, complained when he received the 120-volt shock, demanded to be released from the experiment at 150 volts, got increasingly emotional as the size of the shocks increased, and screamed in agony at 285 volts. Throughout this process, if the teacher expressed any concern about administering the shocks, the person in the gray lab coat would say, "The experiment requires that you continue."

Milgram conducted this experiment to answer the question, "At what point will the teacher refuse to obey the man in the gray lab coat?" He and others conducted this experiment thousands of times. In the basic form of the experiment that we just described, 65 percent of the teachers obeyed the person in the lab coat until they flipped the very last switch. Every participant flipped at least some of the switches. Many, if not most, of the teachers felt stress over shocking the learners, but none of them refused to participate and most of them obeyed in spite of believing that they were inflicting significant pain on another human being.[4]

Milgram and his colleagues kept track of the professions, level of education, political affiliation, and many other individual differences of all of the teachers. These individual differences had almost no impact on the number of switches people would flip. Clearly something was

different between the 65 percent of the people who flipped all of the switches and the 35 percent of the people who did not. Recently, some scholars have suggested new possible explanations for this difference.[5] We examine why people refused to obey in chapter 6. For now, it is sufficient to note that most people learn to obey authority figures early in their lives, and for many of us the automatic tendency to obey people who look and act like authority figures is strong enough to overwhelm other values, even to the point of hurting others.

Helpfulness

The trappings of authority are one of many contextual influences that can overwhelm people's values. Another influence is the number of people in a situation. John Darley and Bibb Latane found this out in an experiment, the genesis of which came from the story of a woman who was killed by a mugger while bystanders did little to help.[6] Darley and Latane had students from a university in a large city come to their laboratory to participate in a discussion. Participants took turns speaking through a microphone to students in other rooms, but what the students in the other rooms heard were actually recorded voices. On one of these recordings a male voice—identified as a student— mentioned that he found life at a city school difficult, and he sometimes suffered from epileptic seizures. Then, during the student's second turn to speak, the recording indicated that he was having a seizure; he spoke disjointedly and painfully and expressed worry about having a seizure and dying. The experimenters then measured whether the participants would try to get help for the student having a seizure and, if so, how long it took them to seek help.

Darley and Latane hypothesized that participants would be more likely to help the student having an epileptic seizure if there were fewer people involved in the conversation. They argued that when we know that other people are also aware of an emergency, we assume that they are just as responsible for responding to that emergency as we are. This logic diffuses the responsibility among all of the participants. If

responsibility is diffused among many people, one individual does not have much responsibility. Therefore, other concerns such as uncertainty, inconvenience, or fear can overwhelm this lessened sense of responsibility.

The experiment confirmed Darley and Latane's hypothesis. They assigned participants to groups of different sizes. Some participants only talked to the recording of the epileptic student. Some participants spoke to the recording of the epileptic student and one other recording. And some participants spoke to the recording of the epileptic student and the recordings of four other students. The participants who thought they were speaking only to the student with the epileptic seizure came out of the room looking for help faster than those who thought they were talking to more people. Those who thought that they were speaking to five other students came out the slowest. Gender, speaking order, personality measures, and background characteristics had no effect on how quickly the students came out looking for help. The only other factor that influenced the speed at which they sought help was the size of the community in which they grew up: people from smaller communities were slightly more likely to help than were people from larger communities.

Diffused responsibility is one reason people fail to help others, but it is not the only reason. Time pressure is another. Darley found this in a study he conducted with Daniel Batson in which they re-created the biblical story of the Good Samaritan—a story in which three people walked past a man who was beaten by robbers. Only one person stopped to help.

Darley and Batson instructed theology students to each give a sermon in a nearby building. They told some of these students that they were late and others that they had plenty of time. In the path between the building in which the students received their assignments and the one in which they were to give their sermons, an actor was lying on the ground, playing the role of an ailing person. Only 10 percent of the seminary students who thought that they were late stopped to help the ailing person, but 63 percent of those who did not think that

they were late stopped. Ironically, Darley and Batson assigned half of the seminary students in each group to give a talk on the parable of the Good Samaritan, and half of the students to speak on an irrelevant topic. Presumably, if a person is giving a talk about stopping to help ailing people on the side of the road, he or she might be more inclined to stop and help ailing people on the side of the road. Some of them did, but for most participants the impact of being late overwhelmed any impact that valuing helping had on actually helping the actor.

Achievement

The trappings of authority in the Milgram studies, additional bystanders in Darley and Latane's study, time pressure in Darley and Batson's study, and cues related to leadership positions on Ryan's mission are all examples of *context*. A person's context includes the surroundings associated with the situation that the person is in. For example, in the Milgram study the teacher's immediate situation was one of instructing the learner in memorizing word pairs, but the teacher's context included the laboratory and the person in the gray lab coat. The situation in the bystander study was another person's epileptic seizure, but the context included the number of other people who were also aware of the situation. The situation in the Good Samaritan study was the encounter of an ailing person, but the context was the sermon that the students were planning to give and the time at which they were planning to deliver it. In each case people encountered situations that might have elicited compassionate or helpful behaviors, but those potential behaviors were overwhelmed by factors in their contexts.

The potential for context to overwhelm values is not limited to prosocial values such as compassion and helpfulness. Context can even overwhelm values that are primarily oriented toward self-advancement, such as personal achievement. For example, Margaret Shih and her colleagues recruited a number of Asian women to participate in a study in which they examined how well these women performed on a math test.[7] Before taking the test, however, Shih and her colleagues randomly

divided the women into three groups and had each group take a different questionnaire about themselves; one-third of the women filled out a questionnaire that focused on being Asian, one-third filled out a questionnaire that focused on being female, and one-third filled out a generic questionnaire that had nothing to do with race or gender.

After filling out the questionnaire, the women took the math test. Those who answered the questionnaire about being Asian performed the best, followed by those who answered the generic questionnaire. The worst scores were obtained by the women who answered the questionnaire about being female. The difference in text scores had nothing to do with their math skills; the women were randomly distributed. The average differences in their scores depended on whether the questionnaire they took had focused them on their racial or gender identities.

In the United States, people learn early and often that Asians are good at math and women are not. Evidence does not support these stereotypes, but the women in this experiment still responded in the ways that society expected them to, even though they had no conscious reason for doing so and no differences in their math skills. The biggest influence on the extent to which they lived up to the value of personal achievement was not their personal values but the unconscious stereotypes they had learned about themselves.

Automaticity

The experiment with Asian women taking a math test is a useful illustration of the power of context and of how automatically people respond to their contexts. The experimenters did not tell their female participants to "think about being a woman" or "think about being an Asian"; there were no explicit connections made between mathematics and gender or race. The women simply filled out a questionnaire. Even though they had no reason to think explicitly about the stereotypical connections among gender, race, and math, the women who an-

swered a questionnaire about their ethnicity still performed relatively well and the women who answered a questionnaire about their gender still performed relatively poorly.

The study with the epileptic student was similar. When it was over, Darley and Latane asked the participants if the size of the group affected their decision to help. The participants said no—even though the size of the group was the most powerful predictor of whether and how quickly the participants looked for help. In other words, participants made sense of and responded to the cues in their context automatically and without explicit thought.

This kind of automatic response is not unique to Asian women in North America or students in a city university; it is fundamental to human behavior. We all react automatically to cues in our environment, every day, without realizing what we are doing. Questionnaires are just one technique that psychologists use to get people to respond automatically. Francesca Gino and Cassie Mogilner used another technique.[8] In their experiment, participants were asked to perform a series of unrelated activities. For the first activity, they randomly assigned participants to three groups and gave each of them a set of word lists. The sets were the same in all three groups, except for one word in each list. For example, one word list read as follows in each of the groups:

Group 1: sheets the change clock
Group 2: sheets the change price
Group 3: sheets the change sock

In other words, the word lists in group one contained words relating to time, the word lists in group two contained words relating to money, and the word lists in group three contained words relating to neither time nor money. For each list, participants were asked to select three words and write a grammatically correct sentence.

When participants finished writing sentences, they were given twenty dollars and a puzzle involving matching number pairs. They were told to complete the puzzles in five minutes, which was not be enough time to complete the matches. The participants were also told that they should keep a dollar for each number pair they were able to match. The grading system was set up so that participants would think that there was no way for their grades to be checked and no way for them to be identified, but the researchers had included secret numbers on the puzzles that allowed them to check and match the grades with the amount of money the participants took. They knew whether and how much each participant cheated.

The two activities were not, in fact, "unrelated." 87.5% of the people who received lists with words that related to money cheated, 66.7% of the people who received lists with words that did not relate to money or time cheated, and 42.4% of the people who received lists with words that related to time cheated. In other words, the simple inclusion of words related to money rather than time was sufficient to get more than twice as many people to cheat.

Simple cues are often sufficient to have a surprising impact on our thoughts, feelings, and actions. A few words or the decorations in the room in which a person sits can change increase or decrease a person's performance, lead people to act more or less compassionately and helpfully, or even get people to cheat.[9] And when the world around us primes us to perform poorly; to act less politely, compassionately, or helpfully; or to act in other ways that are inconsistent with our values we are like poorly designed wings, unable to lift ourselves or others.

Bargh, one of the world's leading researchers on the automatic processes that our brains use, suggests that about 95 percent of our thoughts and actions are automatic, unconscious processes.[10] If automatic processing is so important to our daily functioning, though, and if our core values are so important to us, why do we not learn thought and action responses that are consistent with our core values?

How We Learn to Act Contrary to Our Values

By the time Ryan's mission president had asked Ryan's partner to be the next president's assistant, Ryan's subtle ways of vying for the position were automatic to him. As with many automatic reactions, Ryan's attention had been so well diverted from the fact that he was vying for the position and acting in ways that were contrary to his values that he had become mostly unaware. People lose awareness of the inconsistency between their values and their actions through at least two processes: self-justification and learning others' justifications. An excellent illustration of this process is the pyramid of choice.

Self-Justification

Carol Tavris and Elliot Aronson describe the pyramid of choice as follows:

> Imagine two young men who are identical in terms of attitudes, abilities, and psychological health. They are reasonably honest and have the same middling attitude toward, say, cheating: They think it is not a good thing to do, but there are worse crimes in the world. Now they are both in the midst of taking an exam that will determine whether they get into graduate school. They each draw a blank on a crucial essay question. Failure looms . . . at which point each one gets an easy opportunity to cheat, by reading another student's answers. The two young men struggle with the temptation. After a long moment of anguish, one yields and the other resists. Their decisions are a hair's breadth apart; it could easily have gone the other way for each of them. Each gains something important, but at a cost: One gives up integrity for a good grade, the other gives up a good grade to preserve his integrity.
>
> Now the question is: how do they feel about cheating a week later? Each student has had ample time to justify the course of action he took. The one who yielded to temptation will decide that cheating is not so great a crime. He will say to himself: "Hey, everyone cheats. It's no big deal. And I really need to do this for my future career." But the one who resisted the temptation will decide that cheating is far more immoral

than he originally thought: "In fact, people who cheat are disgraceful. In fact people who cheat should be permanently expelled from school. We have to make an example of them."[11]

The process by which these two young men come to view cheating as "no big deal" versus "disgraceful" is called *self-justification*. People tend to engage in self-justification when they have two inconsistent thoughts or beliefs, such as "Cheating is an immoral thing to do" and "I just cheated on a test," the inconsistency of which makes them feel uncomfortable. Leon Festinger called this uncomfortable feeling "cognitive dissonance."[12] Because dissonance is uncomfortable, people tend to justify or rationalize their thoughts and actions by telling themselves (and sometimes others) a consistent and worthwhile story about these conflicting thoughts, such as "Hey, everyone cheats. It's no big deal. I really need to do this for my career."

What people do less often when confronted by inconsistent thoughts is admit they are wrong and try to make amends. In fact, not only is it less common for people to admit that they are wrong, but as the research on the confirming evidence bias suggests (see chapter 3), even when people are confronted with evidence suggesting that they are wrong they actually tend to defend their actions more tenaciously, finding even more reasons to justify their position.

When professors teach their students about self-justification, the students are usually surprised by the fact that people believe their justifications. However, self-justification is not necessarily the same as lying to oneself. In fact, justification is seldom effective if the rationalizations we use are not true, or at least plausible enough for us to convince ourselves that they are true. For example, when Ryan would do little things such as draw attention to himself, fail to give credit to another, or engage in other small ways of trying to make himself look good and vie for higher positions in the hierarchy of his mission, he would justify the actions in terms of how hard he was working, how well he obeyed the rules, how well he taught, or how much he cared about serv-

ing the people. These justifications were effective in helping Ryan to hide his motives from himself because they were true: he did work hard; he made every effort to be exceptionally obedient; he was a good teacher; and he did care about the people he was serving.

There were occasional moments in which Ryan became aware that his actions were not consistent with his values, but he could quickly regain his ignorance by smothering those realizations with fresh new waves of self-justification. Some of our justifications are so effective, in fact, that we apply them without realizing we are doing so, as evidenced in the experiment with the epileptic student in which participants believed that the number of people in their group had nothing to do with their decisions even though it was the most significant factor.

We believe our self-justifications in part because of how convincing they are, but also because human memory is imperfect. As time passes, our minds forget or distort the evidence or experiences that might contradict our justifications. Research shows, for example, that people often remember teenage squabbles with their parents or eyewitness accounts in courtroom trials differently from the way the actual events occurred.[13] As a result, the fictional young man who cheated in Tavris and Aronson's pyramid of choice developed a worldview that identifies conditions when cheating is okay. The strength of his justifications and the weakness of his memory made these easy to believe. He could then cheat a little more, which required a little more justification, which provided more circumstances in which cheating was justified. Soon cheating was normal. At that point, everyone could see the young man's dishonesty except for the man himself. It is much easier to see hypocrisy in others than in ourselves.

Learning Others' Justifications

People also come to act in ways that are inconsistent with their values by learning justifications from other people, such as when a person takes a new job and learns "how things are done around here." When this happens we learn both behaviors and justifications for

those behaviors, often without thinking about whether or not those behaviors are consistent with our values. (In fact, this is one reason why leadership that deviates from cultural assumptions can inspire others to follow us: such leadership is often deviating from the values-inconsistent habits we were socialized into adopting.) We learn some of the most powerful beliefs from our parents or primary caregivers. Sometimes these beliefs are justifications for choices that have been passed down for generations, affecting our professional lives as much as our personal lives.

An example of inheriting beliefs that keep people from living their values comes from a colleague of ours named Julie, a manager in a large European company. One day she was participating in a team-building session with the members of her leadership team. They were discussing what it felt like to be part of the team, and Julie decided to be honest. She told the other members that she felt like she was the weakest member, that she was not getting much out of her experience, and that she did not feel like she was adding much value.

Julie's teammates were shocked; each person told her that she was seen as a valuable and important member of the team. This response surprised Julie; instead of returning after the next break, she went to her hotel room and cried for the rest of the day. It was clear that her experience that morning had touched her deeply, but she was not sure why.

Over the next few weeks Julie pondered her experience and learned some principles about how she was preventing herself from living her values. She realized, for example, that she valued being a person of voice, influence, and contribution, but that she had instead been silencing herself. She had learned this from her father without realizing it.

Julie's father was very critical of her from childhood to adulthood. For example, one day when Julie was promoted to vice president for talent in her organization, she called to tell her father. He replied, "What kind of a title is that? Sounds like nonsense to me. And what right do you have to be a vice president? You're just a little pischer."

Julie's father was not the only voice teaching her to silence herself. She grew up as an American in London, and peers in her schools teased her regularly for her "ugly" American accent. As a result, she learned to speak with an English accent, and did whatever she could to hide her "Americanness" from other people. Criticisms such as those she learned from her father and from the children who teased her taught Julie that it was safer to hide her voice rather than to contribute what she had to offer. She carried this belief with her into adulthood. As an adult, her friends and coworkers wanted and needed her contributions and opinions, but she withheld them instead. No one was teasing her about her accent now. She seldom saw her father. In fact, she never encountered her father at work, but this was where she was silencing herself the most.

What Julie did encounter at work was her boss, an austere British man in a powerful role who was also the embodiment of the forces that had silenced her in her childhood. As a child, the categories *male, authority,* and *British* became cues that suggested she was likely to be criticized. When she encountered these cues as an adult, they sparked within her an automatic response to hide anything that might be criticized. As a result, she avoided voicing her potential contributions.

The process of reacting to cues (such as *male, authority,* and *British*) in the same way that we reacted to them as children is called *transference*.[14] The problem with transference is that the reactions that were appropriate in childhood are often no longer appropriate in adulthood. For example, Julie's boss was not her father but, even so, Julie reacted to him as if he were. She failed to share her opinions because she was afraid of being criticized. When people transfer what they learn in childhood to adult contexts, they seldom consider acting differently until they have experiences such as Julie's conversation with her team. Sometimes people need dramatic experiences to see that they can be more internally directed.

From External Direction to Internal Direction

Understanding how we become externally directed can help us learn how to become internally directed. We are externally directed when our automatic reactions to our context are not consistent with the values we espouse or that we expect of others.[15] We create these automatic responses by justifying our actions or learning others' actions and justifications over time. These justifications define how we see the world as well as the cues to which we notice and respond. When our actions are inconsistent with our values, these justifications help us to lose our ability to see these inconsistencies. For example, Ryan's competitiveness and attention seeking and Julie's silence became invisible to them because of their justifications.

Once we know we are being externally directed we can do something about it. For example, when Julie realized she was not voicing her thoughts to her boss, she also felt she needed to share this realization with him. She invited him to have a cup of coffee with her. She told him her story, and to her surprise, he then shared a personal story with her. In other words, she exercised leadership, even if she did not think of it as such. Julie's relationship with her boss changed completely. The two of them began to work together as equals, supporting each other in their work instead of simply giving, receiving, and reporting on assignments.

Julie's personal change did more than just change her boss. As she worked to contribute more, Julie became more willing—even eager—to express her ideas and opinions and to share her knowledge. Now she even talks about such things as "gut feel" instead of worrying that people will think that expressing her intuitions will make her seem "soft." She helps other executives see how their decisions affect other employees. She lifts the people around her to higher motivation, trust, and opportunity. Julie even made peace with her father before he passed away.

IN FLIGHT:
BECOMING INTERNALLY
DIRECTED

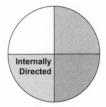

Stephen—a friend of ours—loved basketball, and he was good at it. As a teenager he won awards, dominated the leagues in which he participated, and had some college coaches paying attention to him. When he joined the high school varsity team, however, his coach almost never let him play. Stephen gave his best effort in every practice, followed the rules, outplayed his teammates, and worked constantly to improve, but no matter what he did his coach would not give him any more playing time.

Eventually Stephen and his parents found out that all of the players struggled with the coach—even the kids who started the games. Apparently this coach demoralized his teams every year. He had some of the most talented players in the state, and yet his teams would lose early in the state tournament and his players would say such things as "I cannot wait for the season to end so I can start enjoying basketball again." The coach hardly ever spoke to the players, and when he did he was usually angry, bordering on abusive.

Stephen was a quiet kid, and was a little intimidated by the idea of confronting his coach. In his senior year, however, it became clear that Stephen would probably go through his entire high school experience without ever having a chance to have any significant playing time on a team where he was unquestionably the best player in his position. Stephen's parents could tell how much this hurt him, so they offered to talk to the coach for him. Stephen did not want his parents to talk to the coach, but he eventually agreed to talk to the coach himself. His parents coached him on how to speak effectively in hopes of improving the relationship with his coach as well as improving the situation for everyone involved.

The next day Stephen asked his coach if he could talk to him. The coach looked unhappy and asked him what he wanted. Stephen said that he would like to earn more playing time, and asked the coach if there was anything he could do to improve his skills to make that happen. The coach swore under his breath and walked away. Stephen realized that the coach had no reason for not letting him play more, but the next day the coach put Stephen on the third string, where he was unlikely to ever get any playing time.

Stephen could not stop thinking about how poorly his coach treated him. One night he sat in his bedroom crying. Before going to sleep, he prayed. When he did, he felt an impulse: even though his coach was not a good coach, he was a good man, and he needed to forgive him. When Stephen felt this impulse, he realized that he had grown to hate his coach. Given that he valued love and forgiveness, this meant that he was failing to live his values.

Many of us might be surprised or offended by the claim that we are failing to live our values if we had been treated as Stephen was. After all, if a young person feels hate toward an adult in a powerful position who treats him in ways that are nearly abusive, that hate seems justified. This, however, is the point. Even in a case such as this, where Stephen has done nothing wrong to the coach, he must justify his feelings of hate because they are not consistent with his values. In fact, the research on

cognitive dissonance and the confirming evidence bias suggest that most of us would do exactly that: engage in self-justification. After all, that is what most of the other players on the team were doing.

In contrast, Stephen's impulse helped him to see that even though his justifications were accurate, they did not help him, his team, or his coach. He therefore decided to become internally directed by forgiving his coach. Stephen looked for ways in which his coach was a good man—in spite of being a bad coach. He saw how the coach helped other students in the high school through counseling and administration. He complimented his coach for what he saw, and gradually he felt better about him. He began to get excited about playing basketball again. He practiced hard because he loved playing the game. He quit trying to impress the coach or anyone else. Practice became fun, and Stephen was lifted by his experience.

Stephen's decision to become internally directed did more than lift himself; it also turned him into a leader and lifted others. He made the decision to forgive his coach as his basketball team was winding down its regular season. At this point, his team was following the same pattern it had in its previous years under this coach: even though the team had won eleven of its first twelve games, frustration took over and the team only won two of its last eight games. Players went through the motions, waiting for the season to end. But this year, something different happened.

One of the assistant coaches called a "players only" meeting. He asked if any of the players wanted to express his feelings. The room was quiet. Then, to the surprise of everyone—including himself—Stephen stood up. He talked about the potential of the team and what they could do in the state tournament. He talked about how hard he worked, even though he got hardly any playing time. And then he told them, "I could live with that if the people who get playing time were also working hard." He expressed his honest feelings about how he struggled with the people who were being lazy, and asked them to play hard for the team.

Stephen's teammates were riveted by his words. They committed to work, and they won the first game of the district tournament. The second game was close. In the second quarter, the coach put Stephen in. He had five steals, four points, and a few assists in only a few minutes. They won handily, and also won the district and regional championships. In the first game of the state tournament, Stephen's team lost a close game to a team that was ranked thirteenth in the country.

Stephen never got to play Division I college basketball, though he probably could have. His coach never gave him enough playing time in which college scouts could see and evaluate him. Although he would have liked to have played college basketball, he wonders whether he could have learned how to forgive if he had not had an experience that was that painful to him. He has come to be grateful for the experience, and for the way it developed his capacity to be internally directed. Years later, his youngest brother was on the basketball team in the same high school, and his team made it to the state championship game. When the family arrived at the stadium Stephen saw his old coach, who was now retired and had come as a spectator. To the surprise of some of his family members, Stephen walked straight to his old coach, hugged him, and asked the coach how he was doing. His family realized that they had not forgiven the coach nearly as well as Stephen had, and he inspired them to want to be more forgiving as well.

Changing Our Stories

We propose that Stephen was able to become internally directed because he changed his story: his personal description of who he was and why the events in his life were unfolding as they were. On the night he had the impulse that led him to forgive his coach, he realized that his story so far was a story of hate, and that this story was inconsistent with his values. At that moment he decided to create a new, forgiving story.

Justifications, such as those we discussed in chapter 5, are types of stories. They describe who we are and why we take the actions we take.

When we accept these justifications as truth, they give form to our automatic reactions and can keep us from acting in ways that are consistent with our values (as we discussed in chapter 5). Therefore, one of the most powerful things we can do to help us act in ways that are consistent with our values is to change our stories. Researchers have identified at least two types of stories that we can use instead of justifications: implementation intentions and reasons.

Implementation Intentions

To understand how implementation intentions work, imagine that you are in a room with another person who is quizzing you with flash cards. Each card has the name of a color written on it, but the color in which these names are written is not the same color as the name that is written. For example, a card that has "red" written on it may be written in green ink, or a card that has "blue" written on it may be written in yellow ink. Your job is to name the color of the ink as quickly as you can each time you are shown a card. How much effort would it take for you to name the color of ink on each card correctly each time?

Thomas Webb and Paschal Sheeran posed this challenge to a number of people in an experiment.[1] Naming the color of the ink actually required a fair amount of effort because the participants had to fight the tendency to read the words. Some of the participants had to slog through the task. Others, however, got help. Webb and Sheeran had them state specific intentions for what they would do with each card, such as, "As soon as I see the card I will ignore the word and say the color of the second letter." Simply saying a sentence such as this made a significant difference in how fatigued participants were after performing the task.

Webb and Sheeran measured the participants' fatigue by asking them to solve unsolvable puzzles as a second task. The participants did not know that the puzzles could not be solved. Webb and Sheeran used the amount of time that the participants spent trying to solve the unsolvable puzzles as an indicator of how fatigued they had become from

the color-naming task. They found that participants who had stated specific intentions in the color-naming task persisted longer and made more attempts to solve the unsolvable puzzles than those who had not.

Psychologists have performed other, similar experiments, sometimes in the same order, sometimes in reverse, using different activities or ways of measuring.[2] The results are similar: people grow less fatigued on tasks that require mental effort when they state specific intentions for how they plan to implement their task. Implementation intentions help people override their automatic tendencies (such as reading a color name) before a task so that they do not have to overcome those tendencies during a task. They also help people begin creating new automatic tendencies (such as stating the color of the ink).

Implementation intentions are small stories that describe what we will do in a particular situation. They take the form "If X occurs, I will do Y." If we want to use implementation intentions to be internally directed, then Y needs to be an action that is consistent with our values. For example, we might say, "When I see people who need help, I will stop to help them." Or, "If I feel uncomfortable when someone in authority tells me to do something, I will say, 'I'm not sure why, but I feel uncomfortable about that request. I need to think about it and get back to you.'" Stephen used implementation intentions by telling himself that when he saw his coach at school he would look for things that he admired about him. Implementation intentions such as this embody leadership because they are used to defy cultural assumptions while also developing a plan to live up to our highest values.

The more specific an implementation intention is, the more help it will be in changing behavior. For example, "If my mother says I am inconsiderate, I will think of things I admire about her before responding" will be more effective than "If someone accuses me of a fault I will think positive thoughts." When forming an implementation intention, it may be helpful to ask questions such as "Who?" "What?" "When?" "Where?" and "How?" They identify specific cues to which a person wants to develop a different response and the exact value-consistent

actions that will be taken in response to the cue. A specific description of the context helps people to pause rather than react automatically. A specific description of the new behavior, if implemented over time, can become a new automatic response. Specific implementation intentions become automatic more quickly because we do not have to expend as much energy trying to figure out if a situation matches a specific description.

Reasons

A second type of story we can use to become internally directed is a reason—a story we tell to explain why we should do something. We can see the power of reasons in an experiment conducted by Gregory Maio and his colleagues.[3] These scholars asked participants to (1) write a paper explaining their reasons for supporting or opposing the importance of treating other people equally; (2) perform a word puzzle with such words as *equality, even, same, balance,* and *fair* in it; or (3) do nothing. Thus, one group thought of reasons to treat people equally (or not), one group thought of the word *equality* but did not think of reasons for treating people equally, and one group had no reason to think about equality.

After completing the first activity, Maio and his colleagues divided the participants into red and blue teams and told them that they would play a game of twenty questions—with a twist. The twist was that the participants' teams would get to start the game with some extra points. The way that they determined how many points they would get would be by assigning points to the next group of participants to play the game. They could give the future red and blue teams sixteen points each, or they could give the future team that was the same color as their own team more points than the other team (for example, if the participant was on the blue team, then the participant could choose to give twenty points to a blue player and twelve points to a red player). The participants would get as many points to start with as they gave the future team that was the same color as their own. Thus, the current

participants would have an advantage if they favored the future team that was the same color as their own.

When Maio and his colleagues examined the choices of the people in each group, they found that more of the participants who came up with reasons for treating people equally distributed the future team's points equally than did the participants who unscrambled words or the participants who did not engage in the first activity. In other words, participants were more likely to treat people equally when they had reasons for treating people equally.

The research that Maio and his colleagues conducted suggests that most values, for most of us, are truisms. We learn from early childhood that values are important, but we never spend much time thinking critically about why they are important. As a result, when we encounter cues that make us feel like reacting in ways that are not consistent with our values, we have no reason to resist that impulse other than the existence of the values themselves. In contrast, acting on that impulse is easy and automatic. If participants who have more and better reasons for treating others equally actually treat other people more equally, then all of us might be more likely to live our values if we have more and better reasons for doing so. For example, in a second study Maio and his colleagues found that participants who had reasons for being helpful spent more time helping another person than did those who did not come up with reasons.[4]

Stephen used reasons to help him forgive his coach. He believed that forgiveness would bring him peace, that this peace would prevent him from disturbing others with his anger, that his anger and hate could consume him if he let it, that his anger was pointless (it had no obvious impact on his coach), and that he also had faults and needed forgiveness. These reasons were important, because Stephen had many justifications for not forgiving his coach: his coach had treated him unfairly, was not coaching well, was destroying the team, and was wasting the talent that the boys on the team had to use; and he may have even been damaging some boys' chances to play basketball in college.

Stephen needed strong reasons to forgive his coach in order to over-come the justifications that supported the impulse to hate him.

Stories

Our discussion so far suggests that one reason we recommend us-ing the question "What would my story be if I were living up to the values that I expect of others?" as a way to become internally directed is because implementation intentions and reasons are stories. If we merge implementation intentions and reasons into a single story, we can think of implementation intention as the story's plot and reasons as morals. Implementation intentions are plots because they describe how particular people take particular actions in particular situations. Reasons (and justifications) are morals because they tell us why we should behave that way.

Stories can motivate and direct our actions. Jim Loehr—a psycholo-gist who wrote the book *The Power of Story*—argues that in addition to plots (or "action," as he calls it) and morals (or "purpose"), stories need truth to motivate action.[5] Truth can be found in how honestly we tell our stories. Is the story a justification to make up for the fact that we are not living our values, or does the story represent an effort to live consis-tently with our values in spite of pressures to behave otherwise? Is the story honest about the events that are occurring around us, or are we only including information that confirms what we already believe?

Loehr once told a story that illustrates these principles well. Loehr and his colleagues at the Human Performance Institute train people in how to improve their performance in work and in life by managing their energy. One of Loehr's clients was not managing his energy well; he smoked multiple packs of cigarettes each day. To improve this man's performance in work and in life, they had this man write his story so far and write what the story of his life could be. During this process Loehr learned that this man adored his daughter. She was the most important thing in his life. As they worked with him, he eventually wrote the following story:

It is a beautiful day, and your daughter is radiant. She is eighteen years old. She is at her high school graduation. She looks gorgeous in her robes, and she is smiling at everyone. As the ceremony ends, she runs up to your wife to give her a hug. She thanks your wife for everything your wife did to make this day special for your daughter, saying, "Thank you, Mom. This day was perfect. The only thing that could have made it better was if Daddy hadn't died."

The client went home from the program and never smoked again.

Loehr's client's story has a clear moral and told the truth: "If you don't stop smoking you could miss the most important memories with your daughter." Depriving her (and himself) of those opportunities was more painful for the client than the thought of his own death. Finally, this story has—or at least implies—a plot. It is a hypothetical story about the future consequences of today's actions. It suggests that if the client continued to smoke multiple packs each day, the consequences could be more devastating than death. On the other hand, if he quit smoking he would probably be there with his daughter. The action that he wanted to take became perfectly clear.

What We Expect of Others

Bob: The top management team of a large company once sent all of its senior managers to a famous seminar on quality in hopes that this would improve the company's performance in the marketplace. After the seminar, I sat with these people in a strategic planning meeting. I noticed that they were assuming that their company's quality, productivity, and overall performance would improve as a result of sending their senior managers to the seminar. I was concerned by this assumption, so I told them about another company that I was acquainted with. The senior managers in this other company had been to the same seminar, but three years later there were no observable improvements in that company.

The management team was riveted by my story. They had spent a lot of money sending their people to the seminar. One of them blurted out, "Why did it fail?"

"You tell me," I replied.

The room was silent. Then one of the more senior members of the group spoke quietly. He said, "The leaders of the company didn't change."

I nodded. I told the executives that they were making many assumptions about how other people would change. Then I challenged them: "Identify one time when one of you said that you were going to change your behavior."

The room was silent again. After a few moments, another person asked me for suggestions. I made a few suggestions of simple but significant changes that I had seen executives in other companies make. The group quietly considered these options. They decided to adjourn to think about what they should do.

It is easy to judge these executives for expecting their employees to live up to standards that they themselves were not living up to. But we should also remember that we all have a tendency to justify the gaps in our integrity. Hypocrisy is easier to see in other people than it is in ourselves. Fortunately, the fact that we can see hypocrisy in others suggests a way for us to see it in ourselves. If we think that others' actions are hypocritical, it means that we do not think they are living certain values that we expect of them. And if we think that it is important for others to live those values, then it is important for us to also live them if we do not want to be hypocrites. The phrase "if I were living the values I expect of others" helps us to see this. We need more than stories. We—like the executives who sent their employees to the quality seminar or like Stephen with his coach—need to create stories about living the values we expect others to enact.

To understand the values you expect of others, pay attention to your emotions. People have emotions when their expectations are violated. For example, we might experience happiness when an employee's performance exceeds our expectations. Or we might experience frustration if a coworker fails to deliver on a promised commitment. The fact that we feel emotion when expectations are violated tells us what we value in others. We may be happy about exceptional performance

because we value performance or because we value other people's growth and achievement. We may be frustrated about a failed commitment because we value reliability or integrity to one's promises. Whatever our emotions reveal about our values should be applied to our own story if we want to live with more integrity and less hypocrisy.

The question "What would my story be if I were living the values I expect of others?" does three things for us if we answer it honestly. First, it helps us to identify what values are important to us by noticing what we expect of others. Second, it helps us to critique ourselves with regard to how well we are living those values. And third, it helps us to create a story with a plot, a moral, and truth that will help us to become more internally directed.

Internal Direction: Moments of Dignity

Before Stephen chose to forgive his coach, his story was about being mistreated by the coach and having the joy of basketball stolen from him. Stephen was the object rather than the subject in most of the sentences of this story, and most of the verbs in the story were passive. Those are characteristics of an externally directed story.

After Stephen chose to forgive his coach, his story changed. Stephen appreciated the good he saw in the man; he practiced hard, he improved his skills, and he enjoyed the game. He was the subject rather than the object of most of the sentences in this story, the verbs were action verbs, and the moral of his story was values-driven. Stephen was internally directed. He was energized by basketball and by life, he quit trying to impress the coach, and he focused on interacting positively with his coach and on playing hard, fun basketball.

Energy, focus, and clear direction are elements of internal direction that are similar to being purpose-centered. They are similar because a value is a type of goal—a principle that we feel strongly that we should strive to live[6]—and stories are composed of plots that enable characters to achieve goals.[7] Values are more than just ends that we strive to

achieve, though, and stories are not just descriptions of what people do. Values are also personal and societal ideals and stories are illustrations of characters who live (or fail to live) those ideals. When we live our highest ideals and the highest ideals of the societies we live in, we experience what Joshua Margolis, a business ethicist, calls a "moment of dignity."[8]

To help us understand what a moment of dignity is, Margolis draws on an observation from Stanley Milgram, the psychologist who ran the experiments in which participants were asked to shock another person if the other person did not answer his word-pair questions correctly (see chapter 5). These experiments have occupied the minds of ethicists for many years because they raise the issue of whether people are actually responsible for their actions. After all, if humans are hardwired to react automatically to cues in their contexts, how can they be responsible? And if they are not responsible, then how can we claim that their actions are ethical or unethical?

Milgram began to answer these questions himself. After he had published findings from his early research on the topic, many people criticized Milgram's experiments, saying that they should have been discontinued at the first sign of stress or discomfort in the participants. Diana Baumrind (whom Milgram called "the critic") was one of these; she used language that suggested that Milgram *made* the participants shock the victims.[9] In response, Milgram wrote,

> The critic feels that the experimenter *made* the subject shock the victim. This conception is alien to my view. The experimenter tells the subject to do something. But between the command and the outcome there is a paramount force, the acting person who may obey or disobey. I started with the belief that every person who came to the laboratory was free to accept or to reject the dictates of authority. This view sustains a conception of human dignity insofar as it sees in each man a capacity for choosing his own behavior. And as it turned out, many subjects did, indeed, choose to reject the experimenter's commands, providing powerful affirmation of human ideals.[10]

The last two sentences of this paragraph help us understand what Margolis means by dignity; it is the "capacity for choosing [one's] own behavior." The 35 percent of the participants who thought for themselves and chose to do what they felt was right in spite of the demands of an authority figure (some sooner and some later) affirmed human ideals by acting with dignity.

People do not, however, always act consistently with their potential dignity. We presume that this is why Margolis uses the phrase "moments of dignity": because moments of dignity are times in which people choose to act consistently with that which they take "to be of value, and thus worthy of respect, about human beings"—sometimes in contrast to the impulses they feel in the context that they are in.[11] Dignity occurs in moments when people exercise their distinctively human capacity to live their highest values in spite of pressure. It occurs in our moments of leadership. This is the distinctive feature of internal direction. People feel dignity within them when they experience the pleasure of acting virtuously in spite of inclinations to do otherwise and when they are free from the constraints of self-justification.

Strength

A simple way to understand the pleasure of virtuous action is to think of the last time you chose to wake up early, get off the couch, or relinquish your task list to make yourself exercise. Sometimes the thought of crawling out of that warm bed, turning off the television, or trusting that the work will get done seems excruciating. Most of us also know from experience that if we can make ourselves do this we will feel good about it when we are done. Sometimes just standing up and beginning the process brings a little boost of pleasure.

Christopher Peterson and Martin Seligman, two leaders of the positive psychology movement, made a similar argument in their book *Character Strengths and Virtues: A Handbook and Classification*.[12] Peterson, Seligman, and their colleagues compiled this book as an

alternative to such books as the American Psychiatric Association's *Diagnostic and Statistical Manual of Mental Disorders*, which focuses exclusively on disease, disorder, and pathology as the primary means for diagnosing the human condition.[13] Peterson and Seligman argue that strengths—which include values such as wisdom, courage, humanity, justice, temperance, and transcendence—are just as diagnostic of the human condition as disease, disorder, and pathology, and that these strengths have not received sufficient attention in psychology. They compiled this classification as a step toward fixing this imbalance.

Peterson, Seligman, and other psychologists tend to conceive of such character strengths as wisdom, courage, and temperance as traits that people can develop over time. Moments of dignity, in contrast, occur in situations when people use these strengths, and especially when their automatic impulse is to act in ways that are not consistent with their values. The choice to exercise is often a moment of dignity because it involves exercising the virtue of self-regulation in spite of the impulse to stay in bed.

Self-regulation involves the process of using one's conscious mind to inhibit one's automatic response to the situation and to replace it with a controlled response. We use self-regulation when we choose to exercise; Stephen used self-regulation to look for the good in his coach. The participants in Webb and Sheeran's experiment used self-regulation to say the color of the ink instead of reading the names of the colors on the cards. Webb and Sheeran focused on how people can increase their self-regulation. Other research has shown that when people exhibit self-regulation, their natural emotional reaction is to feel happy.[14]

Stories with specific plots, morals, and truth can reduce the effort needed to exercise self-regulation and help us retrain our automatic reactions, but even with good stories, some degree of effort will always be needed. For example, the research on implementation intentions suggests that implementations only have a "medium-size" effect on people's behaviors.[15] This means that when the automatic reactions

we are trying to replace are weak or only moderately strong, implementation intentions are usually strong enough to change those reactions with relatively little effort. If we have engaged in the same strong, automatic reactions for a long time, however, then even if we use implementation intentions we will still need to exercise self-regulation, and probably for quite a while, before our new stories become automatic.

Self-regulation requires effort, but it feels good when we are successful. Carl Rogers, one of the most influential clinical psychologists of the twentieth century, recognized this experience in the people he worked with. Rogers spent his career helping patients to live lives that were more consistent with their deeply held values and with the emotions they experienced; he wanted to help people be honest with themselves so that they could experience an authentic life. His study and practice led him to describe the feeling of authenticity as a "sense of strength which is experienced in being a unique person, responsible for oneself."[16] Moments of dignity, then, are characterized by feelings of strength, authenticity, and happiness.

Freedom

Rogers also observed that in our moments of dignity we experience freedom from the justifications that keep us from living our values. If we could live with such integrity, he noted,

> We would be much more comfortable, because we would have nothing to hide.
>
> We could focus on the problem at hand, rather than spending our energies to prove we are moral or consistent.
>
> We could use all of our creative imagination in solving the problem, rather than in defending ourselves.
>
> We could openly advance both our selfish interests, and our sympathetic concerns for others, and let these conflicting desires find the balance which is acceptable to us as a people.

We could freely change and grow in our leadership position, because we would not be bound by rigid concepts of what we have been, must be, or ought to be.[17]

This is the freedom that comes when we identify what values are important to us, critique ourselves with regard to how well we are living those values, and act out a new, value-driven story with a plot, a moral, and truth.

We have experienced and helped others to experience this freedom many times, but one of the best illustrations of this principle that we have seen comes from Oprah Winfrey when she was still running her daytime talk show.[18] On her show Winfrey had endorsed James Frey's book *A Million Little Pieces*. Shortly afterward, a website, the Smoking Gun, published evidence that much of Frey's book, which he had published as a memoir of his life, was fictional. Larry King hosted Frey on his show after the Smoking Gun published its exposé, and while he was interviewing Frey, Winfrey called in. Instead of admitting that her endorsement was a mistake, she justified her endorsement, saying that the publisher should have done more to check the facts and that the message of the book still resonated with her even if the story was not true.

What happened next was unusual. Winfrey devoted an entire show to apologizing for her telephone call to King. Her show may have been self-motivated, or may have been driven by her publicists. But even if she was pressured to apologize, she had a choice. As Tavris and Aronson observe, the response "mistakes were made" (implying that they were made by someone else and not by oneself) is much more common that publicly announcing that "I was wrong" and "I am deeply sorry" on national television.[19]

The reason we find Winfrey's story to be a compelling illustration of the freedom that comes in a moment of dignity is because of the contrast between two comments that she made during the show on which she apologized. The first occurred when she confronted Frey and said,

"It is difficult for me to talk to you, because I really feel duped." The second occurred toward the end of the show, when a visitor on the show told her, "The hardest thing to do is to admit a mistake." Given her first comment, no one listening would have been surprised if Winfrey had agreed. Instead she replied, "It really wasn't that hard." This is an interesting change, and one that anyone who has had to apologize can recognize. When we are externally directed, apologies often seem daunting because admitting our mistakes makes us feel embarrassed and foolish. Then, after we do it, we become internally directed, and we are often surprised at how easy it was. The difficulty diminishes as we experience the freedom that Rogers described: we have nothing more to hide and no need to defend ourselves. We are free to experience comfort, focus, creativity, balance, and growth. We are often surprised by the leadership exhibited in an apology.

The Leadership of Internal Direction

Stephen was like Oprah Winfrey in her decision to apologize on TV, or like a person choosing to exercise. He exercised self-regulation to look for the good in his coach rather than give in to the temptation to focus on what was wrong with him. By acknowledging that his hate was inconsistent with his values, and by looking for the good in his coach, Stephen experienced moments of dignity. Free from the justifications that held him captive to destructive feelings and actions, he was able to have fun playing basketball again, even if he did not get to play much in the team's games. And with the added strength and freedom he felt, he surprised even himself by standing up and challenging his team. His internal direction was leadership that lifted his team, his family, and others by elevating them, calming them, and enhancing their performance.

Elevation

Stephen's telling his teammates to work harder is similar in many ways to a story that Kurt, an engineer, wrote in a study conducted by Monica Worline and her colleagues.[20] Kurt and his team were developing a new product for their company, and other employees kept asking the team to add features to the product. Eventually, Kurt's manager took a stand. He said that he would not let any new features creep into the product. Many employees were unhappy with him, and tried to force him to add features, including the "war team" and the manager's boss. However, Kurt's manager knew that the product would not ship on time if they added more features, and that this was more important to the company than adding features, so he held his ground. Kurt thought his manager was courageous. He respected him and said that, since seeing this, he has tried to take a stronger stand whenever he felt like it was the right thing to do.

After collecting and analyzing dozens of stories such as Kurt's, Worline and her colleagues found that when people observe courageous action it affects their beliefs about what they can do, their relationships, and their understanding of their groups. Kurt saw himself as more capable of taking action that he might have been scared to take previously. He had more respect for his manager. And he was more committed to doing what was right for his organization.

The kind of impact that the test manager had on Kurt occurs when people observe any action that they think is virtuous. When we see virtuous action, we tend to experience an emotion that Jonathan Haidt, a psychologist at New York University's Stern School of Business, calls "elevation."[21] Elevation involves a warm, open feeling in the chest and a desire to live one's values more fully. Haidt's research suggests that people feel elevated when they see virtuous action in person or in videos, when they remember it, and when they read about it. His interviews with people from other countries suggest that this is true around the world.

When Stephen started enjoying basketball again, practiced hard even though he knew he had little chance of playing, and challenged his teammates to play hard in spite of the coach, they were elevated by his integrity, courage, and commitment to the team. They started practicing harder and playing more as a team. When Stephen hugged his coach at his younger brother's championship game, his family was inspired to become more forgiving themselves. When we are internally directed, we have a similar impact on others.

Calmness

Our actions can inspire others when we are internally directed, and our emotions can calm them. Consider the story of Oprah Winfrey. As she apologized, she became internally directed. What seemed hard before ("It is difficult for me to talk to you") became easy ("It really wasn't that hard"). She was stronger and freer. The tension she felt went away and she became calm. In Carl Rogers's words, she felt comfortable because she had nothing to hide or defend. The comfort and calm we feel when we are internally directed can be contagious. And if we are calm and comfortable in a situation in which people expect us to be tense, then those people need to make sense of our emotions. Stephen's teammates would not have been surprised if he had expressed anger at them or at their coach, and they probably would have dismissed anything Stephen said in anger. The fact that he could speak about their poor work ethic and the coach's toxic behavior without animosity was more powerful than any anger or yelling could have been. Stephen's serenity made it believable that they could be calm, play well, and enjoy the game in spite of a coach who did everything possible to make the game miserable.

Performance

When we understand the research relating to internal direction and performance, it is not surprising that Stephen's team played better. Elevated and calmed by his internal direction, they were now more ca-

pable of freeing themselves from their externally directed justifications. As Carl Rogers put it in the quote above, now that the basketball team did not feel like they had to hide or defend their actions, they could devote their creative energies to the activities at hand.

Research supports this claim. Psychologists Kennon Sheldon and Andrew Elliott found that college students who set personal goals that were consistent with their personal interests and core values performed better on those goals than on goals that were not consistent.[22] Walter Mischel and his colleagues gave marshmallows to preschool children and told them that if they did not eat them for a few minutes they would get more marshmallows. The preschoolers who regulated their marshmallow-eating performed better in academics, had better social skills, and coped better with problems years later.[23] There is even some evidence to suggest that businesses that employ virtuous practices might outperform businesses that do not.[24] And, similar to the effect of the purpose-centered characteristic, when an internally directed person performs effectively, other people notice. Higher performance makes the actions of the internally directed person seem more legitimate, so people want to participate in and learn from what they see.

When Internal Direction Is Unappealing

Of all of the stories we included in the first edition of this book, none of them has led to more questions and debate than Stephen's. In all of these questions and debates, the central concern was "How can you say that Stephen lifted others—that he was a positive influence—when the bad coach never got fired and Stephen never got a chance to play Division I basketball? What is positive about that?" Another way of saying this is that people had trouble believing that a situation in which justice was not achieved could possibly be positive.

We empathize with this concern. Justice, after all, is a fundamental human concern, and even chimpanzees try to preserve social regularity with behaviors that are strikingly suggestive of a desire for justice.[25]

In his review of the theories of moral philosophy, Michael Sandel suggests that all of these theories in one way or another try to explain goodness in terms of justice.[26] We are all concerned with justice, and for good reason.

In spite of this concern for justice, stories such as Stephen's have led us to wonder if the pursuit of justice is always a positive thing. For example, Ryan once asked a group of executives whether their children ever use the complaint "That's not fair!" The hand of every person in the room who had children went up. He then asked them what they tell their children when they use this complaint. There was a little uncomfortable laughter, and then they admitted that often they tell their children, "Life isn't fair." Implicit in this statement is the realization that a present injustice should sometimes be lower priority than other moral concerns.

A pragmatic explanation for why it may not have lifted Stephen or anyone else to pursue justice in this situation is that such a pursuit may have done more harm than good. Not long after Stephen's coach swore under his breath at Stephen for asking what he could do to earn more playing time, Stephen's parents met with other parents to try to pursue justice. Some of these parents had older boys who had played on previous teams; they told Stephen's parents that the coach had been like this for years. Previous parents had even taken the coach to court multiple times, but had always lost. The coach had argued that the attacks were prejudiced even though many of the parents were of the same race as the coach, and he won with that argument. In the end, efforts such as these had increased the toxicity of their children's experiences and no change had occurred. Life was not fair, and it was not going to be fair. Stephen's only choice was what to do about that.

There are also principle-centered explanations for placing a higher priority on values than on righting a present injustice. For example, Stephen and his parents believed that forgiveness developed virtuous character, treated others well, and led to the greatest happiness for the greatest number of people even if it did not rectify immediate injus-

tice. Stephen would have liked to have developed character, treated people well, and increased happiness while still playing Division I basketball, of course. But given the circumstances he faced, he feels confident that he lifted as many people as he could. Even if internal direction does not achieve perfect justice, it still tends to make things more positive than they were.

The initial decision to become internally directed can sometimes be painful. When people are in an externally directed state, the idea of saying "I was wrong and I am sorry" seldom looks appealing. The longer we have been externally directed, the more we have justified our beliefs, and the more difficult and undesirable it will be for us to admit we are wrong. If Julie (the businesswoman in chapter 5 who was afraid to speak up) cried for an entire afternoon when she realized that people thought her contribution was valuable, then imagine how hard it is for people who have to admit that they caused pain to others, or who are likely to get punished, expelled, fired, or sued if they admit they are wrong. The consequences for most admissions of error will seldom be as daunting as getting fired or sued, but even so, admissions of error can still be quite difficult for people to make. Admitting our mistakes strengthens us, frees us, and increases our dignity, and these are wonderful experiences, but they do not necessarily free us from the consequences of previous bad choices.

Becoming internally directed can be just as hard for others as it is for us. This is why some people are not lifted when we are internally directed. Most people feel elevated when they see others live their values, but there are plenty of examples throughout history of people who demean, ostracize, hurt, or even kill others who are striving to live their values; consider, for example, Mahatma Gandhi or Abraham Lincoln. This does not mean that the influence of the person who was living his values was not positive. More likely, it means that the people who respond negatively to the person who is living his highest values are so steeped in their justifications for their own behavior, and so afraid of admitting that they are justifications, that they would rather demean,

ostracize, hurt, or kill that person who is living his values than admit that their actions have been wrong and that they are sorry.

The fact that people might harm us for trying to live our values could dissuade us from trying. This is why we need compelling stories for living our values. In addition to helping us see how we should live our values and giving us reasons for living those values, stories also take on a life of their own. People who change the world in small or large ways are willing to risk harm for the sake of their stories. They care more about creating and sustaining their stories of a moral world than they care about their own comfort, prosperity, or life. If the stories they are trying to tell live on, they will have given a greater gift to the world than they would have if they had chosen to live below their highest values.

Other problems could also arise if we focus only on being internally directed. What if, for example, a person values hurtful or destructive things? What if people do not know how to live their values in constructive ways? Or what if people focus on only one value and exclude other values? It is because of such possibilities that people also need to be other-focused, externally open, and purpose-centered to experience the fundamental state of leadership. For example, if people are other-focused, they feel empathy toward the people they influence and do not want to hurt them. If people are externally open, they want to learn how to live their values in more effective ways. And if people are purpose-centered, they have a clear view of what the situation is and are better able to judge which values are relevant to managing the situation well. Internal direction lifts us to higher levels of integrity, but integrity alone is not enough. Well-designed wings would not make an airplane fly without air, an engine, and a control system.

Stephen had an extreme experience with internal direction because of an event that happened to him. It is possible for us to become internally directed in the simple experiences of our everyday lives. We can do this by asking ourselves the question "What would my story be if I were living the values I expect of others?" When we do this, we become

internally directed because it helps us identify values that matter, critique the degree to which we are living those values, and develop an honest story to guide us in living our values. We will experience dignity: strength and freedom to act for ourselves. We will elevate others, help others feel comfortable, and inspire them to perform their best.

PRACTICES FOR BECOMING INTERNALLY DIRECTED

When people want to become internally directed they often struggle to recognize their automatic tendencies, have trouble coming up with concrete stories to tell, and give up their self-justifications. The following practices can help:

1. **Ask.** Other people often have less trouble recognizing habits that prevent you from living your values than you do. Choose those who spend time with you regularly, and ask them for honest feedback. You could let them write their answers to you if they have trouble giving feedback directly.
2. **Find people who model the values you want to live and spend time with them.** This can provide learning opportunities and inspiration to help with your effort.
3. **Recite the mantra "No excuses!"** Self-justification is so common and so habitual that it can be useful just to tell yourself "No excuses!" any time you make a decision. Signs with these words on your desk, bathroom mirror, refrigerator, computer, car dashboard, or other places can also help.
4. **Practice future perfect storytelling.** If it is hard to create a story about living your values, try starting at the end of the story. Imagine a title for a newspaper article or an entry in a diary (your own or someone else's) that describes the purpose you have accomplished. Imagine what the article or entry has to say about what you did to live your values as you pursued this purpose.

GROUNDED: BEING SELF-FOCUSED

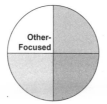

Bob: One day during my childhood, my stepfather sent me to the corner store to buy milk. I moved slowly along the sidewalk, basking in the sun and using the curb as an imaginary tightrope. Just before I reached the store, I heard a blast in the sky. I saw a thick, white trail of smoke and followed it to find the lowest flying jet I had ever seen. I watched for several seconds as the plane moved toward the horizon. The wings fell off and the airplane disintegrated into nothingness. I stood, frozen. I turned toward home. I raced up the porch steps, burst through the front door, and blurted out my story. My stepfather scoffed at me and asked, "Where's the milk?"

Most of my early memories of my stepfather are like the memory of my failure to get the milk from the corner store. He criticized me often and, over time, I hardened.

Years later, when I was a father and Ryan was a baby, I was playing with him on the floor. Suddenly I felt a wave of jealousy. I was surprised, and stopped to reflect. I realized that I was jealous of Ryan because he had what I did not have—a father who loved him for who he was, who cared about his feelings, needs, and desires. Ryan was not an object to me but a human being that I treasured for his own sake. I wished that I had experienced the same thing in childhood.

The contrast between seeing other people as objects, as Bob's step-father saw him, and seeing others as unique and valued human beings, as Bob saw Ryan, was described well by a philosopher named Martin Buber.[1] Buber wrote that humans have two types of experiences in regard to their relationships with others. On the one hand, other people can be objects to us. As objects, they may keep us from or help us to get what we want, but whether they help us or inhibit us, they are still objects to us. When we feel this way about a person, that person becomes an "it" to us. We refer to this state as *self-focused*. On the other hand, when we experience others as human beings with whom we empathize and whom we value for their own sake, that person is not an "it" to us but a "thou." We refer to this state as *other-focused*.

Empathy

Psychologists have studied self-focused and other-focused states. For example, Daniel Batson conducted a number of experiments to examine whether human beings are capable of caring for others for no other reason than to simply care, or if humans only care for others as a means to achieve their own ends.[2] This is an important question because almost all research in the social sciences—psychology, economics, political science, sociology, anthropology—is grounded in some way in the assumption that human beings are motivated by self-interest. (This is part of why empathy exhibits leadership: the act of defying one's self-interest is often a significant deviation from cultural expectations.)

Batson argued that if people help others for self-interested reasons—for example, if they help people who are in pain because they want to stop the pain that they feel when they see others' pain or if they help people because they enjoy the satisfaction they get from having helped someone—they would avoid helping other people if they can get those same benefits in a way that is easier than helping. If people care for the sake of caring, however, then they would help others even if there are easier options for getting satisfaction or reducing pain.

To test this hypothesis Batson conducted experiments in which he presented participants with other people who were in distressing situations. When participants in the experiments encountered the distressed people, they could either help them or choose a second option, such as escaping the situation easily, gaining benefits through other methods besides helping, and so forth. Through all of his experiments Batson kept trying to find alternative motivations for people to help rather than empathetic caring alone. Nevertheless, people continued to help. Based on the accumulating evidence from these experiments, Batson concluded that when people feel empathy they feel with the other person and care for the sake of caring alone.

Some scholars have shown that empathetic caring can still be seen as self-interested because during empathetic caring the people have expanded their conception of themselves to include the other person.[3] To us this seems like an explanation of the phenomenon rather than a contradiction: it is possible to construe anything as self-interest if you want to. For the purposes of understanding the other-focused characteristic of the fundamental state of leadership, we accept Batson's findings that the more empathy a person feels, the more he or she cares about another person for the other's sake alone. Or, in Buber's terms, it is because of our capacity for empathy that we can experience another person as a "thou" rather than an "it." Even so, this capacity is fragile and can be quickly lost, which is one reason why social scientists' predictions of human behavior based on self-interest are accurate so much of the time.

When Buber described the self-focused and the other-focused states, he described them using the terms "I-It" and "I-Thou." He placed the hyphen between the two words to illustrate the fact that who we are is tangled up with, and cannot be separated from, who others are. If we see others as human beings we share their feelings and need their needs to be fulfilled; we want to understand their perspectives, mourn their losses, help when they need help, celebrate their victories with them,

and become secure, calm, trusting, and engaged as well. If we see others as objects, then we not only treat them as objects but we also tend to become insecure, tense, controlling, aloof, selfish, reactive, lonely, suspicious, or defensive. The way we are toward others lifts others up or weighs them down as much as it lifts us up or weighs ourselves down, similar to the way that fluids such as gases and liquids can lift solid objects such as airplanes.

Fluid Dynamics

Daniel Bernoulli studied fluid dynamics 177 years before Orville and Wilbur Wright flew their first powered airplane.[4] He was interested in William Harvey's research on how the heart moves blood through the body, so he used mathematics to study the movement of fluids.

Fluids are made up of molecules that are weakly attracted to each other. Because the attraction is weak, fluid molecules move relatively freely. This means that fluids take the same shape as the containers that hold them. In contrast, the attraction between molecules in solid objects is strong, so solid objects usually retain the same shape in any container.

Bernoulli used mathematics to study the relationship between the speed and the pressure of blood flowing in the body. To do this he poked a hole in a horizontal pipe and put a straw, pointing upward, in the hole. When water passed through the pipe, some of the water would go up the straw, and Bernoulli measured how far the water went. He discovered that he could use this measurement to calculate the pressure of the water in the pipe. Because of this discovery, physicians all over Europe began to measure blood pressure by sticking pointed glass tubes into people's arteries to see how far the blood would rise. (It would be many decades later that scientists found a less painful way to measure blood pressure.)

Bernoulli was less interested in measuring blood pressure than he was in understanding the laws of fluid motion. He knew that the energy

in his pipe-and-straw system did not change. Water molecules need energy to exert pressure and to flow quickly through a pipe. Thus, when he compared the speed and the pressure of the water, Bernoulli realized that its pressure must increase for its speed to decrease and its pressure must decrease for its speed to increase.

This relationship between pressure and speed helps us understand how fluid molecules can lift a solid object up. When a solid object (such as the wing of an airplane) encounters a fluid (such as air) flowing in the opposite direction, the solid object turns the fluid molecules: some of the molecules flow over the wing, and some of the molecules flow under the wing. Whichever way the molecules go, however, they remain in contact with the wing's surface. If the shape and angle of the wing turns the air in the right way, then the air molecules that go under the wing will move more slowly than the molecules that go over the wing. As a result, the slower molecules underneath the wing will exert more pressure on the wing than the molecules on top. The pressure on the bottom will push the wing up. This upward pressure is called *lift*.

Based on Bernoulli's discovery, the Wright brothers knew their wings needed to turn the air molecules to generate more pressure below the wings than above them. In comparison, Buber suggested that if people "turn" their psychological states to empathize with people, they can lift themselves and others. Like a wing moving through the air, we constantly influence others and are influenced by them in return. We cannot stop influencing or being influenced; we can, however, choose what kind of influence we want to be. If we are other-focused, we are like wings that turn the air to create more pressure on the bottom than on the top. We *lift*. This is what Bob did as he played with Ryan. If we are in a self-focused state, we are like wings that do not create more pressure on bottom than on top when they turn the air. We generate no lift, we do not lead. This is what Bob's stepfather did when he scoffed at Bob for not getting the milk.

Self-Focus

> **Ryan:** One day at work, I was in a rush to get to my next appointment. As I walked down the hallway, I passed a woman who looked dejected. For a moment I felt I should stop and ask how she was doing. That feeling was immediately followed by a slew of thoughts such as "I'm in a hurry. She can be pretty negative. And talkative too. If I stop to listen I'll get bogged down and depressed. I really need to get a lot done today." I wavered for a moment, but when we passed each other in the hallway I only said hello. I felt guilty for a moment, but I kept walking to my appointment.

This interaction, which lasted only a few moments, is a rich description of how Ryan chose (and how most of us choose) to be self-focused toward a particular person. It illustrates how we regularly send and receive emotional messages to each other. It also illustrates how our emotions and actions invite others to act empathetically in small or large ways.

Emotional Invitations

When Ryan passed the woman in the hallway, her facial expression, gait, and other emotional cues acted as an invitation: Ryan felt an impulse to show her empathy. We can see why he felt this way when we learn about research that neuroscientist William Hutchinson and his colleagues conducted.[5] They used microelectrodes and an fMRI machine to study how neurons in their study participants' brains registered pain.[6] During the procedure, the scientists provided the participants with sensations such as hot, cold, a pinprick, or a basic touch. One of the neurons that they observed only responded to mechanical stimulation, such as a pinprick. The scientists also observed, however, that when they pricked themselves, and their participants watched the pinprick, the same neuron fired, as if the patient had been pricked instead of the scientist.

Neuroscientists have observed similar neurons and similar effects in other studies. For example, some neuroscientists flashed pictures of angry faces on a television screen for people who were participating in their experiments. The angry faces were replaced so quickly by faces with no emotional expression that the participants' conscious minds did not realize that the angry faces had appeared. Meanwhile, the neuroscientists observed what happened in the participants' brains.[7] Even though the participants did not know that they had seen angry faces, a part of their brain that processes emotion mimicked the emotion that participants saw in the angry faces. Scientists have also conducted similar studies focusing on such emotions as fear and happiness.[8]

Such research suggests that emotional expressions (such as anger) and emotional experiences (such as pinpricks) do more than just communicate a person's emotions to an observer. Because we tend to mimic each other's emotions, emotions and emotional experiences can also be seen as invitations for observers to empathize with, or even to participate in, another person's inner life and experiences. We seldom intend to send others emotional invitations. Initially, emotions are usually experienced as unconscious reactions.[9] But even if emotions emerge unintentionally, they nevertheless act like invitations—invitations to participate in the emotional bonds that human beings share with each other to greater or lesser extents. In other words, when Ryan passed the dejected woman in the hallway at work, her emotions sent him an invitation that empathetic neurons in his brain were inclined to respond to but that he chose to ignore.

Adding Nuance to Empathy

When Ryan passed the woman in the hallway, he felt an impulse to ask her how she was feeling. He does not, however, feel that way every time he sees this woman, every time he sees a dejected person, or every time he sees this particular woman looking dejected. Sometimes he does, and sometimes he does not. What makes the difference?

Neurons in our brain often incline us to mimic the emotions we see in others. But if all our brains did was reflect the feelings of others, then all we would do when we see sadness is get sad, and all we would do when we see anger or happiness is feel angry or happy. Human empathy is much more complex. For example, if we see someone who is happy, we may feel happy, but we may also feel sad (if we have wanted something else to happen), grateful (if the person is happy for us) or indifferent (if the person is happy about something we do not care about). Our responses to others' emotions will not always be empathetic, and even when they are, our empathy can take different forms.

Humans develop more complex empathetic responses over time because we use experience to develop mental models of the world. We are often unaware of our mental models, but as we act, observe, and receive instruction we develop models that enable us to notice more cues and to respond in more nuanced ways.[10] Thus, if we see people frowning (like the woman Ryan saw at work) we may experience different emotions or feel inclined to take different actions.

The emotions we experience and the actions we feel inclined to take may depend on where we are; what we are doing; other people's race, gender, formal position, clothing, words, or nonverbal expressions; our history with these kinds of activities, places, and social cues; or countless other elements of the context.[11] As a result, we may feel inclined to talk to some people, to give other people their space, to offer a sympathetic smile, to give a hug, to inquire further, or to engage in any number of other responses. Our brains use mental models automatically to label and to react to these cues, adding nuance to our empathy.[12]

Mental models can even enable us to feel empathy for people who are not present. Brain imaging studies show, for example, that our brains activate the same circuits when we imagine how others might be feeling as they activate when we reflect on our own feelings.[13]

When Ryan passed the woman in the hallway, the feeling he had was unique, specific to that situation in that moment. In that moment, he

worried that it would be time-consuming if he had to ask her how she was doing and listen to her problems. However, as he got to know the woman better in the years that followed, he realized that many of the assumptions he made to rationalize his behavior when he passed her in the hall were untrue. He now believes that pausing to ask how she was doing would not have taken that long. She does not always need people to stop and listen, and Ryan does not feel an empathetic need to talk to her every time he sees her. Most of the time, it has been sufficient to simply wave, say hello, or smile.

The unconscious invitations for empathy that we receive from others throughout each day are seldom very demanding. And if they are demanding—if there has been personal tragedy or a major struggle— then they are usually demanding for good reasons. Ryan's justifications were only excuses. His choice to ignore his coworker's unconscious invitation to participate for a moment in a social bond was exactly that—a choice. And it was not a choice to lead.

Self-Betrayal

The choice to ignore our impulses to act empathetically is more than a lost opportunity. According to philosopher Terry Warner, it is also an act of "self-betrayal."[14] Warner calls this choice a self-betrayal because we hurt ourselves when we make it. We hurt ourselves because our inaction requires justification (as we discussed in chapter 5), and justifications for ignoring invitations to empathy make us insecure, tense, aloof, selfish, suspicious, or defensive.

To see how our justifications for ignoring the impulses we feel to empathize with others make us insecure, selfish, defensive, and so forth, consider the justifications that Ryan used regarding the woman in the hallway. He justified ignoring this woman's feelings by labeling her as negative, talkative, and depressing. However, after years of interacting with this woman, Ryan learned that, like most people, she sometimes did negative things, often did positive things, sometimes was talkative, and sometimes was not. There was evidence to justify whatever labels

Ryan wanted to use, but he had chosen to focus on the unfavorable ones. By focusing on the negative to justify ignoring her invitations for empathy, he chose to blame her for his lack of empathy. Further, by blaming her for his lack of empathy, Ryan also made himself into a victim—her victim. He was a victim of her negativity, her long-winded descriptions, and her depressing stories. He chose to ignore her feelings, and justified that by blaming *her* for victimizing *him*!

By blaming his coworker, Ryan made himself insecure (because he had defined himself as a victim), aloof (giving this woman only the slightest acknowledgment), selfish (because his justifications created a worldview in which the only person who mattered in this relationship was himself), suspicious (because, being that he was her victim, she could take advantage of him), and defensive (because if we intuit that others may not agree with our justifications we feel a need to defend them). His coworker invited him to be empathetic, helpful, secure, calm, selfless, open, and kind, but Ryan—almost instantaneously, in a nearly habitual reaction—decided to become insecure, aloof, selfish, suspicious, and defensive. He betrayed himself.

This is a frightening idea. It suggests that if people have a bad day and need someone to listen to them for a few moments, we can use their needs as an impetus to turn ourselves into victims and them into our oppressors. This is, admittedly, a stark way to describe self-betrayal, and we will address more nuances as we develop these ideas further, but we begin with a stark description to make the point clear. Even so, whereas there are subtle nuances that we will consider, the story of Ryan's interaction with the woman in the hallway was a minor incident within the realm of ways that people can betray themselves. Self-betrayal can be much worse.

Self-betrayal can have major as well minor consequences on the lives of people who betray themselves and on others. One reason it can have major consequences is that justifications, such as the ones we use to betray ourselves, tend to escalate our commitment to act in particular ways. Barry Staw and his colleagues found this in a study of loan officers

whose jobs require them to justify why they give loans to some people and not to others.[15] Over time, if new evidence suggests that clients will not be able to pay off the loan, loan officers often rely on their old justifications rather than on their new evidence. Each time officers fail to write off a loan they have to justify their decision again. This makes it harder for them to be convinced by new disconfirming evidence, and more likely to fail to write off the loan the next time. Their commitment to keep acting the same way escalates further and further. Because of such findings, most banks now use different loan officers for initiating and managing loans.

Escalating commitment also strengthens self-betrayal. The longer it takes for us to recognize and end our self-betrayal, the more committed we become and the harder it is to stop. When Bob came running into the house to tell his family about the airplane that exploded in the sky, for example, it was a wonderful opportunity for empathy. Here was a child who was excited and would have flourished if a parent had joined in the excitement by listening to the story with rapt attention or by going outside to take a look. Instead, Bob's stepfather ignored any impulse he may have felt to empathize; all he saw was Bob's failure to get the milk, a justification that blamed Bob and made his stepfather a victim. This justification gave his stepfather more reasons to continue acting that way in the future. As a result, he was defensive, aloof, angry, and insecure in his relationship with Bob, causing rifts in the family that took years to heal. Blame and victimization go on and on whenever commitment to self-betrayal escalates, making families dysfunctional, damaging careers, dividing communities, and poisoning organizations.

Anguished Relationships

Imagine that you work in an organization's product development unit. You keep in touch with your customers, and you have shown throughout your career that you have a pretty good feel for the kind of products your customers want. One day you come up with an exciting new idea and you present it to your boss. You think this idea has the potential to make

millions of dollars for the organization. Your boss shows no discernable emotions as he listens to you. When you finish, he hesitates for a fraction of a second, and then, in an emotionless voice, says, "Interesting. Why don't you look into it and see what kind of investment you can come up with." How do you feel after hearing your boss respond?

Our Inability to Hide Our Self-Betrayal

Most people would feel rather deflated after getting such a response from their bosses. As we discussed in chapter 4, we tend to feel energized when the people we interact with express the same emotions that we feel and de-energized when they express different emotions.[16] This is particularly true when we are excited or want to celebrate something. Shelly Gable and her colleagues, for example, studied people in committed relationships and found that when participants failed to share the excitement that their partners felt over positive events, it did more damage to their relationships than the failure to empathize with their partners over negative events.[17] Human beings need to connect with each other on an emotional level.

Now imagine that your boss in the example above actually thought that your idea might be a good one. He felt an impulse to share your excitement, but he also felt fear. Your idea was somewhat radical, and pursuing your idea would require the product development unit to take significant risks and to develop new capabilities, and he was afraid to tell you that he was afraid. So instead of getting excited or confiding his fears to you, he let the opportunity for leadership pass and he betrayed himself. In his mind he blamed you for taking up his time and wanting to do crazy things. He did not say this out loud; instead he tried to hide his feelings. He suppressed his emotion, said you could look for investment, but did not offer to invest in your idea.

In this scenario you would probably feel more than just deflated. Your boss was not just lacking emotion; he was actually suppressing emotion. Emotional reactions, such as the anger, fear, resentment, or worry that come with blame and victimization, are automatic, unconscious

reactions. It takes effort to suppress these. In fact, the attempt to suppress emotion spurs repetitive thoughts about the emotion, making microemotional slips likely.[18]

When our emotions slip out, showing what we really feel for only a fraction of a second, other people pick up on and feel those emotions even if they do not know why. As we saw earlier, when scientists showed angry faces to their participants for only few milliseconds, the participants' unconscious minds detected and mimicked that anger without realizing they were doing so.[19] We may not be aware of it, but we feel and react to other people's emotions. Therefore, when we blame people in our minds, our accusations can still come through unconsciously and damage our relationships, even when we try to suppress it.

Research shows that suppressed negative feelings can inhibit the development of new relationships as well as straining our ongoing ones.[20] Thus, self-betrayal can harm our relationships even when we try to hide our emotions, even when we try to "make" ourselves "do the right thing." If we do and say what we think the right things are, but we do them in a self-focused way, our self-focus seeps out nonetheless.

How Self-Betrayal Becomes Appealing

If self-betrayal hurts others and hurts ourselves, then why do we do it? As we have pointed out, self-betrayal is a choice. If we feel an invitation to empathize, we have an option to respond to that invitation or to ignore it; we are responsible for our choices. If we do not acknowledge that we are capable of choice and responsible for our actions, then we are likely to continue to think of ourselves as victims and to remain in our self-focused state.

It is important to remember that self-betrayal is a choice, even though some circumstances make it harder to respond to the unconscious invitations that others send us to show them empathy. In particular, the degree to which others have empathized with us has a strong influence on how hard it is for us to respond to invitations to show the empathy that we feel. If people fail to provide us with the empathy we need, or

have failed to do so in the past, it becomes easier to justify withholding our own empathy. The need to feel that we belong is fundamental: those who experience significant deprivation of empathy tend to experience physical and psychological illness as well as exhibit dysfunctional thinking and behavior.[21]

> **Ryan:** Early in our marriage, as my wife Amy and I tried to make ends meet, Amy would often figure out ways to rearrange our budget so that we could afford to buy things, such as a new piece of furniture. In many of these cases, the solutions were clever and viable. If I were empathizing with her, I would have listened closely to her explanation and celebrated her idea. Unfortunately, I often failed to do this. I was uptight about our finances and distracted by other things. In those moments Amy would usually withdraw, feeling less inclined to show empathy to me or to the children until she recovered from my lack of empathy.

Amy, like the rest of us, has a tendency to be offended or hurt when people do not show empathy at appropriate moments. Naomi Eisenberger and her colleagues studied the brain activity of people who were excluded from participating in social activities;[22] When this happened it activated the same part of their brains that gets activated when we experience physical pain. Our self-focus can inflict pain on others.

When we feel pain we tend to focus on ourselves: negative emotions demand our attention so that we will try to relieve our pain.[23] And if we are focused on ourselves, it is hard to feel empathy for other people. When Ryan's self-betrayal hurt Amy, she felt a need to focus on her pain rather than on others. In other words, when we betray ourselves, we invite others to betray themselves as well. Mark Leary and his colleagues found this in their research on hurt feelings: when our feelings are hurt our most common reactions are, in order, (1) anger; (2) arguing and defending ourselves; (3) telling the offenders that they have hurt our feelings; and (4) countering with a nasty remark. We often use more than one of these responses. In the long run our relationships are often weakened temporarily or permanently and we worry that they

will be hurt again. We also worry about what others think of us, we experience a decrease in our self-esteem, and we sometimes even experience reoccurring hurt feelings.[24]

The long-term impacts of self-betrayal and self-focus can be more powerful than the short-term impacts. For example, research on childhood relationships suggests that children need empathetic interactions with their caregivers to develop a secure base from which they can venture forth to explore life's possibilities and develop constructive relationships.[25] When people do not develop secure bases, or have weaknesses in their secure bases, those weaknesses surface later in life as insecurities, preoccupations, or dysfunctions that make it harder for them to respond well to the invitations for empathy that others unconsciously send them. As a result, self-focus becomes a habitual response in certain types of situations.

Collusion

If one person's self-betrayal invites another person to betray him- or herself, self-focus has the potential to spread like a disease. The social impact of self-betrayal can be devastating. We can see this in our previous example of the interaction between a boss and an employee in a product development unit. That example was inspired by a true story.

The product development story is about two colleagues of ours, Joe and Micah. One day Joe came up with a new idea for a product that could possibly have made the organization millions of dollars and proposed this idea to Micah. Joe left the conversation believing that Micah had suggested that Joe's idea was not worth investment. Joe felt blame. He left with the impression that Micah thought he was a bother.

Joe was hurt, and he responded by betraying himself. He told his friends and coworkers that Micah was an idiot with no foresight and a poor manager. Joe may have been at least partially right, but by doing this he was blaming Micah, making himself into a victim, damaging the relationship further, and spreading his self-focus to others in the organization.

Although Micah was not willing to invest in Joe's idea himself, he left open the possibility that Joe could try to get other people to invest in the idea, so Joe talked to people in other organizations about his ideas. Some people were interested, and Joe told Micah about it.

When Micah found out that Joe was getting investment from other organizations, he accused Joe of acting against the interests of their own organization, and he told others that Joe was seeking outside investment. Joe and Micah made more and more accusations against each other. Some people in the organization took sides; others avoided these discussions. The cycle continued for years, Joe and Micah had a miserable relationship, and the workplace was poisoned. The organization lost the opportunity to make millions of dollars from Joe's idea (other organizations have since come up with similar ideas and begun implementing them), and the poisoning of the workplace undermined other opportunities as well. This story illustrates how self-betrayal can damage organizations, communities, and even financial opportunities in addition to making individuals miserable and corroding relationships.

The way in which self-focus corrodes relationships is worth further examination. When people betray themselves with regard to others, they need the other persons to betray themselves as well to preserve their justifications for their own self-betrayal. They do not recognize this need, but they act it out nonetheless.

Joe needed Micah to betray himself to preserve his justifications even though he was unaware of this need. For example, if we had asked Joe if he wanted Micah to accuse him of disloyalty, Joe would say, "Absolutely not!" Even so, Joe made himself into Micah's victim by accusing Micah of being an idiot, of lacking foresight, and of being a bad manager. If Micah were to actually give Joe's idea a chance for internal investment, Joe would either have to admit that Micah is not so bad or he would have to find another way to maintain his victimhood. Joe, however, has been so public and explicit about his victimhood that he, like the loan officers who could not write off bad loans, has become

committed to his blame and his victimhood. He needs Micah to continue being a bad manager to maintain his identity as a victim.

Micah needed Joe's self-betrayal as much as Joe needed Micah's. Micah might claim that he wanted Joe to focus on the organization's existing products rather than seek outside investment for his idea, but if Joe stopped pursuing his idea and focused on other products, Micah would no longer have had a reason to blame Joe. He needed Joe to be "disloyal" so that he could use Joe's disloyalty to make his own virtue and victimhood apparent to others.

Our self-betrayal, like Joe's and Micah's, does more than invite others to betray themselves. It also provides them with ongoing excuses for betraying themselves. And their self-betrayal provides us with ongoing excuses for self-betrayal. It is like we are unconsciously colluding to provide each other with excuses. In fact, Warner—the philosopher who introduced the idea of self-betrayal—calls relationships such as these "collusions." They are not intentional collusions, such as groups of business executives conspiring to fix prices. They are unconscious ones in which people, without realizing what they are doing, conspire against themselves.

When people participate in collusive relationships, it is often surprising how easily they can say or do just the right thing to get other people to take offense and react with blaming actions of their own. They do this so easily because people who have betrayed themselves are usually anxious to take offense, even if they do not realize it. This is how Bob was in his interactions with his stepfather. His stepfather felt insecure about measuring up to Bob's deceased biological father. To protect himself, he learned to find fault in Bob. In turn, Bob protected himself by blaming his stepfather through actions such as avoiding, undermining, rebelling, and ridiculing. These actions provided more excuses for Bob's stepfather to see himself as a victim and to find fault in Bob. The cycle of collusion went on. It takes leadership to break a cycle such as this. If we do not break it, it can go on hurting everyone involved.

The End of Self-Betrayal

Sometimes people can break their cycles of collusion in surprisingly short periods of time. For example, we have had students who—after learning the principles in this chapter and chapter 8—have, in a matter of minutes, repaired relationships between business departments or family members that have been warring for years. On the other hand, some collusive relationships take much longer to repair. Joe and Micah never broke their cycle of collusion, but Bob and his stepfather ended their collusion—after many years.

Bob: In my early teenage years my mother, stepfather, and stepsister went through a religious conversion and changed their lives in dramatic ways. They attended church actively, served others, quit working on Sundays, and began to live a healthier lifestyle. It was a wonderful decision that magnified the meaningfulness and joy in their lives. Over time my stepfather even began to make overtures of peace and kindness toward me.

In spite of the wonderful changes that were occurring in their lives, I distrusted their decision and felt embarrassed about those changes. I had spent almost my entire life being treated like an object by my stepfather and treating him as an object in return. He was not a human being to me; he was a threat to my happiness and social survival, and I had years of justification to prove it. Now he was treating me as a unique person with intrinsic value. I could not comprehend treating him that way in return. I was committed to seeing him as a bully who was responsible for my problems. I was so bound by my justifications that they had become part of my identity. When he stopped giving me the excuses I needed to be a victim and to blame him for my victimhood, I did not know who I was or how else to act. I needed him to treat me badly so that I could feel good about acting and feeling negatively toward him.

After my stepfather changed, I could not justify treating him badly any longer because of the way he was treating me. I needed new excuses to blame him for my troubles, and I found one almost immediately. This church my family had joined was an unusual one. Almost no one in our neighborhood belonged to it and it was embarrassing to me that my

family members would join such a weird church. Now I was not only my stepfather's victim but also a victim of my whole family.

It took a long time for me to begin to see my self-betrayal. This is not always the case; sometimes people see and end their self-betrayal much more quickly than I did. But for me, in this case, it took time. It began as I watched my family change. Their lives became increasingly purposeful. I saw this every day, so I could not deny it. And many of the people from my family's new church visited our home. I met them whether I wanted to or not. They were normal people who were trying to live lives of love, service, and purpose. Their lives, and the lives of my family, made it hard to maintain my justifications.

As my embarrassment over my family's decision melted away, I stopped blaming them. But I was still not ready to stop betraying myself in my relationship with my stepfather. I was less antagonistic toward him than I had been in the past, but I did not want to trust him or develop a constructive relationship with him. He was hurt, I think, by my unwillingness to forgive him, but he gave me space to work through my feelings. I got married and had children, and he became a good grandfather.

One day I was listening to a speaker who told a story about forgiving his abusive father. I felt like I was the only person in the room and the speaker was speaking directly to me. He said that the relationship changed when he had an intuition that he should ask his father for help and advice. He did not want to do that, because it would suggest that he respected a man who had hurt him deeply. Eventually he swallowed his pride and asked his father for help and advice. In doing so he began to forgive his father and to build a loving relationship with him.

As soon as I heard this story, I knew I needed to do the same thing. It was just as hard for me as it was for the man I had heard it from. My stepfather was shocked when he received my telephone call, but he treated my request with respect. He even dressed in his best suit when he came. His help and advice was a blessing to me, and I finally reached a point where I could love my stepfather and let him love me. I became other-focused, and being other-focused was a joy.

IN FLIGHT: BECOMING OTHER-FOCUSED

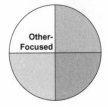

Hugh is a friend of ours who worked as a manager in a research facility at a Fortune 500 company. The company faced a serious recession and threats to its profitability, so its executive team downsized 193,000 of their 244,000 employees in only a few years. Hugh and the other remaining employees were shocked as well as uncertain—even fearful—about their future. Most of them became self-focused—a common reaction when people feel threatened. These employees would have benefited from empathy for each other, but instead some of the employees began to say bad things about each other, sabotage each other's work, and take credit for others' successes before the other people could receive credit. Presumably they did this to make themselves look better than their coworkers; if there was another downsizing, their coworkers would be more likely to lose their jobs than they would.

Once some people began to undermine their coworkers, others did the same thing. Some did it to retaliate; others did it as a preemptive effort to protect themselves. People justified their actions, self-betrayal flourished, trust eroded, performance dropped, and work was not

enjoyable. Hugh agonized over the situation. He did not want to undermine his fellow employees, but he also knew that if he did not protect himself people could undermine him and he might lose his job. Even Damon, a young man whom he had once helped get promoted, had undermined him; Hugh began to think that showing empathy would only make him vulnerable.

During this time Hugh had a conversation with his wife. She empathized with him, offering love and support. She listened to his explanations about the new direction his company was taking. They examined his career prospects; they reviewed their finances, both in terms of daily living expenses and long-term savings, and they decided that if Hugh had to leave his job and they had to get by on a lower income, they could do it (even though it would be difficult).

Knowing that he was loved and supported by his wife, Hugh returned to work and began leading. He refused to see people as objects or as enemies, instead seeing them as people with struggles, fears, hopes, feelings, and needs; and this included Damon. Even though Damon continued to act aggressively and Hugh was tempted to see him as an enemy, Hugh kept looking for the best in him. Hugh told Damon about the good things he saw in him; Damon was suspicious, but Hugh persisted. Eventually Damon was promoted to vice president with Hugh reporting to him, and he treated Hugh as a colleague and friend.

Hugh also called meetings with small groups in his facility. In these meetings he asked people provocative questions such as "What do you want this company to look like in ten years?" Initially Hugh's coworkers were skeptical of him. He was a middle manager; who was he to be asking about the long-term goals and strategies of the company? Hugh persisted, though, and eventually people began to seriously consider and openly discuss their answers to the questions.

Eventually many of Hugh's coworkers acknowledged the need to make themselves and their company more competitive—for their own sake and for the good of the company. They also realized that manag-

ing their careers competitively did not mean that they needed to undermine each other. Many of these employees began to come up with ideas for helping each other develop the skills that they would need to help both their company and their careers. They created a constructive work environment and improved the performance of their facility along the way.

Seeing the Humanity in Others

Hugh lifted himself, Damon, and many others in his organization by becoming other-focused. He changed his behavior, but that change was less important than the change in his psychological state. When Hugh was self-focused, the thought of doing kind things—such as speaking well of others and helping them advance their careers—looked like it would only make him vulnerable. As a result he felt stuck between two bad options: he could undermine his coworkers (which seemed unavoidable if he wanted to protect his career), or he could be kind (and get taken advantage of by his untrustworthy coworkers).

Hugh felt like he had no good options because he was self-focused. He did not want to be kind. Therefore, even if he decided to do kind things his lack of kind feelings would have leaked out in his emotions or actions. His coworkers could have labeled his kind actions as insincere or manipulative. Insincerity would have given them excuses to be manipulative or insincere themselves, and one self-betrayal would have inspired many more.

Hugh did not perform kind actions while he felt self-focused. Instead, with the help of his wife, he became other-focused. Because he was now not focused on himself, he was not worried about people taking advantage of him. Without his self-focused worry, he could empathize with others' needs more clearly. He felt the fear that his coworkers felt about their careers, but he could also sense that they needed to be challenged as well as needing to receive kindness. Because he felt

empathy for his coworkers kindness was no longer an obligation. It was spontaneous. Gathering employees and asking them to envision the future was a natural thing to do.

Empathy is natural as long as we do not impede our empathy with self-betrayal. We can empathize with others by simply imagining how they might feel. Kevin Ochsner and his colleagues showed this by using an fMRI machine to scan the brains of the participants in their experiment while the participants looked at photos.[1] As their participants did this, Ochsner and his colleagues asked them to focus on their own feelings or to judge the feelings of the people in the photos. Ochsner and his colleagues found that whether people were judging their own emotions or others', the same three regions of their brains were activated.[2]

Self-judgments and other-focused judgments also activated other, separate regions of the brain in Ochsner's experiment. The other activated regions of the brain presumably help people to distinguish between different sources of emotion, but the three of the regions that fired in Ochsner's participants' brains do not appear to differentiate between different sources of emotion. Thus, when we imagine others' emotions, we simulate those emotions in the same regions of our brains that would activate if they were our own emotions. Our empathy can be as simple and automatic as mimicking and feeling others' facial expressions.[3]

How Do Others Feel?

The idea that we can become other-focused by imagining how others feel is the basis for the question that we recommend to help people become other-focused: "How do others feel about this situation?" As with the other questions we have introduced, we chose the words in this question carefully.[4] For example, one of the critical words in this question is the word *feel*. By asking how people feel—as opposed to how they think—we open ourselves up to the possibility of receiving invitations for empathy, as we discussed in chapter 7. If we respond to these invitations by empathizing with others we become— or remain—other-focused.

The power of feeling the way others feel about situations can be seen in a story told by Miguel, an anthropologist who was studying Laotian immigrants in Chicago. Most of these immigrants were poor, few of them spoke English, and very few people cared about them. They appreciated the interest that Miguel took in them, and often asked him for help.

One of the most common requests that Miguel encountered was from Laotians who had received eviction notices from their landlords. They struggled to earn enough money to pay the rent, eat, and maintain a living. They wanted to ask their landlords for more time to pay the rent, but they could not speak English. They would ask Miguel to plead with their landlords to not evict them; he did so many times, but he never succeeded.

One day, after reluctantly agreeing to plead with yet another landlord and knowing that he had very little chance of success, Miguel had an idea. It was a crazy idea, but nothing else had ever worked, so he decided that he might as well give it a try. Standing next to his Laotian friend, he knocked on the landlord's door. A gruff man opened the door, looked at the Laotian, and looked at Miguel. Though he knew what Miguel was going to request, he asked harshly, "Whaddya want?"

Miguel put the palms of his hands together in a praying position. He bowed slowly and low. Rising from his bow, he said, "My name is Lithmouthay. I come from the valley of the rising sun. I lived there happily with my wife and children. Then one day the wheeled dragons roared over the hill, spitting fire. We tried to run, but my wife and children caught fire and burned to ashes beside me. I came here because I had nowhere else to go." He put his palms back together, bowed low and slowly again, and then stood silently next to Lithmouthay. The landlord looked at Miguel, looked at Lithmouthay, and then said to Miguel, "Okay. He can stay."

Like Ochsner and his colleagues asking the participants in their experiments to imagine people's emotions, the effect of Miguel's enactment was to invite the landlord to feel the way Lithmouthay felt about

the situation. This was an act of leadership on the part of Miguel. He violated cultural assumptions about how he should behave and he inspired the landlord to follow by prompting the landlord to feel empathy. Even though the landlord did not understand Lithmouthay's language or customs, he felt Lithmouthay's loneliness, pain, and fear, and that empathy was accompanied by a desire to help.[5]

Empathy often inspires help. This is how Hugh's wife felt when she imagined how Hugh felt. She wanted to help him, went through their finances, and offered support. Then, when Hugh imagined how his coworkers' might feel, he also empathized with the fear they felt about their careers and wanted to help them.

When Empathy Is Hard

Troy, a colleague of ours, is a professional mediator who specializes in disputes among environmentalists, the logging industry, and other groups that have an interest in how natural resources are used. Once Troy described a conflict between two of these groups. There was no resolution in sight, until one day when one person from each of the groups happened to bring their children to the same park on the same day.

These two opponents in the park talked about their children and their personal lives. As they did they began to see each other as human beings with legitimate needs, perspectives, and feelings. They quit characterizing each other negatively and instead began to explore things they had in common. They returned to the negotiating table with different and more open-minded perspectives about the other group and shared this perspective with people from their own groups. Other members of their groups began to empathize with their opponents' needs, wants, feelings, and perspectives. As they did they came up with new ways to integrate their interests.

Troy's story is an example of how difficult it can be to feel empathy for others. It is also a story from which we can extract ideas about how

to overcome those difficulties. Sometimes, like the loggers and environmentalists at the negotiating table, we do not want to be other-focused—or at least we do not want to be other-focused toward particular people. Our justifications for disliking them are long-standing and deep-seated, and we vehemently disagree with their beliefs or ideologies. Or, like Hugh in his relationship with Damon, we have been hurt or even undermined by someone we trusted and have always treated well. Why would he want to be other-focused toward people like that?

Questions such as "Why would I want to be other-focused toward someone like that?" are questions that imply blame. They imply that people whose ideologies we find distasteful, or who betray us, do not deserve our empathy. A question of this type suggests that we have not let go of the justifications that make us victims by blaming others. It can be nearly impossible to feel empathy while we cling to such justifications.

What if such justifications are accurate, though? Is it possible that some people really are undeserving of our empathy? We would argue that the question of whether someone is deserving of our empathy is not a useful question. More useful, we believe, is the question "Will my lack of empathy lift me or lift others?" The answer is no. Even if our blame is based on accurate information, the act of blaming makes us insecure, selfish, and defensive and invites others to be insecure, selfish, and defensive as well.

When we blame others, we make ourselves into victims. Our blame inflates their vices and our virtues, giving us a distorted view of the world.[6] Sometimes these distortions are so strong that we cannot empathize: Their vices and our virtues are so inflated that we cannot think of them in any way that is favorable enough to be able to empathize with them. This is one more reason there are four questions for the fundamental state of leadership. Sometimes, before we can empathize with others, we must first deflate our virtue and others' vices. One way to deflate our virtues and others' vices is to ask a question such as the one we proposed in chapter 6: "What would my story would be if we

were living the values I expect of others?" This question assumes that we have gaps in our integrity, even in situations where we have blamed others.

Asking ourselves what our story would be if we were living the values we expect of others helps us to question the justifications we use to convince ourselves we are virtuous and others have victimized us. Once we realize we are not as virtuous as we think, we see our own and others' virtues and vices more accurately. We also have a harder time seeing ourselves as victims, we have an easier time seeing how we might have some responsibility in the situation, and we find it much easier to empathize with others.[7]

Another tool that can help us let go of justifications we are afraid to let go of is our association with people who feel empathy for us. When we enjoy the company of people who are other-focused, the empathy that we feel often makes our self-focused justifications seem less appealing and makes other-focused feelings seem more attractive. The logger and the environmentalist felt this way when they met in the park; Hugh felt this way when he received empathy from his wife. The concern she expressed and her willingness to live on a lower income if necessary was much more pleasant than the suspicion, defensiveness, and tension he felt at work. This idea was the basis of Carl Rogers's research and therapy; he found that empathizing with his clients had a tendency to melt away justification.[8]

Empathy may melt away self-justification, but if this happens, it happens in its own way and its own time. Lithmouthay's landlord's justifications melted quickly, as did the justifications of the logger and the environmentalist in the park. On the other hand, it took weeks before the logger and the environmentalist had this breakthrough, and it took Hugh weeks of talking to his wife and struggling at work before he was able to feel empathy for his coworkers. Some justifications may take years of empathy to slowly melt away. Other justifications, which seem like they would take years to melt away, disappear in moments under

the right conditions. Each justification is different from others. We all carry justifications with us that become our assumptions about how life works. We often do not know which justifications we are carrying with us; therefore we cannot tell when and how those justifications will melt away.

We may not be able to predict when justifications will melt away and we will become other-focused, but we can do things to make ourselves more likely to become other-focused. If we regularly ask ourselves "What would my story be if I were living the values that I expect of others?" we are likely to identify and eliminate many justifications that prevent us from being other-focused. If we regularly ask "How do others feel about this situation?" we are more likely to receive the invitations for empathy that others regularly and unconsciously send to us.

Stakeholders

BOB: In contrast with the story of my relationship with my stepfather in chapter 7, there was another area of life in my teenage years in which I learned to be highly other-focused. This area was basketball. My reasons for beginning to play basketball were self-focused: I just wanted to impress the sixth grade cheerleaders. I quickly learned to focus on others, however.

One reason why I learned to focus on others was because I was the point guard; it was my job to make everyone else on the team better. The way to win the cheerleaders' attention would have been to score as many points as possible, but I was supposed to set up the plays, draw defenders to me so that other people could get an open shot, and make good passes so that other people could score.

In order to play my position well I had to try to understand how my teammates felt and what they needed to succeed. As I began to empathize with their needs and feelings, I found that there was more joy and more success in lifting my teammates than there was in focusing on myself. Eventually I found similar joy in making my coach and the fans

happy as well as my teammates. I felt joy in their success as well as in mine as I empathized with them.

Empathizing with my teammates brought me learning as well as joy. By focusing on their feelings and needs rather than my own, I began to learn how to pass, penetrate, set picks, and run plays in ways that complemented their strengths and helped them to play their best. The more I tried to do this with the different people I played with, the more I learned about how to improve my skills. My teammates also felt this way, and over time we could hardly stand to play with people in self-focused states. They destroyed what was most precious about playing basketball.

Bob's story of learning how to be other-focused when playing basketball is an illustration of why we used the word "others" when we crafted the question "How do others feel about this situation?" We deliberately used the plural "others" rather than a singular phrase such as "the other person" because there may be any number of people who could be influenced in a situation. As Bob learned, the people who cared about a play that he made in a basketball game included more than just the person to whom he was passing; it also included his other teammates, the coach, and even the fans. Anyone who may be influenced by a situation is a stakeholder.

The word *stakeholder* is commonly used with business audiences. For example, Ed Freeman, a business ethicist, writes and teaches extensively about stakeholders. He focuses on employees, stockholders, customers, suppliers, local communities, and even the natural environment as stakeholders. Freeman and his colleagues help business leaders to make more ethical decisions by encouraging them to consider stakeholders perspectives when they make decisions.[9] The question "How do others feel about this situation?" encourages us to think about how different stakeholders feel.

People often worry that empathizing with all of their stakeholders will require them to sacrifice their own benefits or the benefits of some of their preferred stakeholders. Sometimes this is true, but we have also

found that empathizing with all of the stakeholders in a situation often increases everyone's benefits in the long run.

An example of how empathizing with multiple stakeholders can increase everyone's benefits comes from a story of the Bank of Boston. In 1990, the bank faced regulatory pressures from the government (one of its stakeholders) to increase investment in underserved urban neighborhoods (another of its stakeholders).[10] Bank of Boston increased its investment by creating a new bank, First Community Bank. Managers in First Community Bank sought the perspectives of their stakeholders in the urban communities, in nonprofit organizations, and among its own stockholders. It did this so that First Community Bank would be constructive for the communities it operated in, beneficial for the employees and urban clients, and profitable for shareholders. The bank hired managers from local communities, and required managers to attend community events. Their community development officers acted as liaisons with particular ethnic groups, and translated documents into relevant languages for members of these groups. These efforts helped rejuvenate declining communities.

It took five years of investment before First Community Bank made a profit, but it eventually achieved the highest sales in all of Bank of Boston's retail operations. It also generated ideas such as venture capital for inner-city investment, multilingual ATMs, and special products designed for newcomers to banking. These innovations were so successful that they were used throughout the Bank of Boston system for years. By caring about their stakeholders' needs, the leadership of Bank of Boston's employees lifted itself as well as its community stakeholders.

The concept of stakeholders can be useful in everyday situations as well as in business. This is what we see in Bob's story of learning how to play basketball. As he learned the unique feelings and perspectives of each of his teammates, he learned how to play with them in a way that would maximize their talents. Learning to do this improved Bob's talents. And as players learn to play together, new opportunities arise

for the whole team. The uniqueness of each stakeholder provides new opportunities for learning, insight, and action.

High-Quality Connection

Bob's basketball team, Hugh's meetings with his coworkers, Miguel's petition for Lithmouthay, and Troy's clients meeting in a park can each give us insight into what it is like to be other-focused. Empathy, of course, is the most fundamental characteristic of an other-focused state. And closely related to empathy are impulses to act and mutual rapport.

Impulses to Act

Empathy is an emotional experience, and emotions tend to prompt action responses.[11] For example, when we are afraid we want to fight or flee; when we are curious we want to explore; when we are disgusted we want to recoil; and when we feel love, we want to touch.

Empathy involves the experience of others' emotions. Thus, the impulse that comes with empathy is usually an impulse to act for the benefit of others.[12] If a person is struggling, like Lithmouthay, or striving toward a goal, like Bob's teammates, we often feel an impulse to help. If we feel empathy for someone with whom we have been in conflict, as the loggers and environmentalists did, we may feel an impulse to find more collaborative solutions.

Impulses to help can be particularly complex when we empathize with people who are self-focused. If we succeed in empathizing with them, we might empathize with their underlying feelings, such as their insecurity, rather than the feelings they display, such as anger or disdain. Like Hugh with his coworkers, we want to help them alleviate the pain, fear, or hurt feelings that lie beneath their selfishness, defensiveness, or standoffishness.

We also want to act for the benefit of others when others experience positive emotions. For example, if a teammate scores a basket, we might feel an impulse to celebrate with him. When we empathize with people

who are other-focused, we appreciate their empathy and even reverence their dignity. We lift them and are lifted by them in an experience of mutual rapport.

Rapport

If we had observed Hugh's meetings with his coworkers or the negotiations among Troy's clients, we might have noticed the clothes people were wearing, the places they sat in the room, the items they brought with them, and the topics they discussed. We might have noticed patterns in their conversation, or which people were likely to tell jokes and which ones were likely to get distracted. We might also have noticed how facial expressions and tone of voice changed, suggesting distrust, worry, or antagonism in the early stages of the conversations and comfort, interest, and excitement in the later stages. If we had recorded these meetings on video and then watched them in extreme slow motion, we might have seen even more.

Almost thirty years ago, a scientist named William Condon analyzed extreme slow-motion videos of people engaging in conversation.[13] He began by watching four and a half seconds of a dinner conversation over and over again, in frames of 1/45 of a second. After many hours of examining this clip, Condon finally picked up on what his intuition had been telling him all along: the man lifted his hands at the same time that the woman turned her head. Once he saw those movements, he saw other synchronized movements as well—in this video clip and in others. People did not make the same movements, but their movements would begin and end at the same time. One person's shoulder might hunch while another person leaned forward; one person's cheek might rise while another person lifted her eyebrows. These people were moving together in time, and they were moving to the rhythm of their speech, like a dance. Even the volume and pitch of their speech fell into rhythm.

People move together in time when they feel empathy for each other. When they do not empathize with each other their conversations,

expressions, and movements are out of synch and often feel awkward,[14] but when they empathize with each other their minds and bodies join together in rhythmic patterns that reinforce their relationship and feel uplifting.[15] This does not happen when we try to mimic others intentionally.[16] It occurs when our movements synchronize spontaneously because of the empathy we share with each other. It is an experience that Hugh and his coworkers and Troy's clients most likely had because of the mutual empathy they felt as they worked through their differences and shared ideas and as they became excited about new possibilities.

Jane Dutton and Emily Heaphy, organizational scholars, call the rapport that people achieve through mutual empathy a "high-quality connection."[17] Empathy is a high-quality connection because it allows people to express a wide range of emotions, it can withstand the strain of difficult circumstances, it is open to new ideas and influences, and it releases oxytocin and endorphins—chemicals that give people a sensation of relaxed pleasure, or calm energy—in the brains of people who participate.[18] Randall Collins, a sociologist, explains how the energy that people feel in interactions such as these are the motivating force behind the social structures we develop in our societies.[19]

As Hugh and his coworkers envisioned ways to work together to make themselves and their company more competitive, and as Troy's clients came up with ways to collaborate in spite of their conflicting interests, they experienced many, if not all, of the characteristics of high-quality connections. They felt empathy and concern for each other and were inclined to act on each other's behalf. They remained committed to their relationships in spite of facing difficult situations and expressing a wide range of emotion. They listened to each other's ideas, came up with new ideas, created new ways of working together, and got excited about their ideas. They lifted themselves and lifted each other in the process.

The Leadership of an Other-Focused State

People who experience other-focused states can lift others in many ways. We have seen some of these in our discussion so far. When we feel empathy for others, we can help them overcome suffering and increase their performance; melt away their justifications; increase the energy they feel; and help them feel secure enough to consider new ideas, take risks, and explore new possibilities. Here we consider a few additional forms of leading, through energizing others, integrity, resilience, trust, and learning.

Energizing Others

Consider the story of a loan officer told by Wayne Baker:

[Janet's] job was to make loans, and she was evaluated on the volume of loans she produced. One day she experienced a shift of perspective. She stopped trying to make loans and started trying to help. Instead of looking at the person across the desk from her as a loan to be made, Janet saw the person as someone with needs that she might be able to help satisfy. If she thought they didn't need a loan, she would tell them so, even if they qualified for one according to her bank's rules. If she thought her potential customers could do better by getting a loan at a competitor's bank, she would give them the name of a loan officer at the bank. Eventually she engaged potential customers in a broad conversation about their lives, families, and needs, and then worked hard to help them, no matter what kind of help they needed. She even began the practice of sharing cab rides with strangers, just so she could strike up a conversation and see if there was some way she could assist them. What happened? All she helped were so grateful that they did everything they could to help her. Even if they didn't get a loan at her bank, they would recommend Janet to all of their friends, family, neighbors, business associates, colleagues, and just about anyone else. The result was an explosion in Janet's loan productivity. She made more loans—and made more money—than ever before. She had become *extraordinarily*

successful by taking herself out of the equation and helping others without regard to how it might help her.[20]

Janet experienced what sociologists such as Baker call *generalized reciprocity*. Reciprocity occurs when one person gives a gift or a favor in return for receiving a gift or a favor from someone else. We saw some of this in Janet's story: some of the people for whom she did kind things did kind things for her in return. This is *specific reciprocity*.

Reciprocity can also be general. As Janet learned to see people for who they were rather than as loans to be made, she learned their needs and served them whether or not there was a return on her investment. People began to think of her as a person who cared about them. They referred people to her regularly and spontaneously, without keeping track of what she had done for them. Because she gave freely and without expectation, she also received freely and without expectation—and not necessarily from the people for whom she had done things. This is general, rather than specific, reciprocity.

When someone such as Janet sees a person as a human being rather than an object, such practice tends to energize that person. As we discussed in chapter 4, people who energize many other people are often high performers. When we energize others, they usually exert more effort on our behalf, are more open to learning, are more likely to share innovative ideas, and are more likely to share their resources with us.[21] By focusing on others, we often improve our own performance.

Integrity and Resilience

One person's empathy often helps other people be more resilient and act with more integrity because the empathy helps others feel secure. Hugh, for example, was not able to organize his group until he and his coworkers felt secure. His wife helped him feel secure by empathizing with him and helping him, and Hugh's empathy did the same for his coworkers.[22] Empathy is particularly important when people face adversity or other forms of pressure, because people become more re-

silient when they have people who can empathize with them and help them feel secure. When people feel secure, it lowers their anxiety, enables them to make sense of the situation, and helps them find the courage to go on.[23]

The safety and security that other-focused people provide can also help people to act with more integrity. One's integrity can seem like a risk when there are pressures to compromise it. If people feel secure in their relationships with other people, though, they are less likely to give in to these pressures.[24] A good example of this can be found in teenagers who stand up against their peers and refuse to engage in illicit drug use, smoking, alcohol, or early sex. Research indicates that teenagers are much more likely to stand up to pressure when they enjoy secure and loving relationships with their parents. Saying no to peers can feel risky to socially conscious teenagers, but if they are secure in their relationship with their parents, the possibility of losing friends is a risk that they are much more willing to take.[25]

Trust

Safety and security can also be a foundation for trust.[26] Sameer, for example, is a colleague of ours who managed the business books division of Adkar Robbins. Adkar Robbins was acquired by Saline Books. The people in Sameer's company were worried about what would happen to them, to the products they managed, and to their company. As they waited to find out what would happen they felt threatened and only performed their most basic job requirements. Sameer had little control over what would happen, but he made an effort to be other-focused, empathizing with the feelings of his employees, his customers, his peers, and the stockholders.

While attending a conference Sameer heard from a colleague that the Saline Books executives were thinking about closing down many of his product lines and firing many of his employees. Sameer felt that this would be a tragedy; he believed that the people and products in his unit had potential to create significant value for his customers and

his company. He wondered if the managers in Saline Books would alter their plan if they knew the strategy behind the products that Sameer and his employees developed. He decided to talk to Peter, his counterpart at Saline Books. This was risky, because if Sameer shared strategic information with Peter, Peter could use the information to improve his own product line, making Sameer's division redundant.

Sameer exhibited leadership and took a risk. He arranged a meeting and flew to Peter's office, where he began by telling Peter part—but not all—of his division's strategy. Peter understood the sensitivity of the information that Sameer was sharing with him and understood that Sameer was taking a risk by trusting him. He respected Sameer for taking that risk, and shared a little bit of strategic information about his own division in return. Sameer also saw Peter's respect and willingness to share, and opened up further. In other words, the two men saw each other as human beings with legitimate feelings they could empathize with. They developed a rapport with each other, which helped them to feel secure in their relationship.

As the two men shared more information with each other they began to come up with ideas that they could not have come up with before sharing information. For example, they realized that some of their redundant product lines would not be redundant any longer if they sold them internationally. Soon the two men developed a joint strategy and began to implement it, growing their business in new ways. When the executives at Saline Books released their plan for integrating the two companies, the business books divisions were the only divisions that did not have to eliminate lots of people and product lines.

Learning, Experimentation, and Innovation

The story of Peter and Sameer illustrates how empathy and rapport can help people feel secure enough to trust each other, how trust helps people to share information freely, and how people can come up with ideas more easily when they share information. This is true for any type of learning. One illustration of this can be found in a study by

Amy Edmondson and her colleagues, who studied hospitals when they tried to implement a new procedure called minimally invasive cardiac surgery (MICS).[27] Traditional heart surgery involves breaking into a person's rib cage, whereas MICS allows surgeons to operate with only a minor incision in the patient's chest. Surgeons performing MICS do not control all information and decision-making as they had previously, however; surgical teams now have to share information, coordinate, and solve problems together.

Some of the teams that Edmondson and her colleagues studied were successful at implementing MICS and some were not. The teams that were successful did more than share information, coordinate, and solve problems during surgeries; they also spent significant amounts of time talking through procedures after the fact in an effort to learn from them. But teams could only do this if their members felt safe doing so. Many of the team members did not feel safe because they did not feel like they could disagree with a surgeon.

Innovation is similar to learning. Andrew Hargadon, one of the world's leading innovation researchers, has found that innovation occurs when people recombine ideas across social domains.[28] But people are often reluctant to share knowledge with people they do not normally associate with. If they are like Sameer and Peter, it may be because they are afraid that the knowledge may be used against them; or it may simply be that they feel uncertain working across distance or difference. Yet when people build trusting relationships through empathetic interactions they are able to work across social domains and can come up with ideas that benefit themselves and others, like Sameer and Peter or Hugh and his coworkers.

Questions and Concerns about Being Other-Focused

When people are other-focused they tend to lift themselves and the people around them. We become other-focused by asking and answering

the question "How do others feel in this situation?" This can help us to see others as human beings with legitimate feelings and needs, and to feel empathy for them. When we are other-focused we energize people, inspire them to share resources and to invest effort into our projects and theirs, and help them to feel secure. The security they feel can help them be resilient, find the strength to act with integrity in the face of pressure, trust, learn, experiment, and innovate.

When they learn about the other-focused characteristic of the fundamental state of leadership many people worry that being other-focused will interfere with their own legitimate goals. We all have work that we need to get done and activities that we want to enjoy. If we are empathetic toward others, will we get overwhelmed by all that we feel we need to do?

This seldom occurs. In fact, in our experience, being self-focused is more burdensome than being other-focused. For example, we have had experiences in which we felt burdened by overwhelming task lists only to discover that we were being self-focused; when we changed ourselves and became other-focused, the same task didn't feel burdensome anymore because it was no longer a justification of our victimhood that we had to defend. Being other-focused usually requires no more of us than to treat people with respect, say hello, smile, or offer a kind word. This is hardly overbearing. And if invitations to empathy ask more of us, it is usually for good reason. We are unlikely to regret responding to such invitations.

Another issue is the concern over identity loss if we focus on the needs and feelings of others. Again, our experience has proven the opposite: most people find that when they become other-focused they do not lose themselves; instead they become their best selves. They like who they become when they care about others. This makes sense when we realize that our identities are inseparable from our relationships with others.[29] We are social creatures, biologically wired to empathize with each other. Becoming other-focused does not eliminate

our unique characteristics; it draws on our unique characteristics to help us make more of our relationships.

Sometimes people are also concerned that an other-focused state is unprofessional. A reporter may need to record a scene of human distress or a doctor may need to perform a surgery without becoming involved emotionally. It is appropriate to be careful to not let our emotions impair our decision making. However, keeping our emotions from impairing our decision making is not the same thing as betraying ourselves.

A more appropriate way to manage our emotions is to temper them by being purpose-centered, internally directed, and externally open. Reporters are likely to write better stories by using their purposes and values to develop more sophisticated models about how to express the empathy they feel rather than view the people they write about as objects that can advance or impede their careers. Similarly, when doctors feel empathy, patients are more likely to be satisfied with their treatment and medical teams are more likely to contribute meaningfully to surgical tasks.

Finally, might it be easier for someone with negative intentions to take advantage of a person who is other-focused? We do not think this is necessarily the case—a person who is other-focused can also be savvy—but it can happen. Even so, the other characteristics of the fundamental state of leadership can help here. For example, other-focused people are more likely to insist upon arrangements that are beneficial to them as well as to others if they have clear purposes and values. Hugh did this by challenging his coworkers as well as supporting them. And if other-focused people actively seek feedback, they learn how to protect themselves and recognize people who are likely to have negative intention. We turn our attention to the question of whether a person is likely to seek feedback in chapter 9.

PRACTICES FOR BECOMING OTHER-FOCUSED

Empathy can be hard to feel if the people toward whom we are trying to feel it act in unkind or unproductive ways. It can also be hard if our empathy is impeded by justifications. The following practices can help:

1. **Think of stories that explain people's bad behavior as a reflection of their unfulfilled needs.** People can be particularly hard to empathize with if their actions are unkind, manipulative, arrogant, or selfish. People who act like this often do so because they received no empathy during critical moments in their lives. If we ask ourselves what could have happened to these people to lead them to act this way, recently or in their early life, it often becomes easier to empathize with them. Even making up possible stories of what could have happened can help. Asking this does not mean that we should condone their actions.

2. **Ask, "Might I be in the wrong?"** Sometimes we are in the middle of a situation and we want to empathize with someone but we cannot. Our self-justifications are too strong, and we cannot stop the situation to address what our story would be if we were living the values we expect of others. C. Terry Warner offers another question that can be helpful in situations such as these: "Might I be in the wrong?"[1] When we have used this question ourselves, we have always found the answer to be yes in at least some capacity. Acknowledging this makes it much easier to empathize.

3. **Spend time with people who are other-focused.** Being around people who are other-focused tends to melt away our justifications and make us more empathetic ourselves. Remember, though, that empathy is not the same as self-pity; people who reinforce your self-pity will not make you more empathetic.

CHAPTER 9

GROUNDED:
BEING INTERNALLY CLOSED

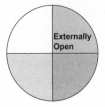

Ryan: After studying Japanese for two years in college, I had an opportunity to spend a year studying corporate strategy and international business at Hitotsubashi University in Japan. I was thrilled and scared. Even though I had studied Japanese, my skills were limited. My ability to read and write the language improved regularly as I studied and practiced, but I did not speak or understand Japanese very well.

Upon arriving in Japan I was embarrassed at my poor ability to speak and understand Japanese. I would try to speak to people, but I usually had to ask them to repeat themselves many times. I felt like I was stupid and I was a burden to the people I was speaking to. For example, if I was in a train station and I did not know which train to take, I would ask someone for directions. The person would give me directions, but I would not understand. Sometimes I would ask people to repeat themselves, but after they had repeated themselves two or three times I would just pretend that I understood and say thank you because I was too embarrassed to ask again. I tried asking other people, but that was embarrassing as well. Sometimes I would spend fifteen or twenty minutes standing by a map with my dictionary trying to figure out what train to get on rather than have to bother more people and humiliate myself further by asking anyone for directions.

I also struggled in school and felt like I bothered my classmates. I would often retreat to my apartment, where I would be alone so that I could practice reading and writing Japanese. I deceived myself, thinking that if I improved my reading and writing, my speaking and listening might improve. It was the opposite of leadership: I questioned no cultural assumptions, and no one chose to follow.

Not long after arriving in Japan, I made two friends who taught me an important lesson about my approach to learning. The first of these friends was a Japanese man who spoke near-perfect English. Although Japanese children take English in high school and most Japanese children become relatively fluent in reading and writing English, at the time I lived in Japan very few Japanese people were fluent at speaking and understanding English. Because it was unusual among the Japanese people I met for someone to speak so well, I asked him if he had ever lived in the United States. He said no. Great Britain? No. Australia? Canada? No. No. How then, I asked him, had he developed such impressive English skills? He told me that he practiced with audiotapes and, more impressively, by standing on street corners giving speeches in English with his friends. When I heard his answer I was embarrassed. Prior to coming to Japan, I was supposed to practice with audiotapes for my Japanese classes. I often felt stupid because of how poorly I did at these audio exercises, so instead I found ways to get the answers I needed for my homework without really working through the audio activities.

The second friend who helped was another exchange student from the United States. He was nearly fluent in speaking and understanding Japanese, and he had developed his speaking skills, he said, by going to restaurants, public baths, newsstands, and other public places and starting up conversations in Japanese with anyone he could. When I compared his approach with my tendency to get embarrassed and quit when I could not understand people, it was obvious why he was nearly fluent and I was not.

Learning Japanese—or anything—is a process of taking action, receiving feedback, reflecting upon and deriving insights from the feedback, and then applying the insights gained by acting again in a different way. Seeking and using feedback, then, is critical for learning; it is also critical for leadership. People seldom choose to follow deviations from

cultural assumptions unless they pay attention to, understand, and adapt to the feedback they get after deviating.

Flying Gliders without Control Systems

Orville and Wilbur Wright understood the importance of acting, getting feedback, and acting again in the designing and flying of airplanes. Prior to the Wright brothers, the people who attempted to build flying machines did not have sophisticated methods (if they had any at all) for using feedback to adapt to flight conditions while airborne. As we mentioned in chapter 2, even Otto Lilienthal (who built and flew so many gliders that people called him "the flying man") came up with no better method for adapting his gliders to flight conditions than to shift his body weight around on the glider. Lilienthal's limited ability to adapt to feedback not only prevented his learning but also led to his death.

In contrast to Lilienthal, the Wright brothers realized that in order to develop a flying machine that could adapt to changing flight conditions in real time, they would need controls that could help an airplane adjust its flight along three dimensions: raising one wing up while lowering the other (the roll), turning the nose of the aircraft right or left (the yaw), and raising or lowering the front and rear of the aircraft (the pitch). Before the Wright brothers, no one had explicitly recognized the need for controls that accounted for all three dimensions.

The Wright brothers developed such controls. They developed controls for roll when Wilbur twisted the cardboard box and came up with his wing-warping idea. To adapt to pitch they used an elevator—a movable, horizontal surface that they mounted in front of the wings. And to adapt to yaw they attached movable, vertical rudders to the back of their wings. They developed different versions of these controls, tested them, and used the feedback that their testing generated to improve them. Eventually they had controls that worked well and that they were proficient at using.

The Wright brothers designed and became skilled at using aircraft controls because they were not afraid to do what Ryan was afraid to do: practice, get feedback, and practice further. When people are afraid of feedback we say that they are *internally closed*; in other words, they focus inward and close themselves to feedback. People are afraid of feedback, according to psychologist Carol Dweck, when they believe that their abilities and attributes are relatively unchangeable.[1] If they believe they cannot change, then feedback does not help them learn; instead it is seen as a judgment of their personal worth. If feedback is a description of our personal worth, and there is a possibility that it might be negative, then the prospect of receiving such feedback is frightening. This was what Ryan struggled with in Japan. He was afraid that his inability to speak and understand Japanese implied that he was not smart, talented, or worthy.

The Belief That We Cannot Change

The idea that people fear feedback because of a belief that their abilities are fixed occurred to Dweck as she studied, with N. Dickon Reppucci, how children learn. In one experiment, two adults asked the children to solve puzzles.[2] One adult gave the children solvable puzzles, and another gave out unsolvable puzzles. After a while, the adults tested the children's puzzle-solving ability with two test puzzles (also solvable). The adult that originally gave the children solvable puzzles gave the children the test puzzles first. Then, a while later, the other adult gave the children the same two test puzzles.

After the children completed the tests, Dweck and Reppucci compared how well each child performed when they were tested by the adult who had given them solvable puzzles with how well they performed when they were tested by the adult who had given them unsolvable puzzles. When the children received the test puzzles from the adult who had given them unsolvable puzzles, they responded in one of two ways. Some of the children solved the puzzles more quickly; after

all, they had seen these puzzles before. The rest of the children took longer to solve these puzzles or did not solve them at all—even though they had solved the same puzzles before! After receiving so many unsolvable puzzles from this person, they now assumed that they could not solve any puzzles this person would give them.

Dweck and Reppucci found that children who solved the second round of test puzzles believed that their abilities could improve with persistent effort and that success depends more on factors that are in their control than on factors that are out of their control. They also found that the children who took longer or failed to solve the second round of test puzzles believed that persistent effort could not do much to improve their abilities and that success depends more on factors that were out of their control than on factors that were within their control.

Dweck, her colleagues, and others who have become interested in this topic found similar results in research with adults, in activities such as taking premed chemistry classes, giving performance appraisals, and managing simulated organizations. When people believe that their ability is fixed, they tend to

- blame failure on lack of ability
- see failure as insurmountable
- underestimate their performance
- expect success to be temporary
- set lower goals
- develop less-efficient strategies
- perform well in repeated activities but poorly when confronted with new challenges
- fail to acknowledge change in other people when their performance improves

This is a list of only a few of the findings from this research.[3] From a leadership perspective, it is useful to ask, "How much would I want to follow someone who exhibits these tendencies?"

Ryan faced many of these problems as he struggled to learn how to speak and understand Japanese. For example, he set lower goals and used less efficient strategies by practicing reading and writing in his apartment instead of going out and practicing speaking and listening. When he ran into challenges—for instance, when he did not understand the directions that people gave him in train stations—he would feel stupid, worry about his ability, and struggle more to understand the next person he would ask. Sometimes he would just give up and read maps or train schedules instead. He was afraid that his ability might be fixed and that he might not be that smart after all.

In spite of his fears Ryan never gave up and never considered the challenge of learning how to speak Japanese to be insurmountable. His ability to speak and to understand the language was not improving quickly, but it *was* improving. He also knew plenty of people—such as his two friends—who had succeeded in developing their speaking and listening skills. There were moments in which he was *externally open* (i.e., he believed he could change and was open to feedback) even though he spent much of his time being internally closed.

Although much of Dweck's research focuses on people's enduring tendencies to be internally closed or externally open, she has also noted that "[p]eople can have different mindsets in different areas. I might think that my artistic skills are fixed but that my intelligence can be developed. Or that my personality is fixed but that my creativity can be developed."[4] In other words, a person can be externally open in one domain or activity and internally closed in another. Further, even if people tend to be externally open in an activity, certain situations or cues can still drive them into an internally closed state—often without them realizing it.

I Can Change—Just Not at This

Ryan: I had an experience with becoming internally closed and not realizing it while I was writing this book. When we began writing we

decided who would write each part, how to share ideas, and how to give each other feedback. When I began my first large chunk of writing, I was externally open. I wanted to write a great book, but I had no idea how to do so. I had a few ideas to start with, and I was sure that I could figure it out along the way. Some of my ideas worked and some did not. When they did not work I appreciated the feedback because it helped me figure out how to write well. I had fun watching this book unfold and loved the feeling of "figuring it out."

While I was working on the book I was evaluated for a contract renewal at the business school where I teach. The school's tenured faculty members reviewed my accomplishments and voted on whether they thought I would earn tenure in three years if they renewed my contract. The vote was positive.

After my contract was renewed, many people congratulated me; they told me how smart I was or how I was an example of the kind of person that we needed at the school. I was moved by their kindness. A few weeks later, though, I noticed a change in my experience in writing this book. It wasn't fun anymore.

I also noticed other changes in the way I was writing the book. I was annoyed by negative feedback. I was worried about how long it was taking to write. Because I was worried about how long it was taking to write, I tried to work harder. But even when I worked harder, I was surprised at how often I was tempted to find other things to do. Somehow, I had become internally closed.

Praise for Ability

To understand how Ryan became internally closed, consider another experiment. This time, Dweck and another psychologist, Claudia Mueller, gave a group of children some problems to solve and then studied the impact that compliments had on the children's beliefs.[5] They focused on two kinds of compliments: praise for effort (such as, "Wow! You really worked hard at that!") and praise for ability (such as, "Wow! You are so smart!"). When they complimented children for their effort, the children wanted to work on harder problems, persisted on those problems, enjoyed their work, and performed well. When they complimented the children for their ability, the children wanted easier problems,

quit sooner, did not enjoy their work, and performed worse; additionally, almost 40 percent of them lied about their performance to others. The only difference was that one group was praised for effort and the other was praised for ability.

Why did praising children's ability make them less likely to take on challenges, to persist, to enjoy their work, to perform well, or to report on their performance honestly? Because praising people's abilities teaches them that their success is dependent on their personal characteristics: you succeeded at this because you were smart, so if you fail you must be dumb. Why would anyone want to take on or persist at challenging tasks if they feel they might fail and thus find out that they are dumb? How can people enjoy their work if there is a chance that they might find out that they are lacking in the essential characteristics they need for success? And why should they tell people the truth about how poorly they performed? That just means that other people will know how deficient they are.

Adults are not that different from children when it comes to praise.[6] Related research and personal experience both suggest that praise for ability can get adults thinking that their ability is fixed. Consider how many leaders in government, business, or other domains surround themselves with yes-men and -women, avoiding even the possibility of receiving negative feedback. Leaders are not the only ones who avoid such feedback, however; entire organizations—employees as well as bosses, according to the research of Danny Miller[7]—have strong tendencies to use past successes as an excuse to ignore negative feedback until it leads them to failure.

People often assume that their successes validate their abilities. They give credit to their abilities, and ignore other factors that also contribute to success, such as particular circumstances or simple luck. Abilities matter for success, of course, but when people give more credit than they should to their existing abilities, they ignore feedback and keep applying the same unchanging abilities repeatedly instead of putting forth the effort to learn new methods and improve their skills. People

and organizations, if they ignore feedback and quit learning long enough, plunge into failure. If the people in the organizations that Miller describes had revered learning from feedback more than they revered the competencies they already had, they might have avoided the major failures that came later.

Ryan became internally closed as he wrote his book, in part because his colleagues praised his abilities. Ryan's colleagues meant only the best when they complimented him for his contract renewal, and Ryan felt wonderful when he received those compliments. As in the case of one of the children in Mueller and Dweck's experiments, however, the idea that he was the kind of person that his colleagues wanted to continue to employ led Ryan to focus on his ability rather than on the effort, learning, and feedback that had made his contract renewal possible. He worried that negative feedback on the book might suggest that he was not the kind of person his colleagues would want to have around, so he avoided work, quit having fun, and did not write as well.

Performance Goals

Ryan's third-year review had one other effect that he did not recognize until later: it changed the kind of goals he was setting.

Ryan: Prior to going through my third-year review, my broad goal was an outcome goal: to write a great book that would help each person who read it to become a positive force in any situation. My daily goals were learning goals: to figure out how to write the section of the book that I was working on in a way that was accessible, enjoyable, useful, and grounded in scientific research. As a result, each day presented a fun challenge to figure out how to write that section. Feedback was welcome; it would help me do a better job.

As I went through the contract renewal process, however, my goals changed without me realizing it. My contract renewal was one step on the way toward earning tenure. When the faculty and administrators at a university decide whether or not to give you tenure as a professor, they judge your work and also ask professors at other universities to judge it. Based on these judgments they decide to offer you permanent employment

or to kick you out of the university. There are only two possible outcomes. Your entire academic career is put on the line for people to decide if what you have done is worthy and whether you merit remaining one of their colleagues. Thinking about my contract renewal got me wondering if I would be worthy of tenure, and that worry changed my goals.

My primary concern as I worried about tenure was not about tenure itself but about how I would look if I did not get tenure. The first three years of my contract had gone well, but my current projects were not progressing as quickly as I wanted them to. I set more aggressive deadlines for completing the book. As a result, as I thought more and more about tenure, my outcome goal (writing a book that would help the people who read it) slowly changed into a performance goal: getting the book done quickly and moving on to my other projects so that I would get tenure and avoid feeling foolish in front of all the people who would know that I had failed. Each day became an effort to get as much done as I could rather than an opportunity to learn to write as well as possible.

In everyday language, the terms *outcome goal* and *performance goal* could mean the same thing, but scholars use these two terms differently to make a point. Outcome goals and performance goals both focus people on outcomes (such as writing a book). In academic research, however, scholars use the term *performance goals* to refer to results that people pursue in order to "perform"—to put on an act. Like actors or actresses on a stage, we want to look good, or at least avoid looking bad. The reason we are pursuing the outcome is egocentric: it focuses on what other people think about us. *Outcome goals*, in contrast, are goals that focus only on the results and do not involve a concern for what others will think of us.

This difference between outcome and performance goals suggests that deadlines such as those Ryan set for himself are not necessarily bad things; they can help us to get work done. In Ryan's case, however, the deadlines were driven by a desire to not look stupid by failing to get tenure. As a result they did not focus him on figuring out how to write,

in a reasonable amount of time, a book that could help other people. Instead they focused him—unintentionally—on the goal of writing a book quickly so as to not look foolish.

When people's goals are oriented toward performing well for the sake of looking good (or not looking bad), they become internally closed.[8] In fact, even if people tend to be internally closed or externally open most of the time, they can still pursue goals that open them to feedback and learning for a specific activity. Gerard Seijts and his colleagues found this in an experiment with MBA students who participated in an exercise in which they ran a simulated mobile phone company.[9] Seijts and his colleagues gave one group of these students a performance goal: to triple the company's market share (the percentage of customers who signed up for their company's services); they gave another group a learning goal: try out six different strategies for increasing market share. The students who were told to triple market share performed significantly worse than those who tried out six different strategies. Seijts and his colleagues found that the type of goal students received influenced their approach to learning in the mobile phone company activity even if the students had general tendencies to learn or to perform.

> **Ryan:** I struggled with writing the book for a couple months before I realized my goals had changed. Once I realized that, I reset my goals. First I reconfirmed that the outcome I wanted was to write an engaging, helpful book. Then I began setting daily learning goals that were focused on what I needed to learn to write well. As I did this, feedback became welcome again, the work became fun, and I could tell that both the quality and speed of my writing had improved.

From Internally Closed to Externally Open

The fear of feedback can prevent managers from learning what is really going on in their organizations; doctors, lawyers, engineers, or other

professionals from improving their practices; employees from advancing their careers; parents from learning how to rear their children well; children from learning from the wisdom that their parents have to offer; and all of us from learning how to deal well with life's challenges. Without feedback we cannot learn and grow; nor can we lead effectively. Feedback is necessary in learning, especially when learning how to deviate in a manner that others will want to follow. A desire to learn from feedback is one of the most important orientations toward life that we can adopt, but doing so is not always easy.

People tend to be internally closed if they believe that their abilities cannot be changed. If they believe that, they do not see feedback as information about how to improve; they see it instead as a reflection of their unchanging and unchangeable abilities. When people are afraid of feedback about their abilities, they perform worse on complex, changing activities, are reluctant to take on challenges (fearing how failure or success might reflect on them), quit easily, expect failure, use less-efficient strategies, lower their aspirations, think others are also unable to change and grow, lose interest in learning, and sometimes even lie about their performance.

There are at least two reasons why people might become internally closed, even if they have a general tendency to be externally open. First, when they receive criticism or praise for their ability, people tend to believe that if they fail it must be because they lack the inherent ability necessary. In an internally closed state, then, people either have or do not have the necessary ability, and there is not much that anyone can do about it.

Second, people might become internally closed because they have goals that focus them on how well they perform relative to others. Performance goals focus people on relative outcomes—on how brilliant or foolish a person looks in comparison to others, not on what he or she can learn from experience.

Ryan: When I lived in Japan I was afraid of looking foolish most of the time. However, from time to time I would overcome my fears and force myself to engage in conversations. With much practice and some embarrassment, I improved enough by the end of my time there to pass the second-highest level of the national examination for Japanese language proficiency. That story has had leadership implications: it has inspired many others to take on international challenges and to try to learn new languages. Even so, sometimes I wonder what impact I might have had if I had more regularly been externally open while in Japan.

IN FLIGHT:
BECOMING EXTERNALLY OPEN

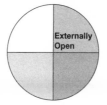

Ryan: My wife Amy teaches piano. One year she set a New Year's resolution for our oldest children, Mason and Katie, to learn how to play. Amy knew that this would not be easy; they would probably resist her efforts. As she wondered how to handle this resistance, she decided that the children needed a role model. If they could see that learning to play the piano was a good thing, that it was hard work for other people too, and that their parents were investing as much into the effort as they were, then they would probably not resist as much. Therefore, Amy decided that their father should also learn how to play the piano. She announced this playfully to Mason and Katie's father. She knew that I knew that I could not expect my children to be externally open if I was not willing to be externally open as well. I had to exhibit leadership by opening myself to feedback.

Amy sat down at the piano to give me my first lesson on January 1. I was a childhood dropout from piano lessons; I knew the basics, but I really had no skill. I listened to her instructions and did the best I could. She assigned me a song named "Cuckoo," and told me to begin practicing.

On January 2, I sat down to practice playing "Cuckoo" for the first time. I was alone; there was not a single person in the house. Even so, as I held my fingers over the keys to begin practicing, I felt a wave of fear

course through my body from my head to my feet. I was shocked. I thought to myself, "This is crazy! There is no one else in this house. Why on earth should I be embarrassed to practice this song?" I understood then that my fear of looking foolish ran deeper than I had thought. I had an unconscious belief that my piano-playing ability was fixed, and there wasn't anything I could do about it.

I may have had an unconscious belief that my piano-playing ability was fixed, but I had a conscious belief that it was not. I knew that I could improve my playing skills by practicing. I reminded myself of that, and I tried to play the first line of the song. I failed miserably, but at least I was pressing the keys. I tried playing only the upper hand, and then the lower hand. I tried playing both hands at the same time. I tried practicing holding one note on one hand for two or three beats while moving my fingers on the other hand after each beat. Then I tried mastering a single measure. By the end of my first practice, I was able to play one measure. By the end of the week I was playing one or two lines. I was starting to feel good about my progress and even found practicing to be fun. After about a month of practicing, I was playing the song pretty well. I told Amy how well I was doing. She told me I needed to play it for her before I could start practicing a new song.

The next day I sat down to pass off the song. With relatively high confidence I began playing, but before I got through two lines I was making mistakes I had not made for weeks. I could not believe it! I had this song down; why was I making such basic mistakes? Amy laughed and said, "That's why you have to play it for me." After five or six attempts I was finally able to play the song well. Amy told me that I had "passed" and assigned me my next song—one that was a little harder. This time there was almost no fear as I began practicing.

Tools for Becoming Externally Open

As Ryan practiced playing "Cuckoo" he became externally open. As he saw evidence that his skills were improving, his assumption that his piano-playing abilities were fixed changed, and he began to assume that these abilities could be improved. As a result he also became more eager to take on the challenge of playing the piano, more open to receiving

feedback about how well he was playing, and even began to have fun when he would practice. The belief that abilities can be learned, a desire to take on challenges, an interest in acquiring and learning from feedback, and the simple enjoyment or fun found in an activity are all characteristics of an externally open state, and they are characteristics that tend to lift the people who experience them. How, then, do we become externally open?

Learning Goals

To see how people who tend to be internally closed can become externally open, it is useful to consider what Gerard Seijts and his colleagues did in the mobile phone company exercise (see chapter 9): they assigned a learning goal to the MBA students by telling them to try six different strategies for increasing market share.[1] By asking for six different strategies, Seijts and his colleagues got even those students who tend to be internally closed to become externally open.

People—such as MBA students learning to run a mobile phone company and Ryan learning to play "Cuckoo,"—become externally open when they have to come up with multiple strategies. For example, as Ryan tried playing with one hand at a time, playing just one measure at a time, and other strategies he first realized that there was more than one way to undertake an activity. Second, he realized that some ways of approaching an activity work better than others, at least at a particular stage. Third, he realized that the only way to know which methods are better is to try them and get feedback. Once a person makes these three realizations, he or she seeks feedback (rather than avoids it) because the feedback is not a reflection of personal worth but an indicator of the usefulness of the strategies. Feedback about strategies is not threatening; it is appealing.

This is why a question such as "What are three or more strategies I could try in learning how to achieve my purpose?" can help a person become externally open. (We use the number three simply to make the

goal of coming up with multiple strategies specific, because people tend to perform better with specific goals. The number could be four, five, or some other number; the exact number is less important than the fact that people are challenged to come up with a specific number of viable strategies.) Once people have three or more unique and viable strategies, they are likely to see feedback on those strategies as desirable and they are likely to see themselves of capable of learning. They must see all of the strategies as viable, however; if they just make up strategies for the sake of answering the question, they are unlikely to be curious about which strategy is best; they will assume that they already know.

Learning and Performance

One of the ironies about types of goals is that when people engage in complex, changing activities, they often perform better with learning goals than they do with performance goals or even outcome goals. Ryan, for example, had trouble playing "Cuckoo" well when he was focused on performing, and the MBA students who had learning goals in the mobile phone company experiment performed better than those who had specific, difficult outcome goals or who were worried about performance. One reason this happens is because humans have a limited amount of attention to spend on any given activity. If we use up part of our limited attention worrying what other people will think of us, we have less attention to spend on actually doing the activity well. Another reason is that if we are not focused on learning, but the requirements of an activity change over time, then we will be less able to see how these changes affect us and less able to adapt. Also, as we mentioned previously, people who are externally open invest more effort, persist longer, look for and use feedback, believe in themselves, and have higher aspirations.[2]

Another reason why learning goals can improve performance is that learning goals require people to break up an activity into smaller components. When Ryan came up with strategies for learning how to play

"Cuckoo," for example, he broke both his learning process and the song he was learning into smaller pieces. This is how people create strategies: by breaking a goal into smaller steps and identifying ways to accomplish each step.[3] People achieve learning goals by coming up with and trying out multiple strategies, or different ways of breaking up and completing an activity. When people focus on components of an activity, the activity seems more manageable, they can draw specific feedback from the activity more easily (updating their strategies along the way), and they stay more committed to their goals.

Research supports the idea that people tend to perform better when they have small, short-term goals as well as larger, long-term goals when they face complex tasks. For example, in another experiment, Gary Latham and Gerard Seijts challenged students to earn money in a toy-making business where the cost of supplies and the prices that customers would pay changed regularly.[4] They gave some students a difficult goal, some students a difficult goal and a number of interim goals, and some students a vague goal. The students who had interim goals as well as a difficult goal made almost twice as much as the students with a vague goal and almost six times as much as the students who only had difficult goals. As we discussed in chapter 4, small goals enable people to achieve small wins that increase people's confidence, make future solutions more visible, and generate resources that can be used in achieving the next win.[5]

Coming Up with Strategies in Real Time

So far we have posed "What are three or more strategies I could try in learning how to achieve my purpose?" as a question we should ask before we start an activity. However, some activities are too uncertain to even begin to guess what kinds of strategies could be employed without actually trying to undertake the activity. And sometimes, even if we think that we understand the characteristics and constraints of a situation, we may not understand them as well as we think we do. In

cases such as these it may be better to wait and ask ourselves to come up with strategies as we perform the activity rather than before we start. This happened to Bob in one of the companies he worked with.

Bob and his colleagues were working with the executives of a Fortune 500 company that was trying to change its culture. They conducted many interviews and analyzed the company and its industry. Using their analyses, they worked with the top management team to design a weeklong workshop that we would run four times, each time with one hundred of the top managers in the company, to begin the process of cultural change. The first two sessions went well.

The third workshop provided a unique challenge: the head of the human resources (HR) department attended. From the employees' point of view his department acted like that of secret police: if someone made a politically incorrect statement in front of an HR person, it could destroy his or her career. As a result, people in the company dreaded having meetings with representatives from HR. The executives told Bob and his colleagues that the third workshop would fail because the attendees would not be candid.

They were right; people were much less forthcoming with their opinions. Bob and his colleagues had trouble making the same progress that they had made in the two previous sessions of the workshop; they began to worry that they were going to fail.

On Thursday morning it was Bob's turn to present. On previous Thursdays this session was a turning point: the groups had collective breakthroughs, but in the third week the attendees were not even approaching a breakthrough. Bob and his colleagues were tense.

Three minutes before Bob was to walk on stage, one of his colleagues told him that they were in big trouble. He said that Bob needed to throw his presentation away. Instead of presenting anything he had ever presented before, he needed to stand in front of the group and do whatever they needed. He was asking for leadership. Throwing one's presentation away before standing in front of a group would certainly

be counter to expectations, and seemed like it would be miraculous if the people in the audience chose to follow. It could only be done by a person who was externally open to receiving feedback.

Bob's first reaction was anger. That was impossible! "What if I stand there and look like an idiot?" he wondered. Who is he to ask me to do this? Would *he* do it?" Bob was internally closed, worried about his ability and how he would look, afraid of feedback and of failure. But the anger only lasted a matter of seconds; Bob, who often taught executives about the need to "walk naked through the land of uncertainty," knew his colleague was right.

Bob nodded his acceptance and walked toward the stage. He focused on being in the present. He would start talking, trying different strategies, until he could connect with the audience in his most authentic voice.

Bob told them that he had left his presentation back on the chair, and that he was standing before them with no organized content. He told them that he was full of fear but he was putting himself in this situation not for money but for the good of the company. He described the success of the two previous workshops and how this one was beginning to look like it could result in failure. He told them that many people had privately predicted this outcome but he could not believe it; he could not believe that mature adults would allow their company to go down the drain because they were afraid of one man in the audience.

The room was in a deep, almost sacred, silence. Bob asked a few questions and, because they had watched him take the risk of opening himself up to criticism, many of the participants were willing to take a similar risk. They gave frank answers in spite of the HR manager's presence in the audience. As Bob stood there he came up with an idea for an activity that would help them assess their true situation and decide if they wanted to confront it. They broke into smaller groups and went into separate rooms to perform the activity. After they left, Bob collapsed into a chair while his colleague congratulated him. The group was going to make it. There were some big issues ahead, but they would act.

Improvisation and Flow

When Bob's colleague challenged him to throw away his presentation, he had no time to come up with a list of strategies. He could, however, start speaking, try strategies as they occurred to him, and trust that he would find the best strategy in real time.

Organizational scholars Christine Moorman and Anne Miner point out that although we usually think of creating strategies and executing strategies as two different activities, done at two different points, people can also bring the creation and execution of strategies together.[6] When they do they are engaging in improvisation. This is what Bob did when he approached the executives in an externally open state: he engaged in improvisation and invited them, implicitly, to join him in improvising.

Initially Bob improvised by taking actions, observing the executives' emotional expressions, and then updating his strategies. For example, as he tried the strategy of comparing their workshop to the workshops of the previous weeks, he could tell by their facial expressions and the way they leaned in their chairs that what he was saying meant something to them. He tried other strategies as he spoke, and in turn received other emotional reactions. Each reaction led him to update and try out even more strategies. Eventually he started asking questions, enabling the audience members to join even more fully in the improvisational exercise, which gave him even more data and enabled him to invent a new collaborative activity for moving the group forward.

Improvisation can lift the people who improvise successfully by giving them a *flow experience*. *Flow* is a word that psychologist Mihalyi Csikszentmihalyi came up with to describe the psychological state that people experience when they perform their best and feel their best.[7] Csikszentmihalyi studied this topic for decades and found that no matter what activity people were doing—either as work or as leisure—when they performed their best at whatever activity they were doing they reported experiencing similar characteristics. These characteristics made the activity feel engaging, exhilarating and, in many cases, fun.

The study we described in chapter 4, in which Ryan studied nuclear scientists and engineers, sorted out these characteristics to see how they relate to each other.[8] He found, for example, that the central feature of the flow experience is the merging of one's awareness of a situation with automatic and appropriate responses to that situation. In other words, flow is the experience of successful improvisation, creating and acting out effective strategies in real time.

Flow requires clear goals and standards to guide people's concentration; it also requires taking on challenges that push the limits of people's abilities and actively seeking feedback. These are characteristics of an externally open state. As people embrace challenge, gather feedback, and develop awareness of an unfolding situation, they come up with strategies for acting in that situation. Then, as they apply those strategies automatically and update them, they begin to experience engagement and even exhilaration, feel an increase in their sense of competence, and lose track of time.

Bob felt flow as he improvised with the executives in the culture change workshop. After a few minutes he could tell that he understood the situation well and that his strategies for handling the situation were working. He felt capable of handling the situation, lost track of time and, as he collapsed into the chair, felt a quiet exhilaration over the experience.

People do not always have to attempt both strategy making and strategy implementation at the same time in order to learn, perform well, and enjoy what they are doing. Sometimes they come up with strategies, implement them, and then update those strategies and reimplement them over longer periods of time. Donald Schön studied architects, engineers, managers, and psychotherapists who approached their work in this way.[9] Their approach was externally open, and they still learned, performed well, and enjoyed their activities. The simultaneous creation and execution of strategy that people do in improvisation and flow may be an "optimal" way to experience activities, but it is not the only way.

Flow, like the fundamental state of leadership, is a psychological state, and the two states share many characteristics. Both of them involve goals (being purpose-centered), standards (being internally directed), learning from feedback (being externally open), and positive emotions. The difference between flow and the fundamental state of leadership, however, is that lift is also other-focused. A person may experience flow, for example, while robbing a house, but people who steal are unlikely to be other-focused. Csikszentmihalyi, in the final chapter of his best-selling book on flow, acknowledged this; he described how people can experience flow in such activities as art, science, tennis, or chess, but can be miserable people when they stop engaging in those activities. Csikszentmihalyi argued that people should develop an integrated goal for their lives that would bring meaning to all of their activities: a goal that is "generalized to other people, or to mankind as a whole"[10]—in other words, a goal that is other-focused.

We agree that a unifying, other-focused goal for a person's life can be of great worth. However, as we explained in chapter 8, focusing on others can also be part of a person's psychological state. Empathizing with others in one's immediate psychological state is important (as we discussed in chapters 7 and 8) because people who do things for others without actually feeling empathy for them can often weigh them down rather than lift them up. We can often sense when other people do not feel empathy for us, even if they are doing things for us. And even if people have broad life goals that are "generalized to other people, or to mankind as a whole," they can lose track of those goals in their day-to-day lives. Flow is a wonderful experience, but if we are to lift others as well as ourselves in the moments of our lives, we would do well to be other-focused as well as purpose-centered, internally directed, and externally open.

The Leadership of an Externally Open State

External openness—like other characteristics of the fundamental state of leadership—also has the potential to lift others as well as to lift oneself.

One way externally open people lift others is by freeing them from labels that might otherwise constrain them; this is a way of inviting others to be externally open. External openness can also lead others by winning legitimacy through artful and adaptive performance, generating knowledge that can be shared, and freeing people to celebrate others' successes as well as their own.

Freedom from Labels

Bob: I was once invited to a six-day retreat with twenty-two spiritual leaders from many different religious backgrounds. I felt a little fear when I thought about going to this retreat because I suspected that there were some people in the group who came from religious traditions that had a history of making public attacks against my religious tradition. There seemed to be a real possibility of having to deal with intense negative feedback, so my first instinct was to stay home.

My administrative assistant noticed what was going on. With an impish grin she asked me if I was afraid; she knew she had me. I groaned and told her to order the plane ticket. I was inclined to be afraid, but at least I recognized it and began making the effort to become externally open.

In the first hour of the retreat I was on edge. Without fully realizing it, because I felt vulnerable, I felt a strong urge to protect my self-esteem. The simplest way to do that would be to judge and label other people before they could judge and label me. However, as the first judgmental thoughts entered my mind I recognized them and knew I had to get out of that state. I chose to change.

One by one, each of us took the risk of opening our hearts and telling personal stories of trial, failure, and triumph. The conversation became intimate. One man spoke of developmental rituals in the wilderness and accounts of his personal transformation. Another man told of enduring brutality while participating in demonstrations in the 1960s; he saw his efforts change the racism of people he thought would never change. A woman spoke of her service in the midst of violent gangs and of occasional sacred moments when anger was turned to love. As I listened to others' stories I became curious about how they became the people they were today. I saw in them some of the growth that I had experienced in my life. We all stopped thinking about each other in terms of our

religious denominations and instead began to see how each of our religious strivings had made personal growth possible. We saw less of what was different among us and more of what we had in common.

The temptation to impose judgmental labels on others (and on one-self) comes when people are internally closed, not externally open; it comes from the belief that people's fundamental character, abilities, and intelligence cannot change. We can see this in research conducted by Peter Heslin and his colleagues, who asked people to take on the role of managers evaluating their subordinates.[11] After measuring the people's beliefs about how fixed or changeable people's personalities and abilities are, they showed them two video clips of "one of their employees" at work and asked them to evaluate that employee's performance. Then they showed two more video clips of the same employee and asked the participants to rate the employee again. In one experiment they showed two clips of the employee performing poorly and then two clips of the employee performing well. In another experiment they showed the clips in reverse order.

When the participants saw the videos, those who believed that people can change adjusted their performance ratings more than those who believed that people cannot change. In other words, when participants who thought that people cannot change saw a person perform poorly, they labeled that person a poor performer and were reluctant to change that label. If they saw a person perform well, they labeled that person a good performer and were reluctant to change. In contrast, the participants who believed that people can change did not label the employees as good or bad; they rated them according to how they performed.

Professionals, parents, teachers, spouses, coaches, and the rest of us behave similarly to the "managers" in Heslin and his colleagues' study. When we label people, they have to deal with the fact that many labels become self-fulfilling prophecies. Without realizing or intending to, people often constrain us to act out the stereotypes that they place upon us. For instance, managers who believe that people have fixed abilities

provide less coaching toward improving employees' performance.[12] This makes sense, because if you think that people cannot change, why would you bother investing time and energy to help them improve? By neglecting to coach their employees, however, they contribute to their poor performance and blame it on the employees' lack of ability. This could hardly be called leadership.

Even positive labels can be damaging, because they praise people for their ability rather than their efforts. This makes it more likely that people will avoid future challenges and feedback.[13] For example, employees with managers who saw their abilities as changeable were free to act without the constraints of their managers' labels, learn from feedback, and improve their performance. Similarly, Bob could build relationships with the people he met at the retreat, and they were able to learn from each other, because they were not constrained by the labels that they might otherwise have placed upon each other. They were all lifted as a result.

Modeling Openness to Challenge and Feedback

Ryan: On my second day of piano practice, I was so struck by the fear that I felt when I tried to play "Cuckoo" that I kept thinking about it. Prior to feeling that fear course through my body, I had no idea how much I feared feeling stupid. The next day at dinner, I told the story to my family. When I finished describing the fear that I felt, I asked our children why they thought I felt that fear. Mason knew the answer instantly: I was afraid of feeling stupid because I was not any good at playing the piano. He could relate to my fear.

When I saw how quickly and easily Mason was able to answer my question, I felt grateful that Amy had decided that I would learn to play the piano with the children. I realized that by learning how to play I was showing them that I was willing to do the same thing that was being asked of them and I was also showing them that it was okay to do something that might make you feel stupid for the sake of learning and growing. By doing something at which I was not skilled, I was also implicitly giving them permission to do something in which they were not skilled. Perhaps if their father—a person who provides for their

needs, helps them to learn the answers to life's questions, and lays down many of the rules of the household—is willing to fail, take negative feedback, and feel foolish for the sake of learning, then it is okay for them to take on challenges for the sake of learning as well.

This is the same thing that Bob did for the executives in the culture change workshop. As they saw his efforts to be externally open for their sakes, with the risk of failing and looking foolish, it gave them the courage to say things that they had avoided saying all week.

The subtle cues we encounter are just as capable of prompting us to become externally open as they are of prompting us to become internally closed. Just as both praise for ability and performance goals incline us to be internally closed, praise for effort, learning goals, and cues that imply these kinds of praise or goals incline us to become externally open. Stuart Bunderson and Kathie Sutcliffe saw this in a study they conducted with teams that manage the business units of large companies.[14] These teams became more open to learning by noticing their teammates' behavior and following it.

Four things need to happen for people to learn from the behaviors that other people model. Learners have to (1) notice the behavior being modeled; (2) have a label for the behavior that will help them to remember it; (3) be able to translate the behavior into action (perhaps through practice); and (4) be motivated to put that behavior into action.[15] When Ryan started practicing the piano with his children, he gave them new and unusual behavior for them to notice. The children had labels for what he was doing because Amy was teaching them as well. Amy also helped them put their labeled behavior into action by having them practice each day. And Ryan set an example of having fun while learning.

Ryan's continued ability to lead and lift his children remains an open question; he eventually let his work and other activities crowd out his piano practice. Yet as he worked on the second edition of this book and encountered this story again, he realized that he needs to be more

internally directed (i.e., more persistent about doing what he asks his children to do) as well as externally open if he wants to continue modeling external openness for his children. He found his old songbook, opened it to "Cuckoo," and got back to work.

Performing Artfully and Adaptively

Ryan's wife Amy is an excellent model of external openness. When Ryan and Amy bought their first home, Amy was excited about furnishing and decorating it. After they moved in, however, she could tell what she did not like but had no idea how to make it look better. She was frustrated over her inability to make the house look the way she wanted it to, but she approached decorating the home in an externally open state. Her learning process is an excellent example of how external openness lifts others through artful performance and collective mastery.

Amy learned how to decorate by reading books, watching home and garden shows on television, hiring an interior designer to teach her (not to decorate for her), hanging different colored paint chips on the wall, and repainting one room more than twenty times until the shade was just right. She tried reupholstering furniture; she tore down cupboards and ceiling fans; and she learned how to install a sink. She tried multiple strategies for every challenge.

Two years later, Ryan and Amy moved again. To Ryan's amazement, when they first went to see the home that they would eventually buy, Amy rattled off a list of specific things that would have to be done to make it look nice. It was like she had become a different person; she no longer struggled to explain what she liked about the interior design of a home but knew exactly what to do.

Amy's road from novice to expert in interior design is the same road that architects, engineers, managers, psychotherapists, and other professionals take. Donald Schön studied such professionals to see how they learn,[16] and found that the best professionals perform their craft artfully by reflecting on their work while they're doing it. In other

words, they are externally open while they work. They come up with strategies, try them out (in their minds or in actuality), judge their quality (by extracting feedback from the tasks), and update their actions as they go along. When they are externally open they develop a more accurate understanding of the situation in which they are acting,[17] they adapt their work more closely to the needs of the immediate situation,[18] and they innovate, coming up with creative new ways to do the work.[19] This process, Schön argued, is what gives professional work its quality—what makes it artful. The same can be said for leadership.

The road to mastery that externally open people take can lift and lead others by producing innovative and artful outcomes that inspire them. The poem "High Flight," which we included in the introduction to this book, is an example of an inspiring outcome. The road to mastery can also lift others when we invite them to walk the road to mastery with us. When groups of people such as Schön's architects, engineers, managers, and psychotherapists do their work together in an externally open way, they can develop a collective mastery in a particular domain. Research suggests, for example, that groups and organizations can develop collective capabilities in such technical domains as cardiac surgery, chemical adhesives development, and distributed organizing,[20] as well as in such moral domains as courage and compassion.[21]

Collective mastery is not limited to formal groups. Amy often shares her growing mastery of interior design with others, and learns from others as well. She continues to watch, read, and talk to others. Whether formal or informal, communities of practice can lift each other by taking on challenges, being open to feedback from those challenges, and working together.

Sharing Knowledge and Celebrating Others' Successes

About a year after Mason and Katie began playing the piano, Amy challenged Katie with a difficult piece. She asked Katie to start working on the song "Cuckoo." From Katie's effort to play it, Ryan learned two more ways in which our externally open states can lead others.

Katie's first day of working on "Cuckoo" did not go well. Later in the evening Amy told Ryan that it might have been too soon to ask Katie to play it. Ryan wondered if he could help Katie figure out how to play it, because he had struggled to learn it himself.

The next day, while Amy was out, Ryan told Katie that it was time to practice the piano. Katie did not want to; her new song was too hard. "Katie," he said, "did you know that this was the first song that your mother had me learn how to play?"

"No," she said. She became slightly more interested.

"It was. And it was hard for me too. But I can show you how I learned how to play it."

Katie was willing to try that out. Ryan showed her how he broke the song up into pieces and practiced a few notes at a time. He played those first few notes for her. He asked her to play the first few notes ten times. She did it, and did it pretty easily. They added a few more notes. After fifteen minutes, she had learned to play the first line and was proud of her accomplishment.

The next day Ryan said to Katie, "Hey Katie, why don't you show your mom what you learned yesterday?" Katie walked proudly to the piano and played the first line of "Cuckoo." Amy was delighted and said, "Katie, that's wonderful! You did great! How did you learn that?"

"Daddy taught me!" she said.

That earned Ryan some brownie points, and Amy immediately got to work helping Katie learn the rest of the song. Within two weeks Katie had it down, and she played it proudly at every opportunity for weeks afterward.

Because Ryan became externally open as he learned to play "Cuckoo," he was able to lift Katie in two ways. First, he shared knowledge. We cannot share knowledge that we do not have. And we gain knowledge through learning, which happens most effectively when we are in an externally open state. By learning to play "Cuckoo" and then teaching it to Katie, Ryan helped her become a better piano player. More im-

portant, perhaps, he helped her become more confident in her ability to learn, which should lead her to be externally open more often.

Helping Katie learn to play the song also gave Ryan an opportunity to celebrate Katie's success with her. People are less likely to share in others' successes when they are internally closed because they tend to feel diminished by the others' successes. If our abilities cannot change, then other people's successes make us less exceptional or more of a failure by comparison.[22] If we are externally open we worry less about comparison, so we can celebrate others' successes. This strengthens our relationship with them, as we discussed in chapter 8.

The Love of Performing

People can become externally open by asking themselves (either before or during an activity), "What are three or more strategies I could try in learning how to achieve my purpose?" External openness lifts us because we believe that we can grow and improve, we can take on challenges, we can learn from feedback, we can perform better in complex or uncertain activities, and we can have fun. It also tends to lift others, because when we are externally open we free others from our judgmental labels, act in ways that invite others to also be externally open, learn together and develop collective competencies, gain new knowledge we can share, and become more likely to celebrate other people's successes with them.

An externally open state is a wonderful thing, but sometimes life requires us to focus on outcomes. What if we need to accomplish a goal now and we do not have time to learn how to do it better? Or what if we need to make an ethical decision? If it is a question of right or wrong, then wouldn't it be wrong to approach the situation open to the possibility of failure?

These are legitimate questions. For example, in the study we mentioned earlier in which Bunderson and Sutcliffe studied business unit management teams, being externally open was only a good thing for

these teams to a point.[23] Too much of a focus on learning led to a decrease in performance, presumably because these teams needed to emphasize using knowledge as well as gaining knowledge. Similarly, when Anne Miner and her colleagues studied improvisation in the product development activities of companies, they found that sometimes people continued to work on the designs of their products when the company needed them to freeze the design process and to begin to manufacture and sell the products.[24] And sometimes ethical decisions need to be made, not deliberated on. Generally we know we should not lie, cheat, or steal. Seeking feedback is not likely to shed additional light on straightforward ethical situations.

There are limits to how much challenge people should tackle and how much feedback should be sought. Even so, we would argue that becoming externally open is still important for at least two reasons. First, when activities are complex and changing, people actually perform better in an externally open state. In a world that seems to be growing more complex and ambiguous by the moment, we are likely to encounter more complex and changing activities. Learning may not be necessary for simple decisions, but with technology, terrorism, shifting demographics, globalization, and countless other forces affecting both our personal and professional lives it seems that the questions of our day are growing more—rather than less—complex. If we believe our character is fixed and we avoid feedback because of this, then we will be ill-equipped to handle the challenges coming our way.[25]

Second, experiencing an externally open state is important because we can take advantage of the benefits of such a state and avoid its disadvantages if we take into account the other three characteristics of the fundamental state of leadership. For example, purposes can include deadlines that tell us when to stop gathering feedback. Values such as efficiency or punctuality can help us know when to put the seeking of feedback on hold. And some of the stakeholders we empathize with are likely to push us to focus on execution when the time is appropriate. The four characteristics of the fundamental state of leadership help us

to avoid taking any particular characteristic too far. Thus, having discussed each characteristic individually, it is now time to explain how these characteristics fit together to help the practice of leadership become a natural part of our lives.

PRACTICES FOR BECOMING EXTERNALLY OPEN

When people want to become externally open, it can be difficult to come up with strategies or to stop worrying about impressing others or looking foolish. The following practices can help.

1. **Restate the praise or criticism you receive from others.** When people praise or criticize your inherent ability, reframe their comments to focus on effort and strategy.
2. **Get input.** If you have trouble coming up with strategies, ask others for stories of how they succeeded in similar activities, or read books, articles, or blogs for suggestions.
3. **Name your fears.** When we feel pressure, stress, or fear we can reduce that fear by naming it. Identifying and acknowledging fear reduces uncertainty and makes it easier to accomplish something.
4. **Set learning goals for your extraordinary purposes.** Sometimes when we think about a result that we want to create, we focus on what others will think about it. We can focus on this less by setting goals for ourselves right after asking what result we want to create.
5. **List things you are grateful for and recall personal development journeys.** Thinking about times when we have overcome difficulties or developed new abilities can help us see that we can overcome challenges or develop abilities this time as well. And if we focus on what we are grateful for, in those journeys and in our lives now, we can reduce our concern over what others think. Gratitude does this by helping us think of our successes more humbly (so we are less likely to attribute them to our own ability), and by focusing us on factors that helped us succeed (which promotes learning).

BECOMING A POSITIVE FORCE IN ANY SITUATION

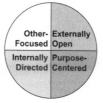

After Orville and Wilbur Wright's successful flight in Kitty Hawk, North Carolina, they announced to the press that the age of the flying machine had come. Even so, their airplane had flown only in straight lines, landing on the soft sands of the North Carolina beach. Therefore, in 1904, the Wright brothers began flying their new airplanes in a cow pasture in Ohio. They added weight to the front of planes to improve stability and moved the elevator farther forward so that it would be less sensitive. Finally, on October 20, 1904, they flew their first circular flight for one minute and thirty-six seconds. By 1905 they built an airplane that flew for thirty-nine minutes. This airplane could be used for practical purposes, so the Wright brothers sought a patent and began looking for customers. By building a machine that could (1) propel itself forward, (2) use properly designed wings to (3) turn the air appropriately, and (4) adjust to changing conditions, they harnessed the

aerodynamic force of lift. Their invention changed the world, but they did not stop trying to improve upon it.

As we have suggested, principles for using the fundamental state of leadership are analogous to the principles the Wright brothers used to harness the aerodynamic force of lift. When people are (1) purpose-centered, (2) internally directed, (3) other-focused, and (4) externally open, they tend to lift themselves and others. Like the Wright brothers, who learned from such people as Daniel Bernoulli and Otto Lilienthal, our work on the fundamental state of leadership builds on the work of people who came before us. For example, Bob drew on the work of people studying organizational effectiveness when he and John Rohrbaugh developed the competing values framework, and Ryan added to the work of people studying psychological states when he studied flow. And, like the Wright brothers, both of us continue to enhance our understanding of the fundamental state of leadership through continued research, teaching, and practice. In fact, the need for practice is illustrated well in the following experience.

Ryan: I was lying in a hotel bed in Athens, Greece, and I could not sleep. I had spent the day training a group of managers from a global company on innovation. The morning had gone well, but in the afternoon I asked the managers to split up into groups to work on an idea-generating task. As I explained the task to them their facial expressions showed little enthusiasm. I convinced myself that they would see the value of the task after they did it, so I pressed on.

A few of the managers asked questions. They were polite, but it was clear that they did not think that the exercise was relevant to them. One of the managers expressed his displeasure vocally; I expressed sympathy and told him that if he performed the task he would see its value. He stood up, said the exercise was ridiculous, and walked out of the room. The room went silent, and everyone felt tense. The rest of the group performed the exercise, but as I walked among the groups I received many forced smiles and few signs of true interest.

Eventually the manager who walked out came back and joined his group. I talked to him, and he explained his point of view more calmly now. I acknowledged the legitimacy of his concerns and expressed appreciation for his willingness to come back and try the activity anyway. When the training session ended, the atmosphere was still tense and there was definitely no enthusiasm.

I wallowed in my problems as I lay in bed. "They need to learn how to come up with ideas," I told myself. "That's a fundamental step in innovating. The executives who hired me wanted me to train them on that. Why can't they trust me? I have expertise in this; that's why they hired me. If these managers rate me poorly, I'll lose this job. That would be so embarrassing. The executives who hired me will never trust me again, and I'll look stupid. Maybe I'm not that good at teaching after all." My imagination ran wild.

Eventually I got control over my thoughts and emotions. I knew I was being comfort-centered, externally directed, self-focused, and internally closed. Fortunately, I also knew what to do about it. I told myself that I had wallowed enough. I had a half day of training left with the group in the morning. Focusing on this half day, I asked myself the four questions.

1. What result do I want to create? At the end of my last half day with them I wanted the managers to be able to walk out of the room with clear ideas about what they were going to do differently to help their company be more innovative, and I wanted them to be excited about implementing those ideas.

2. What would my story be if I were living the values I expect of others? I had been expecting these managers to respect me for my expertise. However, I had not shown them the same level of respect. They had expertise in their jobs; they knew where innovation was needed in their units. I needed to respect their expertise, and I began imagining a story for how I might do that. When I began teaching in the morning, I would ask them what they wanted to know about innovation. I would respect their opinions and figure out how to help them learn the things they needed to learn and how to apply those ideas in their situations.

3. How do others feel about this situation? As I thought about how the managers in my class must feel, I realized how frustrating it must be to have real innovation problems that you want to work on but be receiving training that does not address those problems. I empathized with

their frustration and wanted to do a better job for them—not just for myself.

4. What are three or more strategies I could try to learn how to achieve my purpose? To learn more about their expertise and about what they wanted to know, I came up with different ways I believed could be good for beginning and teaching the class. But I did not know which way would work best. I tried to imagine how each approach might turn out, and then I made adjustments. I knew that in the morning I would have to try one approach, adapt it as needed and, based on how the managers responded, figure out how to teach the class in real time. The curiosity I felt about the strategies reduced the intimidation I was feeling.

The next morning I opened the class by saying, "Yesterday afternoon I asked you to participate in an idea-generating activity that many of you did not want to do. If I understand correctly, those of you who did not want to do the activity feel like generating ideas is not an issue for you in your jobs. I believe in adapting my teaching to the needs of the people I am working with, and I failed to do that yesterday. I am sorry. This morning I want to work together with you to create a training session that will be maximally useful to you for innovating successfully in your jobs. To do that I need to know what you need to know. So, to start out this morning, please tell me what you need to know in order to innovate successfully in your organization."

When I said this the managers in the room raised their hands. Each of them told me what he or she wanted to know, and I wrote all of their answers on a flip chart. When they finished, it was clear that they all had the same issue: they had no problem coming up with ideas that could help them in their work, but they had trouble getting their ideas implemented. In one form or another, each of the managers wanted to know how to influence others in ways that would help them get their best ideas implemented.

Now that I knew what they needed, I paused and thought for a moment. Then I decided to skip over dozens of slides. Instead I selected twelve slides that focused on how to get innovations implemented in organizations. As I presented them, the managers became increasingly enthusiastic. Given how much they liked the concepts I was presenting, I suggested that each person select one of the concepts that I presented, break into groups, tell the other people in the group how they might apply that principle to get one of their own ideas implemented, and then get suggestions from

others in the group about how they could improve their efforts even further. The groups buzzed with energy as they discussed these ideas.

The time flew by. At the end of the morning, managers announced to each other the things that they were going to do differently when they returned to their offices. After we finished, the manager who had walked out on my training session the previous afternoon came up to talk to me. He shook my hand and said, "Thank you. That was fabulous. If our company could do what you did this morning, we would not need any training in innovation." I went on to deliver this training for other branches of the company in Costa Rica, Turkey, and the United States.

Even though Ryan studies, understands, writes about, teaches, and practices the principles of the fundamental state of leadership, he still fell short of this ideal when he was teaching idea generation to the executives. We have found that living these principles takes continual practice. But this story suggests at least two other observations as well. First, it illustrates how the concepts we reviewed in chapters 3–10 become integrated in the fundamental state of leadership. Second, it illustrates the thesis of this book: when people experience the fundamental state of leadership they become a positive force in any situation.

In this chapter we discuss each point in this thesis: What is it about these four characteristics that make the fundamental state of leadership so *positive*? What is it about these four characteristics that help a person become a *force*, or an influence, upon others? Do these four characteristics really apply in *any* situation? And why is this focus on *situations* so important? As we discuss these questions, we also explain how to integrate these principles so that they can work together for maximum benefit.

Becoming Positive

The first step in understanding how the four characteristics of the fundamental state of leadership work together is to summarize the principles behind each characteristic; this is shown in table 11.1. The titles

TABLE 11.1

Summary of the Four Characteristics of the Fundamental State of Leadership

	Purpose-centered	Internally directed	Other-focused	Externally open

Thoughts and feelings that define this state	1. Specific, positive, challenging, self-chosen goals
	2. Energy
	3. Focus
	4. A clear definition of the situation that directs action and gives meaning
		1. Dignity
		  a. Strength
		  b. Freedom
		  c. Stories that describe how and explain why a person should act consistently with personal values
		2. Calmness, comfort
		3. A more complex understanding of the situation
			1. Empathy
			2. Rapport
			3. Energy
			4. Calmness
				1. A belief that people's abilities and characteristics can be developed
				  a. Desire for challenge
				  b. Interest in feedback
				2. Confidence
				3. Enjoyment (fun)

Obstacles to being in this state	1. Expectations learned in previous situations or learned from others	1. Automatic responses to cues in a person's context
		2. Self-justification
			1. Ignoring invitations to empathize
			2. Self-justification
				1. The belief that people's abilities and characteristics are relatively fixed
				  a. Praise for ability or characteristics
				  b. Competitive goals

Question that helps people experience this state and influences that this state has on others	What result do I want to create?
	1. People think more complexly and creatively
	2. People attribute more importance to the situation
	3. People get energized
	4. Energy attracts (and creates) resources
	5. Higher performance creates legitimacy for the purpose being pursued
		What would my story be if I were living the values I expect of others?
		1. Elevation—the desire to live according to one's own highest values
		2. Comfort
		3. Higher performance creates legitimacy for the purpose being pursued
			How would I feel if I were experiencing this situation from other people's points of view?
			1. Security/safety
			2. Increased willingness to take risks:
			  a. Acting with integrity
			  b. Resilience
			  c. Trust
			  d. Learning and experimentation
			3. Higher performance creates legitimacy for the purpose being pursued
				What are three or more strategies I could try in learning how to accomplish my purpose?
				1. Freedom from labels
				2. Openness to challenge and feedback
				3. Higher performance creates legitimacy for the purpose being pursued
				4. Communities of practice
				5. Knowledge to share
				6. Joy in others' success

across the top are the four characteristics. The rows include the thoughts and feelings that make up the four characteristics, the obstacles that prevent people from experiencing each characteristic, a question that helps people experience each characteristic, and the influence that people who experience each characteristic usually have on others.

To see how the four characteristics work together, imagine that Ryan had not clarified his purpose before his final half day in Athens. Instead, imagine that he spent the night trying to solve the problem of how to teach idea generation to managers who did not think they needed to learn it. In this case, even if Ryan respected the managers' expertise (internal direction), he would have tried to figure out how to adapt his teaching on idea generation rather than figure out what they needed to know to innovate successfully. Even if he had empathized with their frustrations (being other-focused), he probably would have tried to find a way to make his training on idea generation less frustrating. And even if he came up with multiple strategies for teaching (external openness), they would have been strategies for how to teach idea generation.

Clarifying our purpose lifts us out of our problems and gives us meaning, direction, and energy for our activities. No matter how much integrity, empathy, and artfulness we use, if we let our problems define our situation we are unlikely to see the opportunities that come when we focus on purpose. We may even exacerbate the problems.

Similar problems arise with each characteristic of the fundamental state of leadership. If Ryan had clarified his purpose, empathized with the managers, and tried out different strategies without developing a story about living his values, he might have regressed into the automatic patterns of hierarchical teacher-student relationships. If he had clarified his purpose, thought through how he would act consistently with his values, and tried out different strategies without trying to empathize with the managers, his effort to teach to their needs might have felt forced or contrived to them. And if he had clarified his purpose, thought through how he would act consistently with his values, and empathized with the managers' frustration without trying out

different strategies, then he might have been more intimidated by feedback and less able to adapt to their needs and deliver them the training that was most useful to them.

Integrating the Experiences

Excluding any one characteristic of the fundamental state of leadership can dampen or even destroy the positivity of our experience. In contrast, when we experience all four characteristics, they collectively reinforce the positive effects and lessen the negative effects of the individual characteristics, both in terms of influence and in terms of a person's psychological state. This occurs whether we are leading a board meeting, repairing a car, visiting a neighbor, stating our earnings, or doing any other activity.

For example, Ryan's purpose—helping the managers be successful at and excited about innovation—reinforced his desire to enact his values because his purpose made the activity more meaningful. After all, if we think a purpose really matters, we want to do it well—and with integrity. The purpose also made it easier for Ryan to experience empathy because it defined the stakeholders with whom Ryan should empathize. It also helped him to identify strategies, seek feedback, and learn, because a purpose tells people what they are developing strategies for and what feedback is relevant.

As with clear purposes, each of the individual characteristics can reinforce the other three. For example, as Ryan became more internally directed, the clarification of his values helped him to become clearer about what his purpose should be, questioning his justifications made it easier to empathize with the managers he was training, and his values served as standards that he could use to help him extract feedback. As Ryan became other-focused his motivation to get the feedback he needed to understand the managers' needs increased, his desire to accomplish his purpose of helping the managers succeed grew stronger, and his respect for the managers (which was one of his values) grew. Finally, as Ryan became more externally open, he learned how to refine

his purpose, he tailored his respect to the managers' situations, and he understood more fully how to empathize with the managers.

Integrating the Influence

Ryan's experience with the managers in Greece also illustrates how integrating the four characteristics of the fundamental state of leadership enhances the positivity of a person's influence. For example, each characteristic—for different reasons, as discussed in chapters 4, 6, 8, and 10—tends to improve a person's performance. This could be seen in the way that Ryan's participants ended the training session excited to implement what they had learned, that the manager who had walked out the day before wanted to compliment Ryan, and in the company retaining Ryan for additional training.

Ryan achieved these results in part because he had a clear, energizing purpose and worked to enact his values, the managers could tell how much he cared, and he adapted to meet their needs. As Ryan's performance improved for each of these reasons, it drew more positive attention, increased people's interest in trying out his ideas, enhanced the legitimacy of his proposals, and helped him find and create new resources, such as coming up with new teaching activities or acquiring additional training opportunities.

Although performance is influenced by all four characteristics of the fundamental state of leadership, it is not the only way in which people who experience the state exert influence. For example, the manager who had walked out on Ryan was inspired as much by the way Ryan adapted to his situation as he was by the outcome of Ryan's training because, as we described in chapter 6, people who see internal direction tend to feel elevated. However, people such as this manager are even more likely to act on the elevation that they feel if the person who elevates them also empathizes with them.

The empathy of others helps us to feel secure and be more willing to take risks. Elevation and security motivate us to take value-laden action,

but this action is more likely to be nuanced or well thought through if the person who elevates us and helps us feel secure is also purpose-centered; the uniqueness of his or her purposeful action will have a tendency to make us think more complexly. And finally, if the person who makes us feel elevated and secure, and who causes us to think complexly, is also externally open, the effect will often be to make us feel like we are part of a learning community that can discover together how to succeed and to grow.

The managers in Ryan's training session did this. When he asked them to break into groups and think of ways to use the implementation tools, they spoke with animation, developed sophisticated plans, and expressed more security and confidence about taking the risks that their initiatives implied. The last column of table 11.1 summarizes the forms of influence we have discussed. When combined, the complementary effect can sometimes be dramatic.

What Is Positive

Elevation, security, complexity, learning, performance, and the other means of influence can often be positive, but we cannot argue that the simple existence of these types of influence ensures that influence will be positive. Any of these forms of influence could end up exerting a negative influence. In fact, given that people have different perspectives on what is positive, it seems possible that some people might think a person's influence is negative even if most people see it as positive. For example, when Ryan trained the managers in Greece, there may have been a few of them who did not think the training was positive. The positivity of a person's influence is a value judgment. If everyone has different values, then it seems like there must always be trade-offs with regard to how positive a person's influence is.

It is because of this potential for trade-offs that the integration of positive opposites in the fundamental state of leadership is so important. The fundamental state of leadership requires us to focus on what

others feel as well as what we want; it requires us to hold ourselves up to enduring values and standards while also using feedback to adapt to unfolding situations. We believe that these positive opposites, and the effort it takes for us to integrate the trade-offs they imply, suggests that we need to think about influence differently.

Normally, when we use the word *influence* we tend to think of it as flowing in one direction, from the influencer to those being influenced. However, if a person is other-focused and externally open, then it may be better to think about influence as a conversation. In a conversation people can influence each other reciprocally or even simultaneously. For example, Ryan clearly influenced the managers he was training in Athens, but because Ryan was other-focused he influenced the managers in a way that took into account their desire to understand implementation. In other words, Ryan was influenced by the managers as much as the managers were influenced by him; influence flowed in both directions. The more our influence integrates different people's perspectives, the more people will consider that influence to be positive.

Becoming a Force

We have just described how, when people experience the fundamental state of leadership, their influence is both reciprocal and inclusive. Their influence also happens in ways that are both intentional and unintentional. They exert unintentional influence because their psychological state influences the nonverbal signals they send to others and also subtly influences the way they take the actions that they take. They also exhibit intentional influence because, as they change their state, they have new insights into their situation, enabling them to make explicit choices about how to act and what purposes to pursue. Therefore the influence is direct and indirect, intentional and unintentional, reciprocal, inclusive, and ongoing.

Even when we are intentional in our efforts to influence others, the people we try to influence still choose for themselves how to respond to

our influence. Thus, when we experience the fundamental state of leadership we may *become* a force, but we seldom, if ever, force other people to think or act in a specific way. We may take aggressive action; we may try to persuade others to adopt our point of view or to take particular actions. But even if we are aggressive or persuasive, our empathy will usually prevent us from trying to control or manipulate. Our desire to learn makes us unlikely to assume that we have sufficient knowledge to force others to do what we want. And our desire to enact our values—especially if those values include such virtues as respect or freedom—will also often prevent us from forcing our will upon others.

There are some exceptions in which we may use force when we experience the fundamental state of leadership. For example, if people try to hurt themselves or others, we may use force to try to stop them. For most people, events such as these are relatively uncommon. When we experience the fundamental state of leadership we may enact negative consequences for actions that other people take, but this will generally be done to help them learn, not to force their behavior. When we experience the fundamental state of leadership we try to be our best selves, allowing this to inspire others to think and act in positive ways; or we seek to learn about others and see how their interests can be integrated with our own in a mutually beneficial way. For example, when Ryan's training session went poorly, it was at least in part because he tried to force the training that he had planned upon the managers in Athens. In contrast, when he experienced the fundamental state of leadership, he tried to learn their perspectives, integrate their desires with his, and exemplify the kind of innovating that he hoped to inspire in them.

If the influence of the fundamental state of leadership is found in the thoughts, feelings, actions, and outcomes to which others interpret and respond, then our influence is separate from the way that other people respond to us. We discussed this briefly at the end of chapter 6. In that discussion we mentioned people such as Mahatma Gandhi and Abraham Lincoln who tried to act in ways that were consistent with their values and were killed for doing so. These men often exerted

positive influence; they thought, felt, acted, and generated results that invited others to respond in positive ways. Other people, however, chose to interpret and respond to their actions in negative ways. This does not mean that Gandhi's or Lincoln's influence was negative, even though some people's responses to their influence were negative.

Sometimes when we experience the fundamental state of leadership our influence may have unintended negative outcomes. For example, a colleague of ours shared a story with us about how he placed adhesive, nonstick tape on the treads of the wooden stairs at his back door to make the stairs less slippery and thus safer. However, when the weather got cold, the tape contracted and pulled the paint off of the stairs; once when he walked down those stairs, he tripped on the loose tape and slid down the stairs on his back. In other words, the actions that he took with the intention to make the stairs safer actually had the opposite effect. His influence in this situation was negative even though the intended influence was positive.

The influence of our colleague's actions may have been negative (even if it only affected himself, though it could easily have affected others), but this influence was short-lived. Because our colleague was externally open, he paid attention to the feedback he received about the safety of his tape (as he fell down the stairs) and took action to remedy his mistake. His immediate influence upon the situation may have been negative, but his openness to feedback made his long-term influence positive. This is one reason why being externally open is so important. If a person experiencing the fundamental state of leadership has unintended negative influence on others, that person's willingness to receive and use feedback will tend to make even his or her unintended influence positive in the long run.

Any Situation?

Another question we could ask is whether the fundamental state of leadership will really have a positive influence in any situation with-

out exception. Although it would be impossible to prove that it works in every situation, and there may be exceptions, we know of no situation in which it has been applied by us or anyone we know in which it has not helped people to exert a more positive influence. We believe that this has been the case, at least in part, because the principles upon which the fundamental state of leadership rests are drawn from a fundamental understanding of attention, cognitive processing, social relationships, and moral philosophy.

In the early drafts of the first edition of our book we considered using the subtitle "Becoming a Positive Force in Every Situation." We decided to use the word "Any" instead of "Every" because we realize that there is an array of forces that tend to push us into comfort-centered, externally directed, self-focused, and internally closed states without us even realizing it. It is probably unrealistic to expect a person to be a positive force in every situation. Even so, we can become a positive force in an increasing number of situations, and it is certainly possible to be a positive force in *any* situation.

The Importance of Situations

Our use of the word "Any" instead of the word "Every" in the first edition's subtitle also highlights another important distinction in how we think about influence and behavior. To claim that people can experience the fundamental state of leadership in every situation would imply that this state is an enduring personality trait rather than a psychological state. Traits, as many people use the term, are patterns of behavior that are consistent across situations.[1] States, in contrast, tend to change from situation to situation.

This is not a book about patterns of behavior that are consistent across situations. Identifying consistent behavioral patterns can help people gain personal insights, but with that also comes a danger: when we label ourselves or others as engaging in the same behavioral patterns across situations, we can get trapped in those behaviors without realizing it.

Consider, for example, the commonly used Myers-Briggs Type Indicator. This instrument classifies people into categories such as introverted (I) versus extroverted (E) and judging (J) versus perceiving (P). People who use instruments such as this to train others usually say that these categories are general tendencies rather than universal descriptions. Our experience, however, is that once people receive this training they tend to treat these labels as universal descriptions. We have sat in meetings in which people who disagree will say something like, "Well that's because you are a P and I am a J." When people do this, they are usually trying to be open-minded by accounting for differences in other people. These kinds of comments have another effect as well, however: they exhibit the internally closed belief that "Our traits are fixed; there's nothing we can do about it, so we'll just have to try to find some way to work around it."

> **Bob:** An alternative to fixed labels is to think of ourselves in terms of temporary states. For example, one day I was designing a course with Phil, a colleague of mine. As we began to discuss the logistics of the course, Phil threw his hands up in the air and said, "I'm not very useful when it comes to these kinds of things; I'm just not detail-oriented enough."
>
> "That's interesting," I said. "I would tend to disagree."
>
> Most people who knew Phil would agree with this. (In fact, his wife and his administrative assistant would both warn you to avoid having him deal with details at all costs!) Phil generally excels at "big picture" work and not at detailed work.
>
> In surprise, Phil asked, "Really?"
>
> "Yes," I said. "For example, I've seen you when you compose music. When you do that, your attention to detail is extraordinary. That suggests to me that if you really care about something, you are entirely capable of taking care of even the finest of details."
>
> Phil looked at me for a second and then said, half jokingly, "I hate it when you do that."

Phil hates it when Bob points out examples that contradict his claims about what kind of person he is because Phil has learned to use labels

for his personality traits as a way to get out of doing things he does not like to do. Much of the time that is fine because Phil excels at "big picture" activities. Sometimes, however, people need him to focus on details. If Bob did not point out that Phil's labels are only labels, then we would lose out on the value of what Phil has to offer in these situations. If we focus on states rather than trait-based labels, we keep our opportunities for impact open.

I Am Part of My Situation and My Situation Is Part of Me

Phil's orientation to detail when he works on musical compositions illustrates a principle that we discussed in chapter 5, where we reviewed such studies as the Good Samaritan exercise and the experiments in which people administered shocks to others. Studies such as these remind us that who we are at any moment—the thoughts and feelings that compose our psychological states—depends in part on our situation. A situation is a combination of the circumstances we encounter and the sense that we make of those circumstances; we cannot separate our psychological state from our situation. Studies such as the Good Samaritan exercise and stories such as the one about Phil's musical composition suggest that our thoughts, feelings, and behaviors are driven at least as much by situation as they are by personality.

Often we respond to particular types of situations with automatic responses. These responses can make it difficult to choose alternative behaviors. The four questions of the fundamental state of leadership can change this. Asking these questions can change our definition of the situation in the short run, can change the specific circumstances that make up our situation in the medium or long run and, in the process, can change who we are. For example, when Ryan asked the four questions about the managers he was training in Greece, the situation changed from one in which students were resistant and displeased to

one in which they were providing Ryan with useful information. Simultaneously, Ryan changed from a frustrated trainer to a curious and engaged facilitator. He was no longer stuck with automatic responses and no alternatives; instead, he had options, opportunity, and creative insight.

Some of the insights we may acquire when we ask ourselves the four questions will be intuitive rather than reasoned. For example, in chapter 1 we told the story about how Ryan's son Mason became angry and irritable after beginning kindergarten. In a bad moment, when Mason hoarded the food on the table, Ryan used the principles described in this book and experienced the fundamental state of leadership. When he did, a thought popped into his head: "Read to him anyway." This thought seemed bizarre. Why should Ryan reward Mason for bad behavior? What would that teach him? The thought felt right, though, so Ryan acted on his intuition. Mason melted, apologized, hugged him, and began behaving better.

Intuitions such as the one Ryan had with Mason depend on our situation. Research on intuition suggests that when we experience intuition, our unconscious minds pick up on relevant cues in our situation, associate those cues with similar situations we have experienced, and give us a feeling about what an appropriate response to the current situation might be.[2] Our unconscious minds may or may not be correct, however.

Whether or not our unconscious minds are correct depends on factors such as our definition of the situation (and therefore what kind of cues we notice), the quality and frequency of feedback, how much practice we have in this kind of situation, the complexity of our understanding of the situation, and the degree of judgment involved. Much research remains to be done before we fully understand intuition, but it is interesting to note that many of the factors that affect the appropriateness of a person's intuition are captured in the four characteristics of the fundamental state of leadership. Purpose defines the situation. Stories suggest new ways for us to practice behaving. Empathy for people

affected by the situation increases the complexity of our understanding. And a belief that our situation-relevant abilities can be improved increases the quality and frequency of the feedback we receive about the situation.

In general, the four characteristics of the fundamental state of leadership dispose us to receive intuition that is high in purpose, integrity, love, and learning. We suspect, as a result, that intuition received when a person is experiencing the fundamental state of leadership is likely to be intuition of high quality. This appears to have been the case in Ryan's experience with Mason, and it also appears to have been the case when Ryan felt intuitions about how to change the innovation training in Greece.

Teaching and Learning

To summarize, people tend to become a positive force in any situation in which they experience the fundamental state of leadership because the fundamental state of leadership (1) integrates competing ethical considerations into our psychology and social relationships; (2) is inclusive of others' free will; (3) helps people adapt over time to unintended negative consequences; (4) applies to most—if not all—of the situations we may encounter; and (5) does not impose labels on us that constrain us to particular patterns of action. It is, therefore, a rather liberating and empowering experience. This is another way in which it is similar to the Wright brothers' creation of a flying machine: it opens possibilities to us that we could not have imagined before. However, as Ryan's story in Greece illustrates, learning to apply the principles of the fundamental state of leadership on a regular basis takes practice—a topic to which we will turn in chapter 12.

LEARNING THE FUNDAMENTAL STATE OF LEADERSHIP

Bob: I could hardly hear Maria when she first arrived in my class because she would look away from me, speak hardly above a whisper, and seem reluctant to state any opinions. It soon became apparent that she behaved this way in most of her interactions. So I could hardly believe it when—five weeks into my class—she told me a story about how, when one of the executives made a decision that her coworkers all resented but dared not challenge, Maria set up an appointment with her and constructively but directly explained why she thought it was a bad decision.

I should not have been surprised. I have heard some amazing stories from students who take my leadership class, yet after years of experience with watching people become leaders the process never ceases to amaze me.

Maria did more than challenge the executive one time. She turned her into an ally, advisor, and confidant. After their meeting she patiently worked with managers throughout the company until a poorly designed program to which the CEO was emotionally attached was eliminated. She became a de facto leader in her company.

Maria's story, though unique to her, is emblematic of the kind of change we see in the classes in which we teach the fundamental state

of leadership. Our classes include many traditional elements, such as case studies, experiential activities, lectures, discussions, reading assignments, and writing projects. But our classes also contain a unique personal development process focused on success that accounts for much of the change we see in our students. We have begun to use this process in organizational interventions as well as in classrooms. To streamline and scale the process, we have developed a tool named Breakthrough that can be found on a social media platform called Lift Exchange (http://www.liftexchange.com/breakthrough). As we use this technology (and other, related tools, such as the Positive Organization Generator) with different organizations and groups, we are beginning to see new and exciting applications. This chapter describes this process.

Learning from Success

Ryan: I was not expecting to become as engaged as I did when the chair of my dissertation committee suggested that I might be interested in attending a seminar on appreciative inquiry in the early 2000s.[1] Appreciative inquiry is a method for organizational change, developed in the field of organization development. It is built on the premise that by asking positive questions we create positive outcomes. Appreciative inquiry typically begins with a steering group that crafts unconditionally positive questions. Participants then ask each other these questions as a way to learn about the best of their organizations and how to spread these good things more broadly. The questions may focus on compassionate patient care, exceptional return on investment, high-functioning work relationships, error-free operations, or any other type of performance people want to improve.

After attending an appreciative inquiry seminar I was so intrigued that I started collecting data on the process. I wanted to understand whether, when, and to what extent it was an effective method for organizational change. Soon I encountered a different organizational procedure—lead user process[2]—that was strikingly similar to appreciative inquiry. Lead user process was developed in the field of operations management as a way to make the innovation process more effective. It

involves identifying the technological area in which you want to innovate—such as enhancing the effectiveness of pharmaceutical remedies, improving ease of use in employee management systems, or increasing safety in automobiles—and finding people who are at the cutting edge of that field and using their knowledge to develop new technologies.

A few years later I discovered another process that was similar to appreciative inquiry and the lead user process: positive deviance,[3] which is a technique for learning about and spreading exceptional practices for alleviating social problems, usually in third world countries. I also discovered that educational professionals have proposed a similar method for public school administrators and that solution-focused therapy uses a similar approach in clinical psychology.[4] All of these procedures involved an explicit effort to find, learn from, and spread successful practices. Although this was engaging, these processes seemed to contradict what I had learned in my statistical training about how to draw reliable inferences from a population of events.

One of the basic principles that scholars learn in their research methods classes is to never sample on the dependent variable. One way to sample on the dependent variable is to ignore failure and focus solely on success. When people sample on the dependent variable like this, they unnecessarily restrict the data from which they can learn. This tends to bias any inferences they may make. This raised the question: were all of the many professionals who use appreciative inquiry, lead user process, and the other techniques sampling on the dependent variable, or could there be wisdom hidden in these techniques that I was unable to see?

I and my colleagues Bret Crane and Jared Harris analyzed the data I had been collecting. We found that learning processes that focus on success are likely to be effective when the learning conversations follow a pattern that mirrors natural selection. In natural selection, "successful" plants or animals—the ones whose genes give them features that make them more likely to survive—get to reproduce; other plants and animals do not. As a result, their species as a whole only learns from success. And under the right circumstances, this learning can be quite effective. For example, researchers and engineers have created computer models of natural selection and used these models to find impressive solutions to problems such as figuring out how to manage airline revenue,[5] designing

molecules,[6] matching faces in forensic analysis,[7] and producing popular music.[8] As we analyzed appreciative inquiry and the other social learning methods we saw that they bore eerie similarities to natural selection. We concluded from this research that the effectiveness of these processes is likely to depend, to a large extent, on how well these processes mirror key elements of natural selection, and we identified which elements are most important for effective learning.[9]

We have incorporated this process into our teaching and our work with organizations. For example, when Maria took Bob's leadership class she had assignments each week that involved developing plans to practice experiencing the fundamental state of leadership in concrete situations from their daily lives and then reporting on how well those plans went. Each week the best reports in the class were selected. The students would then use ideas from these reports to help them in developing their plans for the next week. Table 12.1 contains four abbreviated examples of reports on practicing the fundamental state of leadership.

Initially, many people struggle with the learning process. Many students only do it because it is a class requirement. However, if people stick with the process, it becomes more natural. Some even report asking themselves the questions everywhere they go. After all, Maria was challenging an executive in her company after five weeks, and eventually became someone who people habitually turned to for leadership.

Challenges

People who engage in this learning process may struggle with it for a number of reasons. For example, some struggle to come up with episodes in which they can practice the comments; some feel awkward about pausing to reflect; and some feel like it takes too much time. Some of these concerns vanish if a person is persistent enough to engage the process for a few weeks. For other concerns, we have developed ways to help people address them.

TABLE 12.1

Fundamental State of Leadership Reports

The situation	Insights from planning and asking the four questions	The results
CEO: A member of my senior team was technically indispensable and interpersonally toxic. He was sucking the energy out of everyone. He felt untouchable and would not listen to anyone. I went through the questions.	I had been denying reality and I knew I had to make a tough decision. I worried about the impact of losing him, and the reaction of his peers in seeing him go.	I fired him. Every one of his peers responded positively. They asked me why I waited so long. The senior team is becoming more cohesive. I will not let anything like this happen in the future.
Middle manager: I was asked to make a presentation to senior management on the progress of a project I have been managing. It has been a troubled effort. In the past such presentations have not been pleasant. I had a sense of dread.	The first two questions were helpful but then I got to the one about being other-focused. I tried to identify the deepest needs of the senior people, what were their fears and desires?	In my presentation I put my ego aside and kept my focus on what would best serve the audience. It was probably the best presentation I have made, and while they were still tough with me, I got the most positive feedback that I can remember.
New manager: I joined a group of more experienced managers, all engineers. A project had blown up and we were meeting to discuss it. The intense conversation was going nowhere. Everyone was blaming someone else.	Personally I now use the questions all the time but I was not sure how to use them with others. I decided to just ask them the first question.	I asked what result we were trying to create. They tried to ignore me. I just kept repeating the question. Finally they took it seriously. When we agreed on our purpose, we were able to focus and the conversation became more productive. Next time, I will speak up sooner.
Daughter: I applied the FSL [Fundamental State of Leadership] concept a number of times, but I kept putting off the biggest issue in my life. For years I have blamed my mother for my problems and I cut her off.	When I finally got up the courage I asked the four questions and knew what I had to do.	I called her. I told her I loved her. I owned my behavior and told her I wanted a new relationship. In seven minutes I reignited a connection that had been broken for years.

One concern for which we have developed a tool is that of coming up with opportunities for practicing the fundamental state of leadership. The tool is a list of over sixty examples of episodes in which people have experienced the fundamental state of leadership (see table 12.2). The list is not exhaustive, but even so, it gives people ideas, and all of these ideas are grounded in actual experiences. You may want to keep the list handy. On the surface, many episodes may not seem like leadership opportunities, but people who have practiced the fundamental state of leadership have turned them into leadership opportunities.

Note that the opportunities in the left-hand column are different from those in the right-hand column. The opportunities in the left-hand column are events: discrete moments in time that can be scheduled into one's calendar, recorded on a to-do list, or anticipated and prepared for in some way. The opportunities in the right-hand column are problems rather than events, though people can transform them into discrete events. For example, if a person feels like he or she is afraid of rejection, gets angry easily, or has given up on dreams, asking a simple question can make these opportunities discrete: When is the next time I am likely to experience this but would be better off if I could respond differently? We discuss this process more in chapter 13.

Other challenges that people face when trying to apply this learning process include concerns about time pressure and authenticity. We have found that for most people these concerns can disappear over time if they are persistent. The concern that this process will take too long is an example of this: over time, people get faster at using the process and worry less about the time it takes.

Some people experience an even more profound insight about their use of time. For example, one of Ryan's students was a manager whose billing process was not capable of handling the increasingly larger and more sophisticated organizations that his company was serving. The billing process constantly caused problems, but this student felt he could not do anything about it because people in his department had antagonistic relationships with the department that controlled pricing

TABLE 12.2

Opportunities to Practice the Fundamental State of Leadership

As you go into the next week, will you face any of the following challenges?	Are you currently having any of the following experiences?
• There is a task I am dreading	• I am not taking care of myself
• I will have an important meeting	• I am exhausted
• I will have to persuade my boss	• I am not sleeping
• I will face an intimidating senior person	• I cannot give 100%
• I will have to make a presentation	• I have given up on my dreams
• I will have to do a performance review	• I am losing my sense of direction in life
• I will meet with a difficult customer	• I am denying reality
• I will hear negative feedback	• I do not know who I am
• I will have an overwhelming workload	• I easily get angry
• I will face distractions	• I am behaving selfishly
• I will make a decision without data	• I give direction but I do not listen
• I will deal with a major failure	• I have become a curmudgeon
• I will have an underperforming person	• I suck the energy out of people
• I will work with an unethical person	• I do not want to take risks
• I will deal with a vulnerable person	• I stay within my comfort zone
• I will have people who feel unheard	• I have limited power or influence
• I will have peers not carrying their load	• I need to be liked
• I will deal with peers in conflict	• I cannot challenge people
• I will deal with an intergroup conflict	• I am suffering from a bad habit
• I will experience organizational politics	• I feel like a fraud
• I will have people acting like victims	• I am behaving unethically
• I will be in cynical conversations	• I feel unappreciated
• I will be in an abusive environment	• I am losing confidence
• I will deal with an abusive person	• I am procrastinating
• Someone will treat me like an object	• I am making imprudent decisions
• I may have to think about a job change	• I am making mistakes
• I will have no time for my family	• I am living in fear of failure
• I carry resentment for a family member	• I fear that I am going to be rejected
• I will have a conflict with my spouse	• I fear a coming change
• I will need to help a child	• I fear for my job
• I will have a conflict with a child	• I am living for external rewards

data. He and his colleagues would spend hours working with financial spreadsheets that were onerous and unwieldy.

As this student participated in the learning process in Ryan's class, he got better and better at asking and answering the four questions. One day he asked himself the questions with regard to the billing system; this gave him insight into ways that he could shoulder some of the

burden of adding new price points to the system instead of simply getting upset at the other department for not performing its job. He approached one of the women in that department and offered to take on these responsibilities if she would give him the permissions he needed. She did. He concluded, "In a single day I had fixed a problem that my team had been wrestling with for years." By working with this woman to improve the system, Ryan's student made it possible to automate work they had been doing by hand and probably saved himself and his team hundreds of hours each year.

Some people, when they begin the learning process, say that they feel "fake" when they practice the fundamental state of leadership, like they are trying to be someone that they are not. For example, people who like to please others might feel this way if, after they ask themselves the four questions, they feel like they should fire someone. Or if people who are used to a command-and-control style of leadership ask themselves the four questions and feel like they should spend more time listening, these new impulses may seem inauthentic.

Concerns about authenticity also tend to diminish as people spend time engaging the learning process. After a few weeks of practicing the fundamental state of leadership, most of our participants come to believe that the person they are when they experience the fundamental state of leadership is actually their most authentic self; they realize that their concerns of inauthenticity kept them (and keeps others) from embracing experiencing their own growth and continuous improvement.

Accelerating Leadership Development

Ryan: Philippe was an MBA student in my leadership class. He and his classmates began the learning process by reading ten reports from people who had experienced the fundamental state of leadership. The reports included examples such as increasing accountability in the organization by convincing executives to use different metrics for measuring product mix, ignoring a boss's directive to act in a passive-aggressive manner toward another unit of the organization and instead successfully enlisting

its help, creating an entirely new business venture for the company, and helping a grandmother who had been deteriorating for fifteen years find a reason to live. After reading the stories he asked, "Are these stories all written by MBA students?"

Phillipe had not yet finished the first day of my class on leadership, and the idea that he and his classmates could accomplish feats such as these seemed a little unbelievable to him. By the end of a five-week term, however, he and his classmates were accomplishing feats such as redesigning their company's budgeting and strategic planning process, saving projects from failing, motivating underperforming and disengaged employees, solving safety problems that had plagued their company for over a year, and changing their children's eating habits.

A five-week class is not much time for fundamentally changing how people lead, but stories such as these are now relatively common in our classes. And the process does more than just help people develop as leaders. Because it requires people to recombine others' experiences in new and unique ways, the process has the potential to innovate entirely new ways to lead. If people stay engaged in the process after class ends, there is no limit to the learning and innovation that can occur. Three factors appear to be especially important in creating learning and innovation: focusing on success, learning as a community, and learning through a cycle of action and reflection.[10]

How Success Expands Learning Opportunities

Ryan: I once heard a speech by the former global director of the Hay Group, a consulting firm. He described attending a strategic meeting with the business unit CEOs of a large corporation. The financial performance of each business unit was placed on a screen for everyone to see. Upon seeing the data the business unit CEOs started grilling the leaders of the lowest-performing business units about why their performance was so poor. These leaders started defending themselves, and soon progress was stymied.

The global director stopped the exchange; he ignored the discussion about the poor performers and pointed instead at the performance of the most successful firms. He asked why they were so successful, and a deep

and probing discussion ensued. The business unit CEOs identified some effective decisions made by the CEOs of the successful units, but they also identified a lot of environmental factors and even luck that influenced their success.

After the CEOs had differentiated good strategic decisions from other factors in the business units' environments, the global director from the Hay Group allowed them to talk about the low-performing business units again. Now, with a more complex perspective, the group was able to debate the quality of the strategic decisions and the environmental influences on the businesses without anyone feeling defensive. They were able to develop future strategy much more productively.

One of the benefits of learning from success—as illustrated by the global director's story—is that people tend to be less defensive than when learning from failure. People often worry that failure will be seen as indicative of their personal qualities, as we discussed in chapter 9. But they worry less about how they are judged when we focus on their successes. Leadership development is similar: when people share their leadership successes they feel safer and devote their attention to learning rather than to defending themselves.[11]

A focus on success can also reveal new possibilities and provide informative contrasts for everyday experiences. Success reveals new possibilities because it gives people information about what has worked in the past.[12] This is what Phillipe saw when he read other MBA students' reports of successful leadership; he realized that is was possible for him to do things he had not thought possible before. When people focus on problems, they often miss these possibilities because they focus on what is wrong. Problems reveal what we need to learn about, but they are less useful for understanding the realm of possibilities available to a person. Success can enlarge our options, opportunities, and insights and expand our definition of what excellence is.

Successful experiences with the fundamental state of leadership can also expand learning because the state is a relatively uncommon experience for many of us. For example, Philippe's surprise at what his fellow

MBA students accomplished while experiencing the fundamental state of leadership is evidence that these kinds of experiences were unusual to him. Contrasts such as these can expand learning opportunities because learning occurs through contrast: we understand what something is when we compare it to something different. Failed attempts to experience the fundamental state of leadership can also be instructive, but successful attempts may provide more contrast to our everyday experience.

Success can enhance learning because it increases our feeling of safety, our understanding of possibility, and our sense of contrast, but it can impede learning as well. For example, when people are successful they are often less motivated to learn, less comprehensive in their personal reflection, and more likely to be biased about how much they have contributed to their own success.[13] Therefore, success may not enhance learning if these liabilities are not addressed. When we engage clients or students in a process of learning from success, we integrate incentives into the learning process to preserve people's motivation to learn and include specific questions designed to get participants to question their potential biases and add detail to their reflections. We also require participants to try to combine ideas from different successes as a way of promoting innovation over imitation and to model the process after natural selection.

How Community Expands Learning Opportunities

The learning process in which Ryan engaged Philippe could not be modeled after natural selection unless it occurred in a community. Philippe and his classmates could not take ideas from others' reports and recombine them to make new action plans unless there were other people generating reports from which to take ideas. As we explained in chapter 8, innovation is a process of recombining ideas across social domains. Without recombination, people can learn to master a new set of ideas, but they cannot push those ideas into new horizons.

Communities also have the potential to expand learning because the similarity of peers makes it harder to dismiss their achievements, the diversity of peers increase the number and distinctness of experiences from which members can learn, and communities can build cultures of learning and of pursuing excellence. For example, Philippe may have dismissed the reports he read if he thought that they were written by people with more experience or authority; the fact that they were written by other MBA students made them much harder to dismiss. When a community of peers excels, it challenges us to stretch and learn as well.

Philippe's peers were MBA students of approximately the same age, but they came from different states and countries. They worked in different industries and at different business functions; they comprised both genders and a number of ethnicities. Some were married with children, whereas others were single. As a result, their leadership reports involved stories on topics as broad as accounting, product design, negotiation, raising children, and taking road trips, among other unique situations.

This diversity itself expanded Philippe's learning as well as the learning of his classmates; it caused them to consider practicing leadership in activities that they had not considered before and to see new ways of using the four questions to change their states and generate insight. If people reflect only about their own experiences, their learning may be limited to only a few life domains and a few leadership applications. In a community, everyone gets more than they give and has the opportunity to reflect on leadership experiences they have not had themselves.

As people share and reflect upon each other's experiences with the fundamental state of leadership, it can change the culture of the community. Culture is made up of the taken-for-granted assumptions we have about how the world works. The stories that Phillipe read by MBA students applying the principles of the fundamental state of leadership caused him to question some of his assumptions about what it is possible for MBA students to do. Further, as Maria and others do such things as successfully challenge executives, they provide validation for

new cultural assumptions. When people such as Maria and Phillipe read and share their stories, old cultural assumptions weaken and new ones take hold. When new assumptions come from experiences with the fundamental state of leadership, people learn together to be more externally open, internally directed, purpose-centered, and other-focused.

How Reflection Accelerates Learning

The final reason learning that is modeled after natural selection can accelerate leadership development is because it requires people to plan for and reflect upon their experiences. This process of cycling through planning, action, and reflection repeatedly is perhaps the most fundamental model of learning we have,[14] and research suggests that whereas classroom learning is helpful and important, the vast majority of leadership is learned through action and reflection.[15] Even so, most of us seldom stop to reflect when we are engaged in the normal patterns of daily life; instead we cycle again and again through action, with little planning and almost no reflection. Reflection accelerates learning because it transforms unfiltered happenings into informative experiences.[16] When we require people to read others' leadership reports, extract ideas from those reports to use in their own leadership attempts, execute a new plan, and write reports for others, they necessarily engage the planning-action-reflection cycle and accelerate their leadership development.

The Payoff for the Investment

As we were writing this chapter, a physician-manager named Shailaja sent Ryan an e-mail. Shailaja was a student in one of Ryan's executive MBA classes who used the Breakthrough tool in Lift Exchange to go through the process of learning from success. In her e-mail she described how, using what she had learned in class, she had approached one of her staff members who had been performing below his usual standard for the past couple of weeks. He seemed upset, so she asked

him what was wrong. He said he was touched that she had noticed. He confided in her that his teenage son had recently been exhibiting some major discipline problems, and as a result was increasingly spending time grounded or having time-outs in his bedroom, but things were not getting better. His distress about his son was affecting his work.

Upon hearing this Shailaja told her staff member what she had learned about the fundamental state of leadership. She walked him through the four questions. The staff member was skeptical, but she told him, "Just try it. If it doesn't work, then get a counselor for your son."

A few weeks later the staff member ran up to Shailaja and told her that he had done exactly as she had suggested. As a result he learned that his son had been misbehaving because he was being bullied at school for being overweight. The staff member then reported, in tears, that he had encouraged his son, addressed the issue at the school, signed up for a gym membership, and had started working out with and spending extra time with his son. (His performance at work had also returned to its usual high standard.) He had been waiting for the chance to tell Shailaja and she, in turn, could not wait to tell Ryan.

We live for such stories. They lift us in a way that makes it worth every effort to teach people a model of leadership that lifts others. When we help such people as Maria, Phillipe, or Shailaja learn to experience the fundamental state of leadership more often and more habitually, they can then inspire similar leadership in others. Maria inspired people throughout her company to stand up for what was best for the company in spite of powerful leaders who wanted to keep their pet programs. Shailaja inspired her staff member to transform his relationship with his son and to work more effectively. Our hope is that by providing people an opportunity to learn from successful experiences with the fundamental state of leadership, we can spread this lifting far and wide.

CHAPTER 13

SLIPPING THE SURLY BONDS OF EARTH

Shawn Quinn (Bob's son and Ryan's brother) once worked with a woman who told him a story about a project that she was assigned to lead. The project was important to the work of the organization, and required a team with members of different units from within it. However, when Shawn's colleague went to the different units to recruit team members, the unit managers only let her select team members from their "mediocre" employees because they could not afford to lose their best employees.

Shawn's colleague was nervous about this situation. How could she succeed on such an important project with only mediocre employees on her team? However, these mediocre employees surprised and delighted her in every way, delivering a fantastic project. The outcome of the project was wonderful, but the question that Shawn's colleague was left to ponder was quite disturbing: How many of the employees that the organization's performance management system labeled as mediocre had the potential to be exceptional, and how much of this potential was her company leaving untapped?

Our experience is that organizations, communities, and even families leave a staggering amount of human potential untapped. But one of the benefits of studying, teaching, and applying the fundamental state of leadership is that we also get to see and experience moments of human potential that leave us feeling awe. When we see and experience these moments, we feel like John Gillespie Magee Jr. felt when he wrote the poem "High Flight." These are moments in which we "[slip] the surly bonds of earth . . . with silent, lifting mind." Our work as researchers, teachers, consultants, and entrepreneurs is focused on helping people, organizations, communities, and families achieve this kind of untapped potential, particularly by helping them learn to apply—and applying ourselves—the fundamental state of leadership.

In chapter 12 we described a process and a social media platform that we use to help people learn to use the fundamental state of leadership in their lives. In this concluding chapter we offer a more personal perspective. In the years since we published the first edition of *Lift*, as we have continued our research, teaching, consulting, and other work, we have learned to see human potential in ways that we had not considered previously, and we have also learned new things about how to tap that potential. These insights have come as we have learned more about what makes the fundamental state of leadership so fundamental, why it is important that it is a *state*, and what kind of leadership occurs when people experience this state. We discuss each of these in turn.

What Makes This State So Fundamental?

Bob: I was grading the final papers for my leadership class when I had an unexpected experience. I read a paper in which the student indicated that she was a Muslim. She said that for the first two weeks she hated the class because she felt like it was telling her how to live, and she only allows Islam to tell her how to live. Then she made a discovery: she said that the things she was learning in class *were* Islam. She then totally invested in the class and said she loved it.

I was not expecting a story in which a student who initially felt offended would then find deep connections between class concepts and Islamic doctrine; my class was focused on the science and practice of leadership. My intrigue only increased, however, when a few papers later I read a paper in which a student wrote that he was a devout Christian and, as such, he had had some misgivings about what he was learning in class. Then he read the description of the love of God in the Bible in the fifth chapter of Paul's epistle to the Romans. When he read this he suddenly realized that the class was really about pure Christianity.

A few papers later, another student wrote of spending years as an Israeli helicopter pilot. He said that he took Judaism very seriously, and he concluded that the course was a reflection of the spiritual core of Judaism.

By now my head was spinning, but the grading was not over. Toward the end of the pile, I picked up a paper written by a woman who had once been an active Buddhist. During her study in the MBA program, she found that she practiced her Buddhism less and less. After a few weeks in my class, however, she said she concluded that it was about Buddhism and she began attending her temple again.

Bob's experience with grading the papers from a Muslim, a Christian, a Jew, and a Buddhist was a surprise when it first occurred. Over time, however, it became less surprising, and gave us some useful insights into the question of what makes the fundamental state of leadership just that: *fundamental*. The four students in Bob's class who learned to integrate the fundamental state of leadership into their religious or spiritual philosophies were not the only ones to do so. We have had meaningful insights and conversations with people of many denominations and even with atheists on this subject. As we did this, a scholarly article written by Mark Kriger and Yvonne Seng came to our attention and explained this phenomenon to us quite well.[1]

Kriger and Seng examined what Buddhism, Christianity, Hinduism, Islam, and Judaism each have to say about the topic of leadership. Instead of finding difference, they found a high degree of commonality. And, to our surprise, the commonalities that they found overlap strikingly with the fundamental state of leadership.

One of the first observations that Kriger and Seng made regarded the contrast between what these religions had to say about leadership and scientific theories of leadership. Scientific theories of leadership tend to focus on what leaders *have* and *do*. For example, leaders *have* skills, traits, and resources, and they *do* things: they direct, inspire, motivate, and contribute. The religious traditions assert that leadership is as much about *being* as it is about *having* and *doing*.

Being a leader suggests a concern with a person's psychological state, subjective experience, or momentary identity. When it comes to being, the religions all aspire to a state of oneness in which conventional distinctions are replaced by union, love, Nirvana, or transcendence. People achieve this state of oneness through five conditions (summarized in Kriger and Seng's language, rather than in the language of these religions' holy texts):

1. the achievement of collective purpose
2. the establishment of shared values and meanings
3. the emergence of a shared sense of community
4. the establishment of a dynamic perception of the evolving external situation
5. an evolving internal meaning system that reflects the perception and sense of the whole

Note that the first four conditions on this list map almost perfectly onto the four characteristics of the fundamental state of leadership: being purpose-centered (collective purpose), being internally directed (shared values), being other-focused (shared sense of community), and being externally open (dynamic perception of the evolving external situation). Kriger and Seng focus on the collective experience of these conditions, and we believe that this is consistent with our observation that the reason the fundamental state of leadership tends to have a positive effect on others is because human beings are relational creatures. Our states influence others' because as relational creatures we

constantly experience and make sense of each other, and positive states tend to lift ourselves and others into shared positive experiences.

The fifth condition in Kriger and Seng's list is consistent with the idea we have presented that people experience the fundamental state of leadership by integrating these four conditions into a sense of the whole. The meaning system that makes it possible to have a sense of the whole is always evolving because a person who experiences this state makes different and unique meaning out of each situation that he or she encounters. In these moments the person becomes more complex and adaptive, aligning and realigning with the changing realities of life.

Learning how students integrate the fundamental state of leadership into their religious or personal meaning systems, and reading the research of Kriger and Seng, gave us new insight into the question of why the fundamental state of leadership is indeed so fundamental. It is not just a leadership fad, or even solely a scientific idea that emerged through years of research and professional practice; instead it is yet another discovery of what countless pilgrims have discovered on their road to Anuradhapura, Jerusalem, Mecca, or the bodhi tree. These roads may not merge in every sense, but they do seem to merge as far as leadership is concerned; their findings are a fundamental religious discovery as well as a fundamental scientific discovery.

As important as the religious and scientific roots of the fundamental state of leadership are, the reason why humans have spent millennia inquiring into this phenomenon is because of how fundamentally this state influences people on a personal level. Only when one has had the experience of tapping into our hidden wells of potential and "slipping the surly bonds of earth" can one truly understand what makes this statement fundamental. For example, in one of Ryan's leadership classes he explained the fundamental state of leadership and then asked the students if they had ever experienced this, even if they had no name for it. One student raised his hand and described the experience of losing over a hundred pounds; another described her experience as a twenty-three-year-old military commander responsible for the lives of

all of her soldiers for a year in a combat theater. When Ryan asked what meaning their experiences had for them, they both described a feeling that because of those experiences, if any challenge were to present itself, their inclination would be to say, "I've got this." They had experienced a glimpse of their true potential and they were never the same afterward. We may have different reactions to seeing our potential, but these reactions tend to be deep and emotional, as illustrated by the following story from one of Bob's executive education classes.

Bob: I spent a week teaching a wonderful group of executives, organized around four characteristics of the fundamental state of leadership. At the end of the day on Thursday, I gave them a role-playing exercise. I said, "On Monday, when you return to work, imagine that you get on the elevator and the CEO is standing there. He says, 'You just spent a week in Michigan. That cost us a lot of money. What did we get for it?'"

One of the participants responded, "It was really good, and I learned a lot." They all agreed with this response. I asked them to analyze it more deeply. After some conversation, the executives concluded that this response was reactive and self-interested. They were giving a superficial answer so they could get out of the elevator as gracefully as possible, and they were focused on how to avoid embarrassing themselves in front of the CEO. They had not seen the situation as an opportunity to help the CEO build a better company.

I told them that thirty seconds on an elevator with the CEO is a chance to change the world. They thought that was unrealistic. I reminded them that they had four questions they could use to lift themselves and lift the CEO. I put them into groups and I told them that they each had twenty minutes to prepare one person to stand up and role-play with me. The other groups would score their performance on a scale of 1 to 10. I also told them that when I, the CEO, asked them what they got out of this week's program, their first sentence had to be a question, not a statement. I told them three times that a meaningful question would engage the CEO and a conventional sentence would not.

After twenty minutes the first executive stood. I played the role of the CEO on the elevator and asked him the question about the payoffs of the program, but contrary to my instructions, he did not respond with a question; he started to tell me things that did not engage me. The other

three groups gave him a score of 3 and everyone laughed, including him. I continued.

Three out of four groups started with a statement, not a question. Each group received a 3. One group did ask a question, and I, as the CEO, was engaged, so I asked a question back and the person did not know what to say. The other groups laughed at him, but they gave him a 7. Just having a question made him better.

I asked what they learned. They gave some answers and then someone spoke up and said, "What would you do?"

I had one of them become the CEO and ask me the elevator question. I responded to the CEO's question, "Why did you spend all that money on me? What result did you hope to create? My questioner stumbled and finally said, "To make you a better leader?"

I said, "That is an amazing commitment on your part, thank you. You must really care about the development of the people in this company. It turns out that I learned a simple leadership framework and I have been thinking about how we could use it to profoundly increase the leadership capacity of every executive in this company, quickly and efficiently. Would you be interested in talking about how to do that?"

The person playing the role of the CEO did not hesitate. He said, "Yes, come to my office for lunch on Wednesday."

The room was frozen; it was an extraordinary moment. In a matter of seconds I had established a collective purpose with the CEO. I could see the executives' minds spinning. I asked what they learned, and there was an outpouring of insight. Someone finally said, "Wow, we could make a difference!" The whole week seemed to crystallize in these brief moments.

After the session, one participant stopped me. She was crying, and the tears increased as the participant told of a disastrous previous exchange with a senior authority figure. "These last twenty minutes are twenty of the most important minutes I have ever spent," she said. "If I had understood what I understand right now, last week's conversation would not have been a disaster; it would have had an incredibly positive outcome."

This person was conveying deep gratitude. I walked away grateful for the twenty-minute exchange; I learned much. And I was in turn grateful that she was so grateful. I was in an elevated state, and I felt I wanted to be a better teacher. My mind was racing with ideas on how to do more for

this group; I committed myself to getting up at 4:00 a.m. to design a new exercise for the last day of class to help my students more fully internalize the concepts. I did so, and the next day was spectacular.

Note the reactions of the executives in this story. They had an outpouring of insights; their learning crystallized. One effused, "Wow, we could make a difference!" And at least one of them was in tears from the experience. These are fundamental reactions. The fundamental state of leadership is *fundamental*, then, because when people see or experience it their understanding of their own and others' potential is never the same, and they now feel that they can change the world.

Why Does It Matter That We Think of Leadership as a State?

The importance of thinking of leadership as a state was driven home to us in a meeting in which we were developing the business plan for Lift Exchange (http://www.liftexchange.com). We attended the meeting with Shawn and with two of our former students who were working with us on the venture. As we discussed how we could most effectively incorporate learning the fundamental state of leadership into a software product, one of the former students said that it had been one of the most empowering insights of his life when he realized that he could choose his psychological state in any situation. This is an insight that sometimes comes slowly, and often needs to be re-learned because it is not a natural way to think for most of the people we teach. However, once a person truly begins to grasp this idea, it is surprising how it alone—irrespective of the other ideas in the fundamental state of leadership—can help people to see and act on their own potential.

Ryan: I discovered some inspiring examples of these principles when I was asked to be a keynote speaker at the Oklahoma State Department of Education's "Vision 2020" conference. After receiving the invitation I

decided to read about the conference online, and I learned that one of the other keynote speakers was Ron Clark.

Ron Clark was the 2010 Disney Teacher of the Year award winner, had been invited to the White House three times, had been on the *Oprah Winfrey Show* three times. He had an amazing track record of turning around failing public school classrooms, had founded the Ron Clark Academy, was the subject of the TV movie *The Ron Clark Story* starring Matthew Perry, and had authored several books. I was a little intimidated by this, so I bought a copy of Clark's most recent book to better understand his perspective.[2]

I read some of the book's reviews before buying it. Most were positive, but to my surprise, in the negative reviews I found criticisms about the time and energy Clark devotes to his work: people who "have lives" could never do what he does. Clark provides over-the-top classroom activities, goes to students' homes to help families, bakes cookies, takes his students on trips around the world, and so on. There is a temptation, when you read Clark's books or hear him speak, to think that he is a high-energy person and the rest of us either have what he has or we do not.

A closer examination of Clark's book reveals a more nuanced perspective. When Clark provides a television interview, he first describes how difficult it is to convince himself to get out of his Snuggie. When he tried to raise money for his school, talking to rich people was intimidating and he hid behind a plant until a benefactor made him go talk to people. When it was time to mow the lawn, he wanted to watch television instead. Perhaps my favorite story was his description of how he forces himself out of bed after a night with only a few hours of sleep, drags himself to school, and then, just before the students walk in, makes a decision to give them all the energy he has. Every time he does this, he reports, the students give him back all the energy he needs within a minute or two.

Stories such as these help us see the power of thinking of leadership as a state. If we think of Clark as a high-energy person, or as a person who has resources that the rest of us do not have, then many of us are failures by comparison. But if we see how Clark makes decision after decision in which he chooses his state—and has a positive influence because of these decisions—then we, like Clark, empower ourselves to accomplish extraordinary things.

Coincidentally, I found another example of this phenomenon as I delivered my training at the "Vision 2020" conference. As I taught, one participant raised her hand and said, "Every morning I forgive my students." I was struck by this comment. I have often heard people say things like, "I love my students," but when this teacher said that she forgives her students every morning, I imagined that some people would be put off by that comment. Shouldn't you love your students no matter what? What have they done to require your forgiveness?

With a little reflection, I found this woman's comment to be deeply admirable. A negative reaction to this teacher's claim that she forgives her students every day, suggests that one is not thinking of the situation in terms of states. It assumes that love never changes. In contrast, if we assume that love is a state that you acquire again and again through conscious effort and choice, then it may be that the teacher who forgives her students every morning loves her students more than a teacher who claims undying love for her students, making herself blind to the fluctuations in love that can and do occur.

Learning to think in terms of states was not an easy adjustment for us, and is also difficult for many of our students. One of the techniques we have acquired for helping students learn to think this way is to have them extract events from their challenges. As we mentioned in chapter 12, when people come to us with problems such as "I want to earn the trust of my board of directors" or "I want to motivate my employees to accept the strategic changes we have to make" we often ask them to identify an upcoming event that is related to this. For example, we might ask them, "When is the next time you will interact with one of the members of the board?" or, "When is the next time you will interact with one of your employees?" Only after a person is clear about the next event do we then help him or her walk through the four questions of the fundamental state of leadership.

Thinking in terms of events provides at least three benefits. First, events give people a discrete, manageable period of time to transform. Second, events are often more tractable than long-term problems. For

example, if a person has a tendency to fear rejection, it can be difficult to know how to overcome that tendency. In contrast, if a person only has to ask, "Why do I fear rejection in *this* situation?" the problem becomes more concrete and solutions are often easier to find. Even more encouraging, once a person figures out how to address a concrete instance of a general problem, it often gives him or her insights into addressing the problem more generally. A third benefit of focusing on events is that we develop character traits one event at a time. A person is not just born courageous, and does not just decide one day to be a courageous person; he or she becomes courageous by acting courageously in one event after another. As Will Durant said, "We are what we repeatedly do. Excellence, then, is not an act, but a habit."[3]

Focusing on events—or states—opens our eyes to human potential even before we consider the four questions of the fundamental state of leadership because it suggests that there are more choices available to us than we often think we have. Ron Clark and the woman who forgives her students every morning choose repeatedly to love and to pour energy into their students. We find it intriguing that the act of grounding ourselves in concrete events can enable us to "slip the surly bonds of earth."

How Is This Leadership?

Our efforts to slip the surly bonds of earth in our research, teaching, and practice of the fundamental state of leadership have also changed how we view the topic of leadership more generally. As we explained in chapter 1, we have proposed some changes to the standard definition of leadership. One change involves its intentionality. Leadership can be intentional, as when Ron Clark chooses to pour energy into his students, or when Shawn's colleague—the woman who assembled the team of mediocre employees—achieved the outcome she wanted with her project.

In contrast to these intentional outcomes we have learned that leadership often takes us to surprising places, as in the case of Bob's stu-

dent who suddenly felt an urge to start attending the Buddhist temple again after experiencing the fundamental state of leadership, or Ryan's learning from the executives he was training in Greece and making up an entirely new learning exercise as a result (see chapter 11). Many of us think about leadership in terms of expertise and control, but we have learned that drawing on people's untapped potential often requires us to embrace surprises, learning, and opportunities. Sometimes the unintentional outcomes of leadership are better than the outcomes we expected.

Another change we propose to the standard definition of leadership that comes from our experience with the fundamental state of leadership is the idea that it involves deviating from cultural assumptions or social conventions in a way that inspires others to choose to follow. This definition has a number of implications, some of which were discussed in chapter 1. We will illustrate two more implications of this definition by using the story of a young friend of ours whom we will call Ben.

Ben began his career by working in a manufactured-home company, and he was mired in the surly bonds of earth. It was a rough place to work—to the extreme. One of the characteristics of this rough environment was that people swore at each other all the time; another characteristic was that people were mean. For example, if anyone asked for help, they were more likely to have someone shout at them than they were to actually receive any assistance.

Ben was disturbed by this environment and initially felt helpless to do anything about it. He eventually made a decision, however: the next day at work, he said, he would wait for someone to ask for help; then, before anyone could shout at that person, he would get up, run over, and offer help.

Ben stuck with his plan, and when he did it, his colleagues were shocked. At first they just observed. Ben repeated this behavior again and again. As he did, people also began to notice that Ben did not swear. Pretty soon, people stopped swearing around Ben. Then they also started helping each other. Eventually it became normal for everyone

in the office to use positive language and to help each other. When Ben
told this story he ended by declaring triumphantly, "And we make a
lot more money now, too!"

The first implication from the new definition of leadership that is illustrated in Ben's story is the idea that leadership inspires others to
choose to follow. Ben did not have any formal authority. He did not
try to control others' behavior. Instead, he took inspiring action, and
others chose to follow him.

A second implication from the new definition of leadership that is
illustrated in Ben's story is the idea that a leadership experience is, by
definition, a cultural intervention. Ben's choices to refrain from swearing and to help people before others could shout at them definitely
deviated from the company culture. Even so, his choices were more
than just a deviation; they were inspiring. Thus, the fact that leadership moves people away from existing cultural assumptions or social
conventions and toward new assumptions or conventions means that
it is impossible for a person to engage in a true moment of leadership
without having at least some small impact on the relevant culture.

Ben's story also provides a nice illustration of our previous point
about intentionality. His decision to help people before others shouted
at them was only intended to make the workplace more humane.
The additional profitability his intervention brought to the company
was not intended, but it certainly was welcome!

Onward and Upward

Since publishing the first edition of *Lift* we have learned to see human
potential in places we had not considered looking for it before, and we
have continued to learn about how to tap that potential. These insights
help us to understand what makes the fundamental state of leadership
so fundamental, why it is important that it is indeed a *state*, and how
it has refined our understanding of what leadership is. We believe that
understanding this potential—and how to make use of it—is critical

because so many organizations, societies, communities, and families leave this potential untapped.

Tapping this potential, and watching a new world of possibility unfold when we do so, is an exhilarating experience in which everyone should share. Although Magee's "High Flight" was written about an airplane, we know of no poetry or prose that captures the exhilaration of lifting and being lifted by the people in our lives as well as this poem does. That is why we have used the metaphor of flight to describe the fundamental state of leadership. And that is why we close by inviting you, like Magee, to "slip the surly bonds of earth," "join the tumbling mirth," and "with silent, lifting mind," "top the windswept heights with easy grace." That choice will unleash your potential and the potential of those around you.

ACKNOWLEDGMENTS

A fabulous "flight crew" enabled us to launch this book "up the long, delirious blue." First and foremost, we thank our wives, Amy Quinn and Delsa Quinn, for their support, patience, feedback, and inspiration. Our children and siblings—Abram, Andrew, Chloe, Garrett, James, Jessica, Katie, Kristin, Lisa, Mason, Shauri, Shawn, and Travis—have also been an inspiration and a support. When we wrote the first edition of this book Shawn gave essential support throughout the process, Shauri's feedback was enormously helpful, and the book would not have been complete without the timely support of Ryan's mother-in-law, Ellen Burnside. Additions and revisions for the second edition were less intense than writing the first edition, but our families are, as always, a wonderful source of support.

Steve Piersanti, Jeevan Sivasubramaniam, and their colleagues at Berrett-Koehler have been amazing to work with. Many of the ideas in this book could not have come to life without Steve's mentoring and insight. We are also grateful to those, in addition to our family members Shawn and Shauri, who reviewed the book for us: Ed Freeman, Adam Grant, Peter Heslin, Barry Johansen, Chris Lee, Carol Metzker, Walter Nord, Don Schatz, Gretchen Spreitzer, Joe Webb, and Paul Wright; the quality of their feedback was generous. Bob Bruner, Mike Steep, and many of our colleagues at the universities where we work have given precious support.

We could go on and on. We have certainly missed many people; our gratitude exceeds our memory, and we hope you understand. Each of you has lifted us. We hope this book lifts you and many others.

NOTES

Introduction

1. For a brief history of Magee and his poem "High Flight," see "John Gillespie Magee Jr.," http://en.wikipedia.org/wiki/John_Gillespie_Magee_Jr.

2. Magee passed away in a flight accident shortly after writing this poem on the back of a letter to his parents. The original copy is kept in the Library of Congress. In the winter 1982 issue of *This England* magazine, a friend of the Magee family named Dr. A. H. Lankester—with help from members of Magee's family—wrote a tribute to Magee and included the poem. The editors of the magazine added, "We are pleased to grant permission for the article to be reprinted in any other publication, without fee, providing acknowledgment is made to This England and a copy of the publication forwarded to us for our archives; This England, P.O. Box 52, Cheltenham, Gloucestershire, England. GL50 1YQ."

3. The fundamental state of leadership has also been discussed in other publications, such as R. E. Quinn, *Building the Bridge as You Walk on It: A Guide for Leading Change* (San Francisco: Jossey-Bass, 2004); and R. E. Quinn, "Moments of Greatness: Entering the Fundamental State of Leadership," *Harvard Business Review* 83, no. 7 (2005): 74–83. In the previous edition of this book we called the state *lift*. To prevent confusion with the other publications, in this second edition we call it *the fundamental state of leadership* and we discuss how the state lifts ourselves and others.

4. When we tell stories about other people, we generally change the names of the people and organizations involved in order to protect their privacy. Exceptions to this occur if the name of a person in a story is obvious because of a relationship we have with them (such as our wives or children) or if the story is one that is in the public record.

Chapter One

1. See G. Yukl, "Managerial Leadership: A Review of Theory and Research," *Journal of Management* 15, no. 2 (1989): 251–89.

2. Much of the scientific research on influence tends to focus on tactics such as these. Examples of research that examines influence tactics include D. Kipnis and S. M. Schmidt, "Upward-Influence Styles: Relationships with Performance Evaluations, Salary, and Stress," *Administrative Science Quarterly* 33, no. 4 (1988): 528–43;

D. Kipnis, S. M. Schmidt, and W. Ian, "Intraorganizational Influence Tactics: Explorations in Getting One's Way," *Journal of Applied Psychology* 65, no. 4 (1988): 440–52; and G. Yukl and C. M. Falbe, "Influence Tactics and Objectives in Upward, Downward, and Lateral Influence Attempts," *Journal of Applied Psychology* 75 (1990): 132–40. Popular books that summarize such tactics include R. B. Cialdini, *Influence: The Psychology of Persuasion*, rev. ed. (New York: Collins Business, 2006); and N. J. Goldstein, S. J. Martin, and R. B. Cialdini, *Yes! 50 Scientifically Proven Ways to be Persuasive* (New York: Free Press, 2009). Such literature seldom considers the ethics of influence tactics. If it mentions ethics at all, it usually tells readers only to use these principles ethically.

3. This story was recorded first in R. E. Quinn, *Change the World: How Ordinary People Can Accomplish Extraordinary Results* (San Francisco: Jossey-Bass, 2000), 123–24.

4. Research suggests, for example, that when one person speaks to another, listeners receive 12.5 times as much information, on average, from the speakers' nonverbal cues as they do from the speakers' actual words, and that people believe the nonverbal cues more than they believe the verbal ones. This makes unexpected nonverbal cues even more important for people to make sense of than verbal ones. See J. K. Burgoon, "Nonverbal Signals," in *Handbook of Interpersonal Communication*, ed. M. L. Knapp and G. R. Miller, 2nd ed. (Thousand Oaks, CA: Sage, 1994), 229–85; and J. K. Burgoon, "Nonverbal Communication Research in the 1970s: An Overview," in *Communication Yearbook*, ed. D. Nimmo (New Brunswick, NJ: Transaction, 1980), 179–97.

5. Scientists call this emotional contagion. For a description of the process, see E. Hatfield, J. T. Cacioppo, and R. L. Rapson, "Primitive Emotional Contagion," in *Emotion and Social Behavior, vol. 14: Review of Personality and Social Psychology*, ed. M. S. Clark (Newbury Park, CA: Sage, 1992), 151–77.

6. Donald A. Schön, for example, describes how the reflectiveness with which professionals do their work affects how artfully their decisions are made; see Schön, *The Reflective Practitioner: How Professionals Think in Action* (New York: Basic Books, 1983). Alice Isen's research on emotions and creativity suggest that people will make more creative decisions or perform more creatively depending on their psychological states; see A. M. Isen, "Positive Affect and Creativity," in *Affect, Creative Experience, and Psychological Adjustment*, ed. S. Russ, 3–17 (Philadelphia: Bruner/Masel, 1999). Other examples can be given as well.

7. Large and small successes and other extraordinary results draw other people's attention and add legitimacy to what a person is doing; see J. Collins, *Good to Great: Why Some Companies Make the Leap . . . and Others Don't* (New York: Harper Business, 2001); and K. Weick, "Small Wins: Redefining the Scale of Social Problems," *American Psychologist* 39 (1984): 40–49.

8. See, for example, M. Emirbayer, "Manifesto for a Relational Sociology," *American Journal of Sociology* 103, no. 2 (1997): 281–317.

9. For a good description of how intuitions such as these work, see E. Dane and M. G. Pratt, "Exploring Intuition and Its Role in Managerial Decision Making," *Academy of Management Review* 32, no. 1 (2007): 33–54.

10. See K. S. Cameron, J. E. Dutton, and R. E. Quinn, *Positive Organizational Scholarship: Foundations of a New Discipline* (San Francisco: Berrett-Koehler, 2003).

11. See M. E. P. Seligman, *Authentic Happiness: Using the New Positive Psychology to Realize Your Potential for Lasting Fulfillment* (New York: Free Press, 2002).

Chapter Two

1. Our history of the Wright brothers' quest to build a flying machine comes from the websites of the Smithsonian National Air and Space Museum, NASA, Monash University, and *Failure* magazine.

2. R. E. Quinn and J. Rohrbaugh, "A Spatial Model of Effectiveness Criteria: Towards a Competing Values Approach to Organizational Analysis," *Management Science* 29, no. 3 (1983): 363–77.

3. See K. S. Cameron and R. E. Quinn, *Diagnosing and Changing Organizational Culture: Based on the Competing Values Framework* (Reading, MA: Addison-Wesley, 1999); K. S. Cameron, R. E. Quinn, J. DeGraff, and A. V. Thakor, *Competing Values Leadership: Creating Value in Organizations* (Northampton, MA: Edward Elgar, 2006); J. DeGraff and S. E. Quinn, *Leading Innovation: How to Jump Start Your Organization's Growth Engine* (New York: McGraw-Hill, 2007); S. Hart and R. E. Quinn, "Roles Executives Play: CEOs, Behavioral Complexity, and Firm Performance," *Human Relations* 46, no. 5 (1993): 543–74; R. E. Quinn and K. S. Cameron, "Organizational Life Cycles and Shifting Criteria of Effectiveness: Some Preliminary Evidence," *Management Science* 29, no. 1 (1983): 33–51; R. E. Quinn, S. R. Faerman, M. P. Thompson, and M. R. McGrath, *Becoming a Master Manager: A Competency Framework* (Hoboken, NJ: Wiley, 2003); and R. E. Quinn, H. W. Hildebrandt, P. S. Rogers, and M. P. Thompson, "A Competing Values Framework for Analyzing Presentational Communication in Management Contexts," *Journal of Business Communication* 28, no. 3 (1991): 213–32.

4. See P. R. Lawrence and N. Nohria, *Driven: How Human Nature Shapes Our Choices* (San Francisco: Jossey-Bass, 2002).

5. S. H. Schwartz, "Universals in the Content and Structure of Values: Theoretical Advances and Empirical Tests in 20 Countries," in *Advances in Experimental and Social Psychology*, ed. M. P. Zanna (San Diego: Academic Press, 1992), 25: 1–65.

6. K. Benziger, *Thriving in Mind: The Art and Science of Using Your Whole Brain* (New York: KBA, 2004).

7. A. P. Fiske, *Structures of Social Life: The Four Elementary Forms of Human Relations* (New York: Free Press, 1993).

8. K. Wilbur, *A Theory of Everything: An Integral Vision of Business, Politics, Science, and Spirituality* (Boston: Shambhala, 2001).

9. Our understanding of the fundamental state of leadership continues to evolve and will continue to do so over time. Ryan's specific research project with Ned and Bret builds on the research reported throughout this book by examining the phenomena in specific leadership content and in reference to specific leadership theories. This

project was not complete as we were writing this second edition of the book, but the initial wave of data has been collected and analyzed. We developed experimental manipulations that mirrored asking the four questions and found that three of the four manipulations, in fact, increased the likelihood of participants experiencing the predicted psychological states. We are certain that with some minor adaptations to the manipulation we could induce the fourth state as well. The psychological states, in turn, predicted intentions to enact specific leadership behaviors. We are now in the process of expanding this to a field study to examine momentary leadership states in corporate work teams.

10. Perhaps some of the most prominent works for describing these philosophies are Plato, *Phaedo*, ed. C. J. Rowe, (Cambridge: Cambridge University Press, 1993), on teleology; Aristotle, *Nicomachean Ethics*, trans. T. Irwin (Indianapolis: Hackett, 2000), on virtue ethics; I. Kant, *Groundwork of the Metaphysics of Morals*, trans. H. J. Paton (New York: Harper Torchbooks, 1964); M. Buber, *I and Thou*, trans. W. Kaufmann (New York: Simon and Schuster, 1990); and J. Dewey, *Human Nature and Conduct: An Introduction to Social Psychology* (New York: Henry Holt, 1922), on pragmatism.

Chapter Three

1. R. Fritz, *The Path of Least Resistance: Learning to Become the Creative Force in Your Own Life* (New York: Fawcett, 1989).

2. J. T. Noteboom, "Activation of the Arousal Response and Impairment of Performance Increase with Anxiety and Stressor Intensity," *Journal of Applied Physiology* 91 (2001): 2093–2101.

3. M. H. Ashcraft and E. P. Kirk, "The Relationships among Working Memory, Math Anxiety, and Performance," *Journal of Experimental Psychology: General* 130, no. 2 (2001): 224–37.

4. B. M. Elzinga and K. Roelofs, "Cortisol-Induced Impairments of Working Memory Require Acute Sympathetic Activation," *Behavioral Neuroscience* 119, no. 1 (2005): 98–103.

5. The effects of tension on performance can be summarized by what has come to be called the Yerkes-Dodson Law; see R. M. Yerkes and J. D. Dodson, "The Relation of Strength of Stimulus to Rapidity of Habit-Formation," *Journal of Comparative Neurology and Psychology* 18 (1908): 459–82. The law suggests that the relationship between the tension that people feel and how well they perform in their activities is shaped like an upside-down U. In other words, people initially perform better as their tension increases. Once the tension that they feel passes a certain threshold, however, more tension leads to a decrease in performance. How much tension they feel about an activity depends, of course, on how good people are at performing that activity. When people experience high levels of tension their performance decreases because of hyperfocus, jerky or erratic behavior, habitual behavior, decreased working memory, the fight-or-flight response, rigidity in the face of threat, and so forth. Additional research on this law and on the effects of high levels of tension includes R. P. Barthol and N. D. Ku,

"Regression under Stress to First Learned Behavior," *Journal of Abnormal and Social Psychology* 59 (1959): 134–36; P. L. Broadhurst, "Emotionality and the Yerkes-Dodson Law," *Journal of Experimental Psychology* 54 (1957): 345–52; W. B. Cannon, *Bodily Changes in Pain, Hunger, Fear and Rage: An Account of Recent Researches into the Function of Emotional Excitement* (New York: Harper and Row, 1963); G. Mandler, *Mind and Body: Psychology of Emotion and Stress* (New York: Norton, 1984); B. M. Staw, L. E. Sandelands, and J. E. Dutton, "Threat-Rigidity Effects in Organizational Behavior: A Multilevel Analysis," *Administrative Science Quarterly* 26, no. 4 (1981): 501–24; and R. E. Thayer, *The Biopsychology of Mood and Arousal* (New York: Oxford University Press, 1989).

6. For a detailed analysis of the impact that tension had on the events that unfolded at the Los Rodeos airport, see K. E. Weick, "The Vulnerable System: An Analysis of the Tenerife Air Disaster," *Journal of Management* 16, no. 3 (1990): 571–93.

7. Mandler, *Mind and Body*.

8. G. F. Smith, "Towards a Heuristic Theory of Problem Structuring," *Management Science* 34 (1988): 1489–1506.

9. M. Snyder and W. B. Swann, "Hypothesis-Testing Processes in Social Interaction," *Journal of Personality and Social Psychology* 36, no. 11 (1978): 1202–12.

10. C. Lord, L. Ross, and M. Lepper, "Biased Assimilation and Attitude Polarization: The Effects of Prior Theories on Subsequently Considered Evidence," *Journal of Personality and Social Psychology* 37 (1979): 2098–2109.

11. D. Westen, B. Pavel, K. Harenski, C. Kilts, and S. Hamann, "Neural Bases of Motivated Reasoning: An fMRI Study of Emotional Constraints on Partisan Political Judgment in the 2004 U.S. Presidential Election," *Journal of Cognitive Neuroscience* 18, no. 11 (2006): 1947–58.

12. K. E. Weick, *Sensemaking in Organizations* (Thousand Oaks, CA: Sage, 1995), 90.

Chapter Four

1. See H. Garfinkel, *Studies in Ethnomethodology* (Englewood Cliffs, NJ: Prentice Hall, 1967). Other, related examples can be found in E. J. Langer, *Mindfulness* (Reading, MA: Addison-Wesley, 1989); and G. R. Salancik, "Field Simulations for Organizational Behavior Research," *Administrative Science Quarterly* 24 (1979): 638–49.

2. R. Thurman, "The Countess and the Impossible," *Reader's Digest* (June 1958): 109.

3. G. A. Nix, R. M. Ryan, J. B. Manly, and E. L. Deci, "Revitalization through Self-Regulation: The Effects of Autonomous and Controlled Motivation on Happiness and Vitality," *Journal of Experimental Social Psychology* 35, no. 3 (1999): 266–84.

4. S. R. Marks, "Multiple Roles and Role Strain: Some Notes on Human Energy, Time, and Commitment," *American Sociological Review* 42, no. 6 (1977): 921–36.

5. See K. H. Moffit and J. A. Singer, "Continuity in the Life Story: Self-Defining Memories, Affect, and Approach/Avoidance Personal Strivings," *Journal of Personality* 62, no. 1 (1994): 22–43; and J. A. Singer, "Affective Responses to Autobiographical Memories and Their Relationship to Long-Term Goals," *Journal of Personality* 58

(1990): 535–63. There are also advantages to negative goals; some researchers have found that negative goals increase vigilance, systematic and analytical processing, and the prevention and detection of error. See J. Brockner and E. T. Higgins, "Regulatory Focus Theory: Its Implications for the Study of Emotions in the Workplace," *Organizational Behavior and Human Decision Processes* 86 (2001): 35–66; and N. Schwarz and G. Bohner, "Feelings and Their Motivational Implications: Moods and the Action Sequence," in *The Psychology of Action: Linking Cognition and Motivation to Behavior*, ed. P. M. Gollwitzer and J. A. Bargh (New York: Guilford, 1996), 119–45. In practice, people often use multiple goals in a single activity. Thurman's superordinate goal, for example, may have been to "mow a five-dollar lawn," which consisted of several subordinate goals, both positive and negative, such as "don't miss any corners" and "trim the walkway."

6. J. Tomaka, J. Blascovich, R. M. Kelsey, and C. L. Leitten, "Subjective, Physiological, and Behavioral Effects of Threat and Challenge Appraisal," *Journal of Personality and Social Psychology* 65, no. 2 (1993): 248–60.

7. For the study in which the data about this scientist was collected, see R. W. Quinn, "Flow in Knowledge Work: High Performance Experience in the Design of National Security Technology," *Administrative Science Quarterly* 50, no. 4 (2006): 610–41.

8. C. E. Cohen and E. B. Ebbeson, "Observational Goals and Schema Activation: A Theoretical Framework for Behavior Perception," *Journal of Experimental Social Psychology* 15 (1979): 305–29.

9. See E. A. Locke and J. F. Bryan, "The Directing Function of Goals in Task Performance," *Organizational Behavior and Human Performance* 4 (1969): 35–42; N. E. Adler and D. Goleman, "Goal Setting, T-Group Participation, and Self-Rated Change: An Experimental Study," *Journal of Applied Behavioral Science* 11, no. 2 (1975): 197–208; J. R. Terborg and H. E. Miller, "Motivation, Behavior, and Performance: A Closer Examination of Goal Setting and Monetary Incentives," *Journal of Applied Psychology* 63, no. 1 (1978): 29–39; W. F. Nemeroth and J. Cosentino, "Utilizing Feedback and Goal Setting to Increase Performance Appraisal Interviewer Skills of Managers," *Academy of Management Journal* 22 (1979): 566–76; E. Z. Rothkopf and M. J. Billington, "Goal-Guided Learning from Text: Inferring a Descriptive Processing Model from Inspection Times and Eye Movements," *Journal of Educational Psychology* 71, no. 3 (1979): 310–27; and E. A. Locke, D. O. Chah, S. Harrison, and N. Lustgarten, "Separating the Effects of Goal Specificity from Goal Level," *Organizational Behavior and Human Decision Processes* 43 (1989): 270–87.

10. Thurman, "The Countess and the Impossible," 109.

11. Ibid., 110.

12. Ibid.

13. K. E. Weick, *The Social Psychology of Organizing* (New York: McGraw-Hill, 1979).

14. G. F. Lanzara, "Ephemeral Organizations in Extreme Environments: Emergence, Strategy, Extinction," *Journal of Management Studies* 20, no. 1 (1983): 71–95.

15. For additional evidence regarding people's tendencies to preserve their expectations, see W. Samuelson and R. Zeckhauser, "Status Quo Bias in Decision Making," *Journal of Risk and Uncertainty* 1 (1988): 7–59, on the status quo bias; and L. Ritov and J. Baron, "Status Quo and Omission Bias," *Journal of Risk and Uncertainty* 5 (1990): 49–62, on the omission bias.

16. S. Moscovici and C. Faucheux, "Social Influence, Confirming Bias, and the Study of Active Memories," in *Advances in Experimental Social Psychology*, ed. L. Berkowitz (New York: Academic Press, 1972), 6: 149–202. See also C. Nemeth and C. Chiles, "Modelling Courage: The Role of Dissent in Fostering Independence," *European Journal of Social Psychology* 18 (1988): 275–80.

17. L. Van Dyne and R. Saavedra, "A Naturalistic Minority Influence Experiment: Effects on Divergent Thinking, Conflict, and Originality in Work-Groups," *British Journal of Social Psychology* 35 (1996): 151–67.

18. Nemeth and Chiles, "Modelling Courage."

19. For a review of the relationship between goals and persistence, see E. A. Locke and G. P. Latham, *A Theory of Goal Setting and Task Performance* (Englewood Cliffs, NJ: Prentice Hall, 1990).

20. J. Pfeffer, *Managing with Power: Politics and Influence in Organizations* (Boston: Harvard Business School Press, 1992).

21. The commonality of emotional cues around the world is limited to facial expressions. The commonality of facial expressions and their meanings across cultures, however, is quite striking. Paul Ekman found these commonalities by traveling to some of the most remote places in the world and comparing facial expressions. The involuntary movements of muscles in the face correspond to particular emotions. For example, the Duchenne, or authentic, smile is a sign of happiness everywhere. See P. Ekman, *Telling Lies: Clues to Deceit in the Marketplace, Politics, and Marriage* (New York: Norton, 1992).

22. See R. N. Emde, "The Representational Self and Its Affective Core," *Psychoanalytic Study of the Child* 38 (1983): 165–92.

23. F. Strack, L. L. Martin, and S. Stepper, "Inhibiting and Facilitating Conditions of the Human Smile: A Nonobtrusive Test of the Facial Feedback Hypothesis," *Journal of Personality and Social Psychology* 54, no. 5 (1988): 768–76.

24. B. L. Fredrickson and C. Branigan, "Positive Emotions Broaden the Scope of Attention and Thought-Action Repertoires," *Cognition and Emotion* 19, no. 3 (2005): 313–32.

25. C. E. Waugh and B. L. Fredrickson, "Nice to Know You: Positive Emotions, Self-Other Overlap, and Complex Understanding in the Formation of New Relationships," *Journal of Positive Psychology* 1, no. 2 (2006): 93–106.

26. K. J. Johnson and B. L. Fredrickson, "'We All Look the Same to Me': Positive Emotions Eliminate the Own-Race Bias in Face Recognition," *Psychological Science* 16, no. 11 (2005): 875–81.

27. A. M. Isen, "Positive Affect and Creativity," in *Affect, Creative Experience, and Psychological Adjustment*, ed. S. Russ (Philadelphia: Bruner/Masel, 1999), 3–17. It is

important to note here that the story of creativity is more complex than just "positive emotions make people more creative." Other factors, including negative emotions, can also play a role; see, for example, J. M. George and J. Zhou, "Understanding When Bad Moods Can Foster Creativity and Good Moods Don't: The Role of Context and Clarity of Feelings," *Journal of Applied Psychology* 87 (2002): 687–97. Our point in citing the work on the relationship between positive emotions and creativity is simply to provide further evidence for the general observation that positive emotions tend to broaden the thoughts and actions that people have available to them and help them build enduring resources.

28. W. Baker, R. Cross, and M. Wooten, "Positive Organizational Network Analysis and Energizing Relationships," in *Positive Organizational Scholarship: Foundations of a New Discipline*, ed. K. S. Cameron, J. E. Dutton, and R. E. Quinn (San Francisco: Berrett-Koehler, 2003), 328–42.

29. Locke and Latham, *A Theory of Goal Setting and Task Performance*.

30. K. E. Weick, "Small Wins: Redefining the Scale of Social Problems," *American Psychologist* 39 (1984): 43.

31. R. I. Sutton and H. Rao, *Scaling Up Excellence: Getting to More without Settling for Less* (New York: Crown, 2014).

32. For a similar argument, see J. Collins, *Good to Great: Why Some Companies Make the Leap . . . and Others Don't* (New York: Harper Business, 2001), 176.

33. R. Fritz, *The Path of Least Resistance: Learning to Become the Creative Force in Your Own Life* (New York: Fawcett, 1989), 135–36.

Chapter Five

1. M. Bazerman and A. E. Tenbrunsel, *Blind Spots: Why We Fail to Do What's Right and What to Do about It* (Princeton, NJ: Princeton University Press, 2011).

2. M. Rokeach, *The Nature of Human Values* (New York: Free Press, 1973).

3. S. Milgram, *Obedience to Authority* (New York: Harper, 1974).

4. Scientists and ethicists have engaged in extensive debates over how ethical Milgram's experiments were, and we will discuss some of this debate in chapter 6. Because of these experiments and others like them, universities and other research institutions now have much stricter controls over what kinds of research can be conducted. Milgram conducted this research primarily in the 1960s.

5. Examples include T. Blass, "Understanding Behavior in the Milgram Obedience Experiment: The Role of Personality, Situations, and Their Interactions," *Journal of Personality and Social Psychology* 60 (1991): 398–413; and S. A. Haslam and S. Reicher, "Beyond the Banality of Evil: Three Dynamics of an Interactionist Social Psychology of Tyranny," *Personality and Social Psychology Bulletin* 33 (2007): 615–22.

6. J. Darley and B. Latane, "Bystander Intervention in Emergencies: Diffusion of Responsibility," *Journal of Personality and Social Psychology* 8, no. 4 (1968): 377–83. The story is that of a woman named Kitty Genovese. A newspaper article claimed that thirty-seven people (the number has been disputed) witnessed Genovese get attacked

three times over the course of thirty minutes, and that none of the witnesses did anything to help her; see M. Gansberg, "37 Who Saw Murder Didn't Call the Police," New York Times, March 27, 1964, p. 1. Evidence found later suggests that the claims of the original article may not be entirely true, but the research it inspired is both rigorous and groundbreaking and has contributed significantly to our understanding of why people who value helpfulness may choose to not be helpful; see R. Manning, M. Levine, and A. Collins, "The Kitty Genovese Murder and the Social Psychology of Helping: The Parable of the 38 Witnesses," *American Psychologist* 62 (2007): 555–62.

7. M. Shih, T. L. Pittinsky, and N. Ambady, "Stereotype Susceptibility: Identity Salience and Shifts in Quantitative Performance," *Psychological Science* 10, no. 1 (1999): 80–83.

8. F. Gino and C. Mogilner, "Time, Money, and Morality," *Psychological Science* 25, no. 2 (2014): 414–21.

9. See, for example, C. Kirchner, I. Völker, and O. L. Bock, "Priming with Age Stereotypes Influences the Performance of Elderly Workers," *Psychology* 6 (2015): 133–37; M. Shih, T. L. Pittinsky, and N. Ambady, "Stereotype Susceptibility: Identity Salience and Shifts in Quantitative Performance," *Psychological Science* 10, no. 1 (1999): 80–83; and F. Gino and C. Mogilner, "Time, Money, and Morality," *Psychological Science* 25, no. 2 (2014): 414–21, for a very small sampling of priming research.

10. J. A. Bargh and T. L. Chartrand, "The Unbearable Automaticity of Being," *American Psychologist* 53, no. 7 (1999): 462–79.

11. C. Tavris and E. Aronson, *Mistakes Were Made (But Not by Me): Why We Justify Foolish Beliefs, Bad Decisions, and Hurtful Acts* (Orlando, FL: Harcourt, 2007), 32.

12. L. Festinger, *A Theory of Cognitive Dissonance* (Stanford, CA: Stanford University Press, 1957).

13. A. Buckley and B. Kleiner, "The Accuracy of Eyewitness Testimony," *Managerial Law* 44, nos. 1–2 (2002): 86–91; B. C. Feeney and J. Cassidy, "Reconstructed Memory Related to Adolescent-Parent Conflict Interactions: The Influence of Attachment-Related Perceptions and Changes in Perceptions over Time," *Journal of Personality and Social Psychology* 85 (2003): 945–55.

14. S. Freud, *An Outline of Psychoanalysis*, trans. James Strachey (London: Balliere, 1940).

15. *External direction* refers to automatic behaviors that are inconsistent with our values. We focus on external direction because it is a "normal" state. It is not normal in the sense that people constantly act in ways that are inconsistent with their values; they also behave in automatic ways that are consistent with their values. It is normal because it happens often—more often than we think. And just as it is possible to act in automatic and unconscious ways that are consistent and inconsistent with our values, it is also possible to act consciously and deliberately in ways that are both consistent and inconsistent with our values. As illustrated by Tavris and Aronson's example of young men deciding whether or not to cheat on a test, these conscious decisions can easily become unconscious patterns of behavior.

Chapter Six

1. T. L. Webb and P. Sheeran, "Can Implementation Intentions Help to Overcome Ego-Depletion?" *Journal of Experimental Social Psychology* 39 (2003): 279–86.

2. The leading researcher on the topic of implementation intention is Peter Gollwitzer. See, for example, P. M. Gollwitzer, "Goal Achievement: The Role of Intentions," *European Review of Social Psychology* 4 (1993): 141–85; P. M. Gollwitzer and V. Brandstaetter, "Implementation Intentions and Effective Goal Pursuit," *Journal of Personality and Social Psychology* 73 (1997): 186–99; P. M. Gollwitzer and B. Schaal, "Metacognition in Action: The Importance of Implementation Intentions," *Personality and Social Psychology Review* 2 (1998): 124–36; and P. M. Gollwitzer, K. Fujita, and G. Oettingen, "Planning and the Implementation of Goals," in *Handbook of Self-Regulation: Research, Theory, and Applications,* ed. R. F. Baumeister and K. D. Vohs (New York: Guilford, 2004), 211–28.

3. G. R. Maio, J. M. Olson, L. Allen, and M. M. Bernard, "Addressing Discrepancies between Values and Behavior: The Motivating Effect of Reasons," *Journal of Experimental Social Psychology* 37 (2000): 104–17.

4. This experiment can also be found in Maio et al., "Addressing Discrepancies between Values and Behavior."

5. For additional evidence on how stories can motivate action, see A. M. Grant, "The Significance of Task Significance: Job Performance Effects, Relational Mechanisms, and Boundary Conditions," *Journal of Applied Psychology* 93 (2008): 108–24; and A. M. Grant, "Employees without a Cause: The Motivational Effects of Prosocial Impact in Public Service," *International Public Management Journal* 11 (2008): 48–66. Participants in Grant's studies increase their effort, persistence, performance, and productivity after hearing stories of how their work benefits others.

6. M. Rokeach, *The Nature of Human Values* (New York: Free Press, 1973).

7. A. J. Greimas, *On Meaning: Selected Writings in Semiotic Theory* (Amsterdam: John Benjamins, 1988).

8. J. D. Margolis, "Responsibility in an Organizational Context," *Business Ethics Quarterly* 11, no. 3 (2001): 431–54.

9. D. Baumrind, "Some Thoughts on Ethics of Research: After Reading Milgram's "Behavioral study of obedience," *American Psychologist* 19 (1964): 421–23.

10. S. Milgram, *Obedience to Authority* (New York: Harper, 1974), 197. Milgram actually defended his research on a number of other points as well. He argued that he and his research assistants took measures to protect participants, they told participants that they could withdraw at any time, the deception in the experiment was necessary to address the research question, they explained the deception to the participants as soon as the experiment was over, and follow-up surveys with participants suggested that participation had not harmed them but in some cases, was life-altering for them in a positive way.

11. J. D. Margolis, "Responsibility in an Organizational Context," *Business Ethics Quarterly* 11, no. 3 (2001): 441.

12. C. Peterson and M. E. P. Seligman, *Character Strengths and Virtues: A Handbook and Classification* (Washington, DC: American Psychological Association, 2004).

13. American Psychiatric Association, *Diagnostic and Statistical Manual of Mental Disorders*, 4th ed. (Arlington, VA: American Psychiatric Publishing, 2000).

14. See·G. A. Nix, R. M. Ryan, J. B. Manly, and E. L. Deci, "Revitalization through Self-Regulation: The Effects of Autonomous and Controlled Motivation on Happiness and Vitality," *Journal of Experimental and Social Psychology* 35, no. 3 (1999): 266–84.

15. P. Sheeran, "Intention-Behavior Relations: A Conceptual and Empirical Review," in *European Review of Social Psychology*, ed. M. Hewstone and W. Stroebe (Chichester, England: Wiley, 2002), 12: 1–36.

16. C. R. Rogers, *On Becoming a Person* (Boston: Houghton Mifflin, 1961), 122.

17. Ibid., 180.

18. The quotes in this story can be found in the transcript of the *Oprah Winfrey Show* for January 26, 2006. A longer description and analysis of this story can be found in C. Tavris and E. Aronson, *Mistakes Were Made (But Not by Me): Why We Justify Foolish Beliefs, Bad Decisions, and Hurtful Acts* (Orlando, FL: Harcourt, 2007), 213–16.

19. Tavris and Aronson, *Mistakes Were Made*.

20. M. C. Worline, A. Wrzesniewski, and A. Rafaeli, "Courage and Work: Breaking Routines to Improve Performance," in *Emotions in the Workplace: Understanding the Structure and Role of Emotions in Organizational Behavior*, ed. R. Klimoski and R. Kanfer (San Francisco: Jossey-Bass, 2002), 295–330.

21. J. Haidt, "The Positive Emotion of Elevation," *Prevention and Treatment* 3, no. 3 (2000), http://faculty.virginia.edu/haidtlab/articles/haidt.2000.the-positive-emotion -of-elevation.pub020.pdf.

22. K. M. Sheldon, and A. J. Elliott, "Goal Striving, Need Satisfaction, and Longitudinal Well-Being: The Self-Concordance Model," *Journal of Personality and Social Psychology* 76, no. 3 (1999): 482–97.

23. W. Mischel, Y. Shoda, and P. K. Peake, "The Nature of Adolescent Competencies Predicted by Preschool Delay of Gratification," *Journal of Personality and Social Psychology* 54, no. 4 (1988): 687–96.

24. Kim Cameron and his colleagues have begun to study the relationship between virtues and performance; see, for example, K. S. Cameron, D. Bright, and A. Caza, "Exploring the Relationships between Virtuousness and Performance," *American Behavioral Scientist* 47, no. 6 (2004): 766–90. Also relevant to the issue of virtuous business and performance, however, is the question of how well a company and its members engage in self-regulation. Jim Collin's research suggests, for example, that a "culture of discipline" is a necessary condition for companies to move from good performance to great performance; see J. Collins, *Good to Great: Why Some Companies Make the Leap . . . and Others Don't* (New York: Harper Business, 2001).

25. See, for example, F. B. deWaal, "The Chimpanzee's Sense of Social Regularity and Its Relation to the Human Sense of Justice," *American Behavioral Scientist* 34, no. 3 (1991): 335–49.

26. M. J. Sandel, *Justice: What Is the Right Thing to Do?* (New York: MacMillan, 2010).

Chapter Seven

1. M. Buber, *I and Thou*, trans. W. Kaufmann (New York: Simon and Schuster, 1990). We focus on Buber here because his philosophy examined specific psychological states. Immanuel Kant, however, was the philosopher who introduced the idea that morality is dependent on treating the humanity in others and in oneself as an end and never merely as a means. See I. Kant, *Grounding for the Metaphysics of Morals*, 3rd ed., trans. J. W. Ellington (Indianapolis: Hackett, 1993).

2. C. D. Batson, "How Social an Animal? The Human Capacity for Caring," *American Psychologist* 45, no. 3 (1990): 336–46.

3. R. B. Cialdini, S. L. Brown, B. P. Lewis, C. Luce, and S. L. Neuberg, "Reinterpreting the Empathy-Altruism Relationship: When One into One Equals Oneness," *Journal of Personality and Social Psychology* 73, no. 3 (1997): 481–94.

4. D. A. Quinney, "Daniel Bernoulli and the Making of the Fluid Equation," *Plus* (1997), http://plus.maths.org/issue1/bern/index.html.

5. W. D. Hutchinson, K. D. Davis, A. M. Lozano, R. R. Tasker, and J. O. Dostrovsky, "Pain-Related Neurons in the Human Cingulate Cortex," *Nature Neuroscience* 2 (1999): 403–5.

6. The participants in this study were patients who were suffering from psychiatric diseases. They had to go through brain surgery, so they were already undergoing the surgical procedure necessary for Hutchinson and his colleagues to study their brains with microelectrodes. The patients agreed to participate in the study, but they were told that they could withdraw at any time.

7. J. S. Morris, A. Öhman, and R. J. Dolan, "Conscious and Unconscious Emotional Learning in the Human Amygdala," *Nature* 393 (1998): 467–70.

8. P. J. Whalen, L. M. Shin, and S. C. McInerney, "A Functional MRI Study of Human Amygdala Responses to Facial Expressions of Fear versus Anger," *Emotion* 1, no. 1 (2001): 70–83.

9. N. H. Frijda, "The Laws of Emotion," *American Psychologist* 43, no. 5 (1988): 349–58.

10. S. D. Preston and F. B. M. de Wall, "Empathy: Its Ultimate and Proximal Bases," *Behavioral and Brain Sciences* 25 (2002): 1–72.

11. Communication scholars point out that we cannot know what other people's intentions are when we communicate with others. Some scholars, such as François Cooren, explain that even though we cannot understand others' intentions, we get by relatively effectively most of the time because of our ability to use our context to help us interpret people's messages; see F. Cooren, *The Organizing Property of Communication* (Amsterdam: John Benjamins, 2000). We would argue that emotions are often the most important contextual cues that humans have to help them with these interpretations; see, for example, R. W. Quinn and J. E. Dutton, "Coordination as Energy-in-Conversation," *Academy of Management Review* 30, no. 1 (2005): 36–57.

12. Sometimes some of the nuance that we add to our empathy is inaccurate or inappropriate because some element or elements of our mental models are inappropriate.

If this happens, we will often feel inclined to update our mental models to make them more accurate because of the empathy we feel for others. It is important, however, to acknowledge that this system is imperfect, making learning and adaptation as important as empathy.

13. K. N. Ochsner, K. Knierim, D. H. Ludlow, J. Hanelin, T. Ramachandran, G. Glover et al., "Reflecting upon Feelings: An fMRI Study of Neural Systems Supporting the Attribution of Emotion to Self and Other," *Journal of Cognitive Neuroscience* 16, no. 10 (2004): 1746–72.

14. C. T. Warner, *Bonds That Make Us Free: Healing Our Relationships, Coming to Ourselves* (Salt Lake City: Shadow Mountain, 2001). For an excellent application of Warner's ideas to business settings, see Arbinger Institute, *Leadership and Self-Deception: Getting Out of the Box* (San Francisco: Berrett-Koehler, 2002).

15. B. M. Staw, S. G. Barsade, and K. W. Koput, "Escalation at the Credit Window: A Longitudinal Study of Bank Executives' Recognition and Write-Off of Problem Loans," *Journal of Applied Psychology* 82, no. 1 (1997): 130–42. For further research on justification and the escalation of commitment, see G. R. Salancik, "Commitment and the Control of Organizational Behavior and Belief," in *New Directions in Organizational Behavior*, ed. B. M. Staw and G. R. Salancik (Chicago: St. Clair, 1977), 1–54; and K. E. Weick, *Sensemaking in Organizations* (Thousand Oaks, CA: Sage, 1995).

16. See R. Collins, *Interaction Ritual Chains* (Princeton, NJ: Princeton University Press, 2004).

17. S. L. Gable, G. C. Gonzaga, and A. Strachman, "Will You Be There for Me When Things Go Right? Supportive Responses to Event Disclosures," *Journal of Personality and Social Psychology* 91, no. 5 (2006): 904–17.

18. On the difficulty of mental control, see D. M. Wegner, "Ironic Processes of Mental Control." *Psychological Review* 101, no. 1 (1994): 34–52. On the costs of emotional suppression, see E. Kennedy-Moore and J. C. Watson, "How and When Does Emotional Expression Help?" *Review of General Psychology* 5, no. 3 (2001): 187–212. Paul Ekman's work is also relevant here, showing how the face reveals lies in the micro-movements of its muscles; see P. Ekman, *Telling Lies: Clues to Deceit in the Marketplace, Politics, and Marriage* (New York: Norton, 1992).

19. Morris et al., "Conscious and Unconscious Emotional Learning in the Human Amygdala."

20. For research on how emotional suppression inhibits the development of new relationships, see E. Butler, B. Egloff, F. H. Wilhelm, N. C. Smith, E. A. Erickson, and J. J. Gross, "The Social Consequences of Expressive Suppression," *Emotion* 3 (2003): 48–67.

21. R. F. Baumeister and M. R. Leary, "The Need to Belong: Desire for Interpersonal Attachments as a Fundamental Human Motivation," *Psychological Bulletin* 117, no. 3 (1995): 497–529.

22. N. I. Eisenberger, M. D. Lieberman, and K. D. Williams, "Does Rejection Hurt? An fMRI Study of Social Exclusion," *Science* 302, no. 5643 (2003): 290–92.

23. See, for example, G. Mandler, *Mind and Body: Psychology of Emotion and Stress* (New York: Norton, 1984).

24. M. R. Leary, C. Springer, L. Negel, E. Ansell, and K. Evans, "The Causes, Phenomenology, and Consequences of Hurt Feelings," *Journal of Personality and Social Psychology* 74, no. 5 (1998): 1225–37.

25. See M. D. S. Ainsworth, S. Bell, and D. Slayton, "Infant-Mother Attachment and Social Development: Socialization as a Product of Reciprocal Responsiveness to Signals," in *The Integration of a Child into a Social World*, ed. M. P. M. Richards (Cambridge: Cambridge University Press, 1974), 99–135; F. J. Bernieri, S. Reznick, and R. Rosenthal, "Synchrony, Pseudosynchrony, and Dissynchrony: Measuring the Entrainment Process in Mother-Infant Interactions," *Journal of Personality and Social Psychology* 54, no. 2 (1988): 243–53; J. Bowlby, *A Secure Base: Parent-Child Attachment and Human Development* (New York: Basic Books, 1990); T. Field, "Attachment as Psychobiological Attunement: Being on the Same Wavelength," in *The Psychobiology of Attachment and Separation*, ed. M. Reite and T. Field (Orlando, FL: Academic Press, 1985), 415–54; and A. Schore, *Affect Regulation and the Origin of the Self: The Neurobiology of Emotional Development* (Hillsdale, NJ: Erlbaum, 1994).

Chapter Eight

1. K. N. Ochsner, K. Knierim, D. H. Ludlow, J. Hanelin, T. Ramachandran, G. Glover et al. (2004), "Reflecting upon Feelings: An fMRI Study of Neural Systems Supporting the Attribution of Emotion to Self and Other," *Journal of Cognitive Neuroscience* 16(10): 1746–72.

2. The three parts of the brain that were activated were the medial prefrontal cortex, the superior temporal gyrus, and the posterior cingulate.

3. See, for example, W. D. Hutchinson, K. D. Davis, A. M. Lozano, R. R. Tasker, and J. O. Dostrovsky (1999), "Pain-Related Neurons in the Human Cingulate Cortex," *Nature Neuroscience* 2: 403–5.

4. It is also worth noting that in addition to choosing the words of this question carefully, we also were careful about what words we would *not* include in this question. In particular, this question does not ask, "How would *I* feel if I were experiencing this situation from others' perspectives?" This is because Daniel Batson and his colleagues have found that we feel empathy when we ask how another person feels, but when we ask how we would feel in the same situation we feel both empathy and personal distress; see C. D. Batson, S. Early, and G. Salvarani (1997), "Perspective Taking: Imagining How Another Feels versus Imagining How You Would Feel," *Personality and Social Psychology Bulletin* 23(7): 751–57. This is an important distinction, because when we feel empathy, we feel compelled to help other people for their sake, but when we feel empathy and distress, our desire to help those people is motivated by more self-focused desires.

5. See C. D. Batson, *The Altruism Question: Toward a Scientific Answer* (Mahwah, NJ: Erlbaum, 1991); and D. L. Krebs (1970), "Altruism—An Examination of the Concept and a Review of the Literature," *Psychological Bulletin* 73(4): 258–302.

6. For a more extensive discussion of how this process works, see C. T. Warner, *Bonds That Make Us Free: Healing Our Relationships, Coming to Ourselves* (Salt Lake City: Shadow Mountain, 2001), 197.

7. It can also be harder to be other-focused when the expectations that define our situation are self-focused. Nicholas Epley and his colleagues conducted a series of experiments in which they asked participants with competing interests to consider the perspectives of the other participants. Instead of acting more fairly, the participants who considered the other participants' perspectives acted less fairly, even after clearly stating what they believed fair actions would be. Epley and his colleagues found that considering other participants' perspectives led to unfair behavior because participants who considered other participants' perspectives realized that it was in the other participants' interest to act unfairly as well. Considering other people's perspectives in competitive situations, they conclude, makes people more likely to act more selfishly, not less. See N. Epley, E. M. Caruso, and M. H. Bazerman (2006), "When Perspective Taking Increases Taking: Reactive Egoism in Social Interaction," *Journal of Personality and Social Psychology* 91(5): 872–89. Competitive environments certainly make cooperative behavior more difficult. The experiments that Epley and his colleagues conducted could be used to explain the behavior of most of the people in Hugh's company. They quickly realized what other people's interests were and acted selfishly. These experiments do not, however, explain how or why Hugh came to feel and act so differently. At least one major difference between Epley's experiment and Hugh's experience is that Epley and his colleagues did not require their participants to question their own virtue. Virtue was very much an issue for Hugh, and questioning it enabled him to make empathy more appealing in spite of the competitive environment; it helped him to see how he and others were using the environment as a justification to be less virtuous than they wanted to be. It is easier for them to feel empathy for others when they realized that those others were struggling with the same issues with which they had struggled. We suspect that this is why Hugh felt a need to challenge his coworkers as well as to offer his support: he felt a desire to help them free themselves from their faulty justifications.

8. C. R. Rogers, *On Becoming a Person* (Boston: Houghton Mifflin, 1961).

9. R. E. Freeman, J. S. Harrison, and A. C. Wicks, *Managing for Stakeholders: Survival, Reputation, and Success.* (New Haven, CT: Yale University Press, 2007).

10. The story of Bank of Boston and First Community Bank can be found in R. M. Kanter (1999), "From Spare Change to Real Change: The Social Sector as a Beta Site for Business Innovation," *Harvard Business Review* 77(3): 122–35.

11. N. H. Frijda, P. Kuipers, and E. Schure (1989), "Relations among Emotion, Appraisal, and Emotional Action Readiness," *Journal of Personality and Social Psychology* 57: 212–28.

12. Batson, *The Altruism Question*; Krebs, "Altruism." Adam Grant finds that when people feel empathy for others, they exert more effort, persist longer, and engage in more helping behaviors; see A. M. Grant (2008), "The Significance of Task Significance:

Job Performance Effects, Relational Mechanisms, and Boundary Conditions," *Journal of Applied Psychology* 93: 108–24; and A. M. Grant (2008), "Employees without a Cause: The Motivational Effects of Prosocial Impact in Public Service," *International Public Management Journal* 11: 48–66.

13. W. S. Condon, "Cultural Microrhythms," in M. Davis (ed.), *Interaction Rhythms: Periodicity in Communicative Behavior*, 53–76. (New York: Human Sciences Press, 1982).

14. S. Albon and C. Marci (2004), "Psychotherapy Process: The Missing Link," *Psychological Bulletin* 130: 664–68.

15. L. Tickle-Degnan and R. Rosenthal (1990), "The Nature of Rapport and Its Nonverbal Correlates," *Psychological Inquiry* 1(4): 285–93.

16. M. Greer (2005), "The Science of Savoir Faire," *Monitor on Psychology* 36(1): 28–30.

17. J. E. Dutton, and E. D. Heaphy, "The Power of High Quality Connections," in *Positive Organizational Scholarship: Foundations of a New Discipline* edited by K. S. Cameron, J. E. Dutton and R. E. Quinn, 263–78 (San Francisco: Berrett-Koehler, 2003).

18. For more on the physiological effects of a high-quality connection, see J. Panskepp, *Affective Neuroscience: The Foundations of Human and Animal Emotions* (Oxford: Oxford University Press, 1998); and S. E. Taylor, S. S. Dickerson, and L. C. Klein, "Toward a Biology of Social Support," in C. R. Snyder and S. L. Lopez (eds.), *Handbook of Positive Psychology*, 556–72 (Oxford: Oxford University Press, 2002).

19. See R. Collins (1981), "On the Micro-Foundations of Macro-Sociology," *American Journal of Sociology* 86: 984–1014; and R. Collins (1993), "Emotional Energy as the Common Denominator of Rational Action," *Rationality and Society* 5(2): 203–30.

20. W. Baker, *Achieving Success through Social Capital: Tapping the Hidden Resources in Your Personal and Business Networks* (San Francisco: Jossey-Bass, 2000), 22–23.

21. W. Baker, R. Cross, and M. Wooten, "Positive Organizational Network Analysis and Energizing Relationships," in K. S. Cameron, J. E. Dutton and R. E. Quinn (eds.), *Positive Organizational Scholarship: Foundations of a New Discipline*, 328–42 (San Francisco: Berrett-Koehler, 2003).

22. For a description of how empathetic relations can help adults in working environments increase their felt security, see W. A. Kahn (2001), "Holding Environments at Work," *Journal of Applied Behavioral Science* 37(3): 260–79.

23. For research examples of how empathetic relationships help people be resilient and find courage, see R. W. Quinn and M. C. Worline (2008), "Enabling Courageous Collective Action: Conversations from United Airlines Flight 93," *Organization Science* 19(4): 497–516; and M. C. Worline, J. E. Dutton, P. Frost, J. Lilius, and J. Kanov (2008), "Creating Fertile Soil: The Organizing Dynamics of Resilience," unpublished paper, Emory University.

24. C. R. Rogers, *On Becoming a Person* (Boston: Houghton Mifflin, 1961).

25. See J. D. Hundleby and G. W. Mercer (1987), "Family and Friends as Social Environments and Their Relationship to Young Adolescents' Use of Alcohol, Tobacco,

and Marijuana," *Journal of Marriage and the Family* 49: 151–64; B. C. Miller, *Families Matter: A Research Synthesis of Family Influences on Adolescent Pregnancy*. (Washington, DC: National Campaign to Prevent Teen Pregnancy, 1998); and Partnership for a Drug-Free America, *Partnership Attitude Tracking Study* (New York: Partnership for a Drug-Free America, 2002).

26. A sense of security is often needed to trust others because in doing so we make ourselves vulnerable; see D. M. Rousseau, S. B. Sitkin, R. S. Burt, and C. Camerer (1998), "Not So Different After All: A Cross-Disciplinary View of Trust," *Academy of Management Review* 23(3): 393–404.

27. A. C. Edmondson, R. M. Bohmer, and G. P. Pisano (2001), "Disrupted Routines: Team Learning and New Technology Implementation in Hospitals," *Administrative Science Quarterly* 46: 685–716.

28. A. Hargadon, *How Breakthroughs Happen: The Surprising Truth about How Companies Innovate* (Cambridge, MA: Harvard Business School Press, 2003).

29. M. B. Brewer and W. Gardner (1996), "Who Is This 'We'? Levels of Collective Identity and Self-Representations," *Journal of Personality and Social Psychology* 71(1): 83–93.

Chapter Nine

1. C. S. Dweck, *Mindset: The New Psychology of Success* (New York: Random House, 2006). Dweck uses the phrase "fixed mindset" to describe the belief that one's abilities are relatively unchanging and unchangeable, and the phrase "growth mindset" to describe the belief that one's abilities can be grown and developed with effort and time. We like Dweck's phrases, but we use the terms *internally closed* and *externally open* to describe these psychological states because they capture the idea that competing values are necessary to make lift possible. Internally closed and externally open states are the state versions of the traits that Dweck calls "fixed mindset" and "growth mindset."

2. C. S. Dweck and N. D. Reppucci, "Learned Helplessness and Reinforcement Responsibility in Children," *Journal of Personality and Social Psychology* 25, no. 1 (1973): 109–16.

3. See C. I. Deiner and C. S. Dweck, "An Analysis of Learned Helplessness: Continuous Changes in Performance, Strategy, and Achievement Cognitions following Failure," *Journal of Personality and Social Psychology* 36, no. 5 (1978): 451–62; C. I. Deiner and C. S. Dweck, "An Analysis of Learned Helplessness: II. The Processing of Success," *Journal of Personality and Social Psychology* 39, no. 5 (1980): 940–52; R. Wood and A. Bandura, "Impact of Conceptions of Ability on Self-Regulatory Mechanisms and Complex Decision-Making," *Journal of Personality and Social Psychology* 56, no. 3 (1989): 407–15; H. Grant and C. S. Dweck, "Clarifying Achievement Goals and Their Impact," *Journal of Personality and Social Psychology* 85, no. 3 (2003): 541–53; and P. A. Heslin, G. P. Latham, and D. VandeWalle, "The Effect of Implicit Person Theory on Performance Appraisals," *Journal of Applied Psychology* 90, no. 5 (2005): 842–56.

4. Dweck, *Mindset* 47.

5. C. M. Mueller and C. S. Dweck, "Praise for Intelligence Can Undermine Children's Intelligence and Performance," *Journal of Personality and Social Psychology* 75, no. 1 (1998): 33–52.

6. Although researchers have not examined the explicit link between praise for ability and becoming internally closed, they have found that it is not difficult to induce an internally closed state in adults. There is also quite a bit of anecdotal evidence to support the idea that adults, like children, may be similarly influenced by praise for ability. Citations on inducing an internally closed state in adults include J. Aronson, C. Fried, and C. Good, "Reducing the Effects of Stereotype Threat on African American College Students by Shaping Theories of Intelligence," *Journal of Experimental Social Psychology* 38 (2002): 113–25; C.-y. Chiu, Y.-y. Hong, and C. S. Dweck, "Lay Dispositionism and Implicit Theories of Personality," *Journal of Personality and Social Psychology* 73, no. 1 (1997): 19–30; and R. Wood and A. Bandura, "Impact of Conceptions of Ability on Self-Regulatory Mechanisms and Complex Decision Making."

7. D. Miller, *The Icarus Paradox: How Exceptional Companies Bring About Their Own Downfall* (New York: HarperCollins, 1992).

8. See, for example, C. S. Dweck and E. S. Elliott, "Achievement Motivation," in *Handbook of Child Psychology vol. 4: Social and Personality Development*, ed. P. H. Mussen and E. M. Hetherington (New York: Wiley, 1983), 643–91.

9. G. H. Seijts, G. P. Latham, K. Tasa, and B. W. Latham, "Goal Setting and Goal Orientation: An Integration of Two Different Yet Related Literatures," *Academy of Management Journal* 47, no. 2 (2004): 227–39.

Chapter Ten

1. G. H. Seijts, G. P. Latham, K. Tasa, and B. W. Latham, "Goal Setting and Goal Orientation: An Integration of Two Different Yet Related Literatures," *Academy of Management Journal* 47, no. 2 (2004): 227–39.

2. C. S. Dweck, *Mindset: The New Psychology of Success* (New York: Random House, 2006).

3. See, for example, R. C. Shank and R. P. Abelson, *Scripts, Plans, Goals, and Understanding* (Hillsdale, NJ: Erlbaum, 1977).

4. G. P. Latham and G. P. Seijts, "The Effects of Proximal and Distal Goals on Performance on a Moderately Complex Task," *Journal of Organizational Behavior* 20, no. 4 (1999): 421–29.

5. K. E. Weick, "Small Wins: Redefining the Scale of Social Problems," *American Psychologist* 39 (1984): 40–49.

6. C. Moorman and A. S. Miner, "Organizational Improvisation and Organizational Memory," *Academy of Management Review* 23, no. 4 (1998): 698–723.

7. M. Csikszentmihalyi. *Flow: The Psychology of Optimal Experience* (New York: HarperPerennial, 1990).

8. R. W. Quinn, "Flow in Knowledge Work: High Performance Experience in the Design of National Security Technology," *Administrative Science Quarterly* 50, no. 4 (2006): 610–41.

9. D. A. Schön, *The Reflective Practitioner: How Professionals Think in Action* (New York: Basic Books, 1983).

10. Csikszentmihalyi, *Flow*, 233.

11. P. A. Heslin, G. P. Latham, and D. VandeWalle, "The Effect of Implicit Person Theory on Performance Appraisals," *Journal of Applied Psychology* 90, no. 5 (2005): 842–56.

12. P. A. Heslin, D. VandeWalle, and G. P. Latham, "Keen to Help? Managers' Implicit Person Theories and Their Subsequent Employee Coaching," *Personnel Psychology* 59, no. 4 (2006): 871–902.

13. C. M. Mueller, and C. S. Dweck, "Praise for Intelligence Can Undermine Children's Intelligence and Performance," *Journal of Personality and Social Psychology* 75, no. 1 (1998): 33–52.

14. J. S. Bunderson, and K. M. Sutcliffe, "Management Team Learning Orientation and Business Unit Performance," *Journal of Applied Psychology* 88, no. 3 (2003): 552–60.

15. R. Wood and A. Bandura, "Social Cognitive Theory of Organizational Management," *Academy of Management Review* 14, no. 3 (1989): 361–84.

16. Schön, *The Reflective Practitioner*.

17. Dweck, *Mindset*.

18. See J. S. Brown and P. Duguid, "Knowledge and Organization: A Social-Practice Perspective," *Organization Science* 12, no. 2 (2001): 198–213; W. J. Orlikowski, "Improvising Organizational Transformation over Time: A Situated Change Perspective," *Information Systems Research* 7, no. 1 (1996): 63–92; and Schön, *The Reflective Practitioner*.

19. See B. Barnes, "Practice as Collective Action," in *The Practice Turn in Contemporary Theory*, ed. T. R. Schatzki, K. K. Cetina, and E. von Savigny (London: Routledge, 2001), 17–28; F. J. Barrett, "Creativity and Improvisation in Jazz and Organizations: Implications for Organizational Learning," *Organization Science* 9, no. 5 (1998): 605–22; and D. Obstfeld, "Social Networks, the Tertius Iungens Orientation, and Involvement in Innovation," *Administrative Science Quarterly* 50, no. 1 (2005): 100–130.

20. See A. C. Edmondson, R. M. Bohmer, and G. P. Pisano, "Disrupted Routines: Team Learning and New Technology Implementation in Hospitals," *Administrative Science Quarterly* 46 (2001): 685–716; A. Hargadon, *How Breakthroughs Happen: The Surprising Truth about How Companies Innovate* (Cambridge, MA: Harvard Business School Press, 2003); and W. J. Orlikowski, "Knowing in Practice: Enacting a Collective Capability in Distributed Organizing," *Organization Science* 13, no. 3 (2002): 249–73.

21. See R. W. Quinn and M. C. Worline, "Enabling Courageous Collective Action: Conversations from United Airlines Flight 93," *Organization Science* 19, no. 4 (2008): 497–516; and J. E. Dutton, M. C. Worline, P. J. Frost, and J. Lilius, "Explaining Compassion Organizing," *Administrative Science Quarterly* 51 (2006): 59–96.

22. Dweck, *Mindset*.

23. J. S. Bunderson and K. M. Sutcliffe, "Management Team Learning Orientation and Business Unit Performance," *Journal of Applied Psychology* 88, no. 3 (2003): 552–60.

24. A. S. Miner, P. Bassoff, and C. Moorman, "Organizational Improvisation and Learning: A Field Study," *Administrative Science Quarterly* 46, no. 2 (2001): 304–39.

25. Throughout chapters 9 and 10 we have focused on people's beliefs about whether or not their abilities can change. We have not discussed whether people believe they can change their character or personality. We focused on ability because simply learning that one's abilities can be developed can be a groundbreaking concept for many people, but the thought that they can change their character is even harder to grasp. There is, however, a significant research literature on character change that we do not review here. We note that this literature exists, and that many—if not most—of the same principles we discuss in chapters 9 and 10 apply to character change as they do to changing one's abilities. This is especially important when we juxtapose the externally open state with the internally directed state, because becoming internally directed involves recognizing our lack of integrity. This is a hard thing for many people to accept, and some people have trouble forgiving themselves when they discover it. But if we accompany a realization that we have gaps in our integrity with a realization that we are all "works in progress" in the development of our moral character—and that it is okay to be incomplete in the development of our moral character, as long as we are striving to improve—then it is much easier to forgive ourselves for our shortcomings.

Chapter Eleven

1. Although laypeople usually think of *traits* as characteristics that are consistent across situations, this is not necessarily how psychologists use the term. People who have authoritarian personalities, for example, may be domineering when they are in a high-power situation and submissive when they are in a low-power situation. Here we use the more common way of thinking about personality traits simply to make a distinction between thinking of people as responsive to situations rather than consistent across situations.

2. For a review of the research on intuition, see E. Dane and M. G. Pratt, "Exploring Intuition and Its Role in Managerial Decision Making." *Academy of Management Review* 32, no. 1 (2007): 33–54.

Chapter Twelve

1. See D. L. Cooperrider, D. Whitney, and J. Stavros, *Appreciative Inquiry Handbook: The First in a Series of AI Workbooks for Leaders of Change* (San Francisco: Berrett-Koehler, 2005).

2. E. Von Hippel, *Democratizing Innovation* (Cambridge, MA: MIT Press, 2005).

3. R. T. Pascale, J. Sternin, and M. Sternin, *The Power of Positive Deviance: How Unlikely Innovators Solve the World's Toughest Problems* (Cambridge, MA: Harvard Business Press, 2010).

4. See J. R. Garver and J. V. Antonetti, *Focus on Learning: A Process for Personal and Collaborative Reflection* (Phoenix, AZ: Colleagues on Call, 2010). On solution-focused therapy, see C. Franklin, T. S. Trepper, W. J. Gingerich, and E. E. McCollum, *Solution-Focused Brief Therapy: A Handbook of Evidence-Based Practice* (New York: Oxford University Press, 2012).

5. A. George, B. R. Rajakumar, and D. Dinu, "Genetic Algorithm Based Airlines Booking Terminal Open/Close Decision System," (paper presented at the International Conference on Advances in Computing, Communications and Informatics, Chennai, India, August 3–5, 2012).

6. P. Willett, "Genetic Algorithms in Molecular Recognition and Design," *Trends in Biotechnology* 13, no. 12 (1995): 516–21.

7. C. A. Stockdale, "A (R)evolution in Crime-Fighting," *Forensic* (June–July 2008): 30–34.

8. BBC News, "Entertainment: To the Beat of the Byte," (1998), http://news.bbc.co.uk/2/hi/entertainment/123983.stm.

9. R. W. Quinn, B. D. Crane, and J. Harris, "Learning by Sampling on the Dependent Variable: A Normative Model of Search-Based Success," (working paper, 2014).

10. In fact, a 2014 report argues that these accelerating factors are the future of leadership development; see N. Petrie, *Future Trends in Leadership Development* (Greensboro, NC: Center for Creative Leadership, 2014). Historically, leadership development has focused on teaching people about the competencies individual managers need to gain. Its is predicted that in the future this will change, and leadership development will focus on helping people learn together how to take personal accountability for developing collective leadership competencies.

11. Amy Edmondson's work is particularly relevant on this topic. See, for example, A. C. Edmondson, "Psychological Safety and Learning Behavior in Work Teams," *Administrative Science Quarterly* 44, no. 2 (1999): 350–83.

12. R. M. Cyert and J. G. March, *A Behavioral Theory of the Firm* (Englewood Cliffs, NJ: Prentice Hall, 1963).

13. See, for example, A. C. Amason and A. C. Mooney, "The Icarus Paradox Revisited: How Strong Performance Sows the Seeds of Dysfunction in Future Strategic Decision-Making," *Strategic Organization* 6, no. 4 (2011): 407–34; Cyert and March, *A Behavioral Theory of the Firm*; D. K. C., B. R. Staats, and F. Gino, "Learning from My Success and Others' Failure: Evidence from Minimally Invasive Cardiac Surgery," *Management Science* 59, no. 11 (2013): 2435–49; and S. B. Sitkin, "Learning through Failure: The Strategy of Small Losses," in *Research in Organizational Behavior*, ed. B. M. Staw and L. L. Cummings (Greenwich, CT: JAI Press, 1992), 14: 231–66.

14. For an excellent description of the action-reflection cycle, see S. J. Ashford and D. S. DeRue, "Developing as a Leader: The Power of Mindful Engagement," *Organizational Dynamics* 41 (2012): 146–54.

15. See, for example, B. J. Avolio, J. Griffeth, T. S. Wernsing, and F. O. Walumbwa, "What Is Authentic Leadership Development?" in *Oxford Handbook of Positive*

Psychology and Work, ed. P. A. Linley, S. Harrington, and N. Garcea (New York: Oxford University Press, 2010), 39–52.

16. See S. Alinsky, *Rules for Radicals: A Practical Primer for Realistic Radicals* (New York: Vintage, 1971).

Chapter Thirteen

1. M. Kriger and Y. Seng, "Leadership with Inner Meaning: A Contingency Theory of Leadership Based on the Worldview of Five Religions," *Leadership Quarterly* 16, no. 5 (2005): 771–806.

2. R. Clark, *The End of Molasses Classes: Getting Our Kids Unstuck—101 Extraordinary Solutions for Parents and Teachers* (New York: Touchstone, 2012).

3. W. Durant, *The Story of Philosophy* (New York: Simon and Schuster, 2006), 98. This is Durant's eloquent summary of Aristotle's analysis.

INDEX

Ryan and Robert (Bob) Quinn decided to pursue careers as professors of management because of the opportunities it would give them to lift others. Business professors conduct research, teach students, consult with organizations, and serve in the management of the units, committees, and projects of their schools and their professional organizations. Ryan works in the Management Department at the University of Louisville's College of Business. Bob is the Margaret Elliott Tracy Collegiate Professor in the Management and Organizations Department at the University of Michigan's Ross School of Business.

Management is an interdisciplinary topic, so Ryan and Bob draw on such fields as sociology, psychology, and economics in their research. Ryan's research focuses on the social impact of psychological states and on learning from success. Bob studies effectiveness and change; he developed the competing values framework, is one of the cofounders of the Center for Positive Organizational Scholarship at the Ross School of Business, and has published sixteen books, including *Beyond Rational Management, Becoming a Master Manager, Deep Change, Change*

the World, Building the Bridge as You Walk on It, and *Diagnosing and Changing Organizational Culture.* Together Ryan and Bob drew on their complementary expertise to write this book.

Ryan and Bob put into practice the things that they learn through their research by trying to lift the students they teach and the clients for whom they consult. They have taught students in undergraduate, MBA, and executive MBA programs as well in executive education. They have also consulted for Fortune 500 companies, government agencies, and nonprofit organizations throughout the world. Their teaching and consulting focus on leadership and change.

As much as they enjoy their careers and the opportunities they give them to lift people around the world, Ryan and Bob most enjoy lifting and being lifted by their families. Ryan has been married to his wife Amy for seventeen years and has four children: Andrew, Chloe, Katie, and Mason. Bob has been married to Delsa for thirty-nine years and has six children, five sons- and daughters-in-law, and fifteen grandchildren (at the moment).

Berrett–Koehler
Publishers

Berrett-Koehler is an independent publisher dedicated to an ambitious mission: *connecting people and ideas to create a world that works for all*.

We believe that to truly create a better world, action is needed at all levels—individual, organizational, and societal. At the individual level, our publications help people align their lives with their values and with their aspirations for a better world. At the organizational level, our publications promote progressive leadership and management practices, socially responsible approaches to business, and humane and effective organizations. At the societal level, our publications advance social and economic justice, shared prosperity, sustainability, and new solutions to national and global issues.

A major theme of our publications is "Opening Up New Space." Berrett-Koehler titles challenge conventional thinking, introduce new ideas, and foster positive change. Their common quest is changing the underlying beliefs, mindsets, institutions, and structures that keep generating the same cycles of problems, no matter who our leaders are or what improvement programs we adopt.

We strive to practice what we preach—to operate our publishing company in line with the ideas in our books. At the core of our approach is stewardship, which we define as a deep sense of responsibility to administer the company for the benefit of all of our "stakeholder" groups: authors, customers, employees, investors, service providers, and the communities and environment around us.

We are grateful to the thousands of readers, authors, and other friends of the company who consider themselves to be part of the "BK Community." We hope that you, too, will join us in our mission.

A BK Business Book

This book is part of our BK Business series. BK Business titles pioneer new and progressive leadership and management practices in all types of public, private, and nonprofit organizations. They promote socially responsible approaches to business, innovative organizational change methods, and more humane and effective organizations.

Berrett–Koehler
Publishers

Connecting people and ideas
to create a world that works for all

Dear Reader,

Thank you for picking up this book and joining our worldwide community of Berrett-Koehler readers. We share ideas that bring positive change into people's lives, organizations, and society.

To welcome you, we'd like to offer you a free e-book. You can pick from among twelve of our bestselling books by entering the promotional code **BKP92E** here: http://www.bkconnection.com/welcome.

When you claim your free e-book, we'll also send you a copy of our e-newsletter, the *BK Communiqué*. Although you're free to unsubscribe, there are many benefits to sticking around. In every issue of our newsletter you'll find

- A free e-book
- Tips from famous authors
- Discounts on spotlight titles
- Hilarious insider publishing news
- A chance to win a prize for answering a riddle

Best of all, our readers tell us, "Your newsletter is the only one I actually read." So claim your gift today, and please stay in touch!

Sincerely,

Charlotte Ashlock
Steward of the BK Website

Questions? Comments? Contact me at bkcommunity@bkpub.com.

MIX
From responsible
sources
FSC FSC® C113845
www.fsc.org

Certified

Corporation
bcorporation.net